The Oxford Book
of Animal Stories

The Oxford Book *of* Animal Stories

Dennis Pepper

Oxford University Press

OXFORD NEW YORK TORONTO

Oxford University Press, Great Clarendon Street, Oxford OX2 6DP

Oxford New York
Athens Auckland Bangkok Bogota Buenos Aires Calcutta
Cape Town Chennai Dar es Salaam Delhi Florence
Hong Kong Istanbul Karachi Kuala Lumpur Madrid
Melbourne Mexico City Mumbai Nairobi Paris
São Paulo Singapore Taipei Tokyo Toronto Warsaw

and associated companies in
Berlin Ibadan

Oxford is a trade mark of Oxford University Press

Cover illustration by John Butler

A CIP catalogue record for this book is available
from the British Library

ISBN 0 19 278134 0 (hardback)
ISBN 0 19 278160 X (paperback)

Printed and bound in Great Britain by
Biddles Ltd, Guildford and King's Lynn

Contents

3 *Serves You Right* 67

4 *In the Wild* 91

5 *The Hunter and the Hunted* 137

6 *In Field and Home* 231

Introduction

In compiling this collection I have drawn on the work of writers and storytellers from many countries and cultures and on stories first told thousands of years ago as well as those written more recently. The older stories show us something of the beliefs of the peoples who first told them and the societies in which they lived. This is especially true of the myths and legends in the first section, even though they have been translated, retold, and modernized for a different audience from the one they were intended for. The modern reader can still appreciate that these stories reflect distinctive views of the animal world, and humans' involvement in it.

In a collection of stories that sets out to explore the relationship between the human animal and the rest of the animal world, I thought it was important to include such myths and legends, as well as fables and the more lighthearted folk tales, alongside the conventional literary stories of the last hundred years or so. This is not because they are quaint, but because they are different.

The human animal and the rest of the animal world relate to each other in several ways. Early hunters knew that their own survival depended not only on what they caught to eat but on the continued survival of the animals they hunted. They would need to eat the next day, and the following year. More recently some animals have been hunted to extinction, and not always because the hunter was hungry. Hunting is, indeed, at the heart of the relationship between people and animals, and so hunting stories of various kinds have a prominent place in this collection. It is not, however, the only relationship that exists and I have made a point of including stories about domesticated animals too, and about working animals, animals held in captivity for various reasons, and pets.

As well as different relationships, there are also different ways of writing about animals. In folktales animals speak and sometimes wear clothes and live in houses. In fables they not only speak but are used to point morals about human behaviour. A modern writer may give an animal human intentions and emotions, or may tell a story by describing an animal's behaviour from the outside, while being careful to avoid giving human motives to that behaviour. I have chosen stories to show different ways of writing as well as different relationships.

I have also chosen to bring together a collection of *stories* rather than extracts from longer books. The trouble with extracts is that although they may recount a whole incident or episode they are still part of something else, something the reader may not have, and are essentially incomplete. Short stories are quite different. Although they may be based on experience or incidents taken from real life, they have been written with the intention of providing a complete, satisfying experience. If the story is a good one it may amuse you, disturb you, make you angry, bring you close to tears, help you to understand or feel sympathy—but it won't disappoint you.

There are, of course, some obvious limitations to what might be included in an anthology such as this. I could not, even if I wished, include stories about every animal there is—just to list their names would require a longer book—but in making my selection I have cast my net as wide as I could. What I have caught reflects both where I chose to fish—I had to go to places I knew and to others that looked promising—and what's there to be caught. It's a certain fact that there are more stories about mammals than about reptiles and more about either than about insects. What in the end I chose to keep, and put in this collection, are the ones I liked. I hope you will like them too.

DENNIS PEPPER   *September 1993*

Coyote and the Making of the People

Miwok, retold by Robert Scott

When Coyote had finished making the world and the animal people he called a council. All the animals came. There were Grizzly Bear and Brown Bear, Deer and Mountain Goat, Owl and Eagle, Otter and Porcupine – all the animals were there. Mouse sat next to Mountain Lion. Lion was in charge. He was the first to speak.

'Coyote's planning to make human people,' he said, 'and he wants our ideas. Now *I* think they should be covered with fur and have claws and very strong teeth. And a terrible roar, of course. Agreed?'

Grizzly Bear laughed. 'That's ridiculous!' he said, looking at Coyote. 'If you give people a voice like Lion's they will frighten off everything they try to catch. They should be very strong and move silently but swiftly so that they can seize their prey without any noise. I agree about fur, though. They will need to be covered with fur or hair to keep warm.'

Stag spoke up. He agreed with Grizzly Bear that it would be ridiculous to give the people great roaring voices. 'If I created them, I would worry less about their voices and pay more attention to their ears and eyes. They should have ears as soft and silky as a spider's web, ears that can catch the faintest sound and eyes like fire. Of course, they would also need a great pair of antlers to fight with. They would look silly without antlers.'

Mountain Sheep disagreed. 'Great antlers like yours would be a constant bother,' he said. 'People would always be catching them on bushes and branches. It would be better to have big, heavy horns rolled up on each side of the head like mine, then they could butt down anything.'

3

'What people really must have,' said Beaver, 'is a broad, flat tail like mine to carry mud on when they build their houses. And teeth. Long, sharp front teeth so they can cut down trees.'

'Wings,' said Owl, who had been listening quietly. 'People would be useless without wings.'

'And feathers, of course,' added Eagle. 'And a great hooked beak too, for that matter.'

'Whiskers,' squeaked Mouse.

'. . . long bushy tail . . .'

'. . . quills . . .'

'. . . sensitive nose . . .'

'. . . short stumpy tail . . .'

'. . . long ears . . .'

Then Coyote spoke. 'This is madness,' he said. 'Can you imagine what people would be like if they were made with everything you ask for? The trouble is, each of you wants them to be made in your own image. Of course, there is a lot to be said for claws, but there's a lot to be said for fingers, too. Thick fur is very useful in the winter, but it isn't always a benefit. It all

4

depends,' he added, 'it all depends on how people are going to live.'

Coyote went on to say that he didn't think people would need a voice as loud as Lion's, but it should be a good deal louder than Mouse's. Four legs would make them swift, but they should also be able to walk on two legs like Grizzly Bear. If they had hands and fingers they could make things to cover themselves with, so they needn't wear fur all the time.

Coyote stopped and looked round the gathering.

'Well, I think —' began Otter.

'Wait!' said Coyote. 'I want you all to get a lump of clay and make a model of just how you think people should look. Then we can choose the best.'

That was just the thing to do. Why hadn't they thought of it before? Each animal took a lump of reddish clay from the bank close by and started to make a model. They worked long and hard but they still hadn't finished when it was time to sleep. But Coyote didn't sleep. He worked on his model until he had finished. Then he did three things. He went round all the other

5

models and threw water over them so that they were all ruined. He looked at his own model and decided it needed one more thing. 'It will be clever,' he said, 'and quick-witted, just like me. The people will be *smart*.' And finally he gave it life.

When the animals woke late the next morning, Coyote's model was walking about.

'This is the first of the new people,' said Coyote.

The animals looked at what Coyote had created, then they looked hard at Coyote. They shrugged, and sighed, and wandered off to find some food.

That's how the People came to be.

NORTH AMERICA

1
In the Beginning

Sedna, the Woman Under the Sea

Inuit, retold by Joseph Bruchac

Long ago an Inung man and his daughter, Sedna, lived together along the ocean.

Their life was not easy, for the fishing was often not good and the hunting was often poor. Still, Sedna grew up to be a strong and handsome young woman and many Inung men came to ask her to marry. No one, though, was good enough for her. She was too proud to accept any of them. One day, just at the time when the long days were beginning and the ice was breaking for spring, a handsome man came to Sedna. He wore clothing of grey and white and Sedna could see that he was not like other men. He was a sea-bird, the fulmar, taking the shape of a man to woo her and he sang to her this song:

> Come with me, come with me
> to the land of the birds
> where there never is hunger,
> you shall rest on soft bearskins.
>
> Come with me, come with me
> to my beautiful tent,
> my fellow birds will bring you
> all that your heart desires.
>
> Come with me, come with me
> and our feathers will clothe you,
> your lamp will be filled with oil,
> your pot will be filled with meat.

His song was so lovely and his promises so enticing that Sedna could not resist him. She agreed to go with him, off

9

across the wide sea. Their journey to his land was a long and hard one. When they reached the place where the fulmar lived, Sedna saw that he had deceived her. His tent was not beautiful and covered with soft skins. It was made of fishskins and full of holes so that wind and snow blew in. Her bed was not made of soft bearskins, but of hard walrus hide. There was no oil for her lamp, for there were no lamps at all, and her food was nothing but raw fish. Too late, Sedna realized the mistake she had made and she sang this song:

> Aja, my father, if only you knew
> how wretched I am, you would come to me.
> Aja, my father, we would hurry away
> in your boat across the wide sea.
>
> The birds do not look kindly
> on me, for I am a stranger.
> Cold winds blow about my bed
> and I have little food.
>
> Aja, my father, come and take me back home.

So she sang each day as a year passed. Now the ice broke again and Aja decided he would go and visit his daughter. In his swift boat he crossed the wide sea and came to the fulmar's country. He found his daughter, cold and hungry, in a small tent made only of fishskins. She greeted him with joy, begging him to take her back home. Just then, the fulmar returned from fishing. Aja was so angry that he struck the fulmar with his knife and killed him. Then he placed Sedna in his boat and began to paddle swiftly back across the sea.

Soon the other fulmars came back from fishing. They found the body of Sedna's husband and they began to cry. To this day you can still hear the fulmars mourning and crying as they fly over the sea. They decided to find the one who had killed their brother and they began to fly in great circles over the sea, searching him out.

Before long, they saw the boat of Aja. They saw Sedna was with him and knew that he was the one who was the murderer. Then, using their magical powers, the fulmars made a great

storm begin. The waves lifted high above the small boat and
Aja became very afraid. He had seen the birds and knew that
they were causing the storm to punish him for the death of
Sedna's husband.

'You fulmars,' he cried, 'look! I give you back this girl. Do not
kill me.' Then he pushed his daughter out of the boat. But
Sedna grasped the side of the boat.

'Let go,' Aja shouted at her. 'The fulmars will kill me if I do not give you to the sea.' But Sedna still held on to the side of the boat. Then, taking his sharp knife, Aja cut off the tips of her fingers. The ends of her fingers fell into the water and became the whales. Sedna still grasped the side of the boat and now her father cut off the middle joints of her fingers. Those, too, fell into the water and were transformed into seals.

The fulmars, who saw what Aja did, thought it certain that Sedna would drown. They were satisfied and flew away. As soon as they departed, the storm ended and Aja pulled his daughter back into the boat.

Now, though, Sedna hated her father. When they had reached shore and her father had gone to sleep in his tent, she called to her dogs, who would do whatever she said. 'Gnaw off the hands and feet of my father,' she said. And the dogs did as she said. When this happened, Aja cursed his daughter. The Earth opened beneath them and all of them fell deep down to the land of Adlivun, which is beneath the land and the sea.

To this day, that is where Sedna lives. Because the whales and the seals were made from her fingers, she can call them and tell them where to go. So it is that when the people wish to hunt, they have their *angakok*, the shaman, descend in his dream-trance to the land under the sea where Sedna lives.

He combs out Sedna's long, tangled hair, for without fingers she is unable to do it herself. Then he can ask her to send the whales and seals back to the places where the people can hunt them. Thanks to the blessings of Sedna, who is always generous to those who remember to ask her help in the right way, the people no longer go hungry.

ARCTIC REGIONS

How Raven Brought the Light

Crow, retold by Robert Scott

In the beginning there was no light on earth. The darkness was so thick you could almost feel it.

The animal people shivered in the dark and cold because Sea Gull owned all the light. He kept it locked up in a box in his tepee and would not share it with anyone. 'No,' said Sea Gull every time he was asked. 'It was given to me to look after and I'm not going to let you use it all up.'

So the animal people held a meeting to decide what to do.

'It can't go on like this,' said Crow. 'I've flown into things so many times I must be black all over. Now I walk everywhere.'

'That's no better,' said Grizzly Bear. 'I bump into things no matter how slowly and carefully I walk. And I can't see what I'm eating.'

'I don't think there *is* anything to eat,' said Rabbit. 'I don't think things grow any more.'

'And that's not the worst of it,' Fox said sadly. 'My family's waiting for me to come home but I can't find my way back.'

'What about Raven?' said Ground Squirrel suddenly. 'Sea Gull's his cousin so perhaps he can do something.'

'I'm here,' said Raven, who had been listening quietly. 'Sea Gull's my cousin all right, but he won't take any notice of me, either. I've tried to get him to open his box just a little bit, but he won't hear of it.'

The meeting went on for a long time, but no one could think what to do.

Then Raven cleared his throat and everyone was silent.

'I think,' he said, 'I think there may be a way of getting Sea Gull to open his box. Possibly.'

13

They all started talking at once, wanting to know what Raven's idea was.

'Well?' demanded Crow finally, but Raven didn't answer. He had slipped away in the dark.

Sea Gull lived near the sea, of course, and Raven had remembered that the last time he had visited his cousin he had got himself tangled in some thorn bushes that grew near Sea Gull's tepee. Now he flew back, very cautiously, and stripped a number of branches from the bushes and spread them out round the entrance to the tepee and down towards the beach where Sea Gull tied up his canoe. Then he started to shout.

'Hey! Hey, Sea Gull! Your canoe's come adrift. Your canoe's floating out to sea! Sea Gull! Wake up! You're losing your canoe!'

Sea Gull heard him. He knew the tide was going out so, without waiting to put on his moccasins, he dashed out and started down the trail towards his canoe.

'Ah! Aargh! Ow! Oooow! AAARGH!' He stopped in the middle of the thorns and shouted to Raven to save the canoe.

'All right,' Raven shouted back, but he didn't do anything because he knew Sea Gull's canoe was still safely tied up. Instead, he waited a while then made his way – carefully – to Sea Gull's tepee.

'What's the matter, cousin? Are you all right?'

Sea Gull told Raven to come in and started to complain about the thorns in his feet.

' . . . and if I find out who left them there —' he finished angrily.

'Must have been the wind.'

'Wind? What wind?'

'Wind last night. Didn't you hear it? Everyone's complaining about the damage. Anyway, let me have a look at your foot. Perhaps I can get them out.'

And Raven groped about until he caught hold of one of Sea Gull's feet.

'*Aaaaah!* Be careful, can't you!'

'Sorry. My, you do seem to have collected a lot. Never mind. I'll soon have them out.' Raven began to push and pull at the thorns in Sea Gull's foot.

'Oooo! *Aaaargh!*'

'It would be a lot easier if you would let a little daylight out of your box.'

'No! Certainly not! *Ouch! Ugh!* Wait a minute. *Aaaaah!* Stop, can't you? I'm opening it.'

And Sea Gull opened the lid of his box a tiny crack so that a little light slipped out. Raven promptly pulled out several thorns.

'That's better. Much better,' he said, and pushed the next thorn hard into Sea Gull's foot.

'*Eeeyoww!*'

'Oh, I'm sorry. You know, I could see much better if you would give me just a little more light.'

Sea Gull lifted the lid a little more. Raven pulled out more thorns. Then he pushed another one in.

'It's too difficult to see,' he said when Sea Gull had stopped shouting. 'I do need some more light.'

And Sea Gull opened the lid of his box a little more. Raven pulled out some more thorns.

'I've finished that foot,' he said at last, 'but I'm afraid the other one looks much worse.'

'It can't be!'

'I'm afraid it is.'

'I think I'll leave them in.'

'You know you can't do that. Just open your box a bit more. It'll be a lot easier for me to see and then it won't hurt so much.'

Sea Gull opened the lid even further so that the inside of his tepee seemed bathed in bright moonlight.

'That's *much* better,' said Raven, quickly pulling out all but one of the thorns.

'This last one's going to be hard to get at,' he said, pressing it in.

'*Oooo! Aaaah!*'

'I can't get hold of it properly. I'll need some more light for a few minutes.' And he pressed the thorn again.

'There! There!' shouted Sea Gull, opening the lid wide. 'Now get it out.'

And Raven pulled out the last thorn, but as he did so he knocked Sea Gull's box over and all the daylight spilled out and spread everywhere. Sea Gull rushed about trying to collect it all up again, but he was too late. He cried out in anger and frustration. He still flies about the edge of the sea calling for it to come back into his box.

That is how Raven brought daylight to the world.

NORTH AMERICA

How Beaver Stole the Fire

Sanpoil, retold by Robert Scott

In the beginning there was no fire on earth. The animal people shivered and ate their food raw.

'There is fire up in the sky,' Eagle said one day. 'Let's go up and get it.'

So all the animals had a big gathering to decide how they could steal the Sky People's fire. They came – Magpie, Crow, and Grizzly Bear; Coyote, Bat, and Chickadee; Dog and Frog and Beaver – from all over the country. They danced and sang, and then they talked.

'We'll have to fix a road to get up to the sky.'

Of course, they all had bows and arrows. 'Let's try to make a road of arrows and climb up that.' All the big animals tried first. They used up all their arrows, but they couldn't shoot them high enough to stick in the sky.

'Let me have a go,' said Chickadee. All the animals laughed.

'You!' they said. 'You're *much* too small.'

Chickadee stepped forward with his bow and arrows. He took careful aim and shot his first arrow. All the animal people watched. His arrow reached the sky and stuck there. He shot another arrow. It stuck fast in the first one. He shot a third arrow and it stuck in the second. He kept on shooting until he had used all his arrows and they reached almost back to the ground. He borrowed some more arrows to finish the road.

The animals climbed up Chickadee's arrow road to the sky. The last to go was Grizzly Bear.

'I must take some food with me,' he said to himself. 'There may not be any up there in the sky.'

So when Grizzly Bear started up the arrow road he had a big bag of food with him. He was so heavy that he broke the ladder and fell flat on his back. He had to stay behind.

When the other animal people reached the sky, they made Eagle their leader because he was the one who first thought of stealing the fire and bringing it back to earth. It was night time, so Eagle decided to send out spies to scout around.

First he sent Dog and Frog, but they were so lazy they stopped for a rest and fell asleep.

'We didn't see anything,' they said when they came back. 'Not a thing.'

Next Eagle sent Crow and Magpie, but they couldn't stop arguing with each other and soon had a big quarrel.

'We didn't see anything either,' they said, 'but there was a lot of noise going on.'

'This is no use,' said Eagle. 'We'll never get fire at this rate. I'll go myself and I'll take Beaver with me. Come on.'

'Me?' said Beaver.

'Yes,' said Eagle. 'You.'

'All right.'

They set out at once, Beaver swimming along a river while Eagle flew just over his head. They made their plans as they went. When they reached the Sky People's houses, Eagle flew to the top of a big tree. Beaver swam along until he found a trap. He went into it and played dead.

Early next morning one of the Sky People went down to see if he had caught anything in his trap.

'That's a very fine beaver,' he said as he removed Beaver from the trap. 'I could use a nice thick fur like that. I'll take him back and skin him right away.'

Eagle saw what was happening and flapped his wings to attract attention. One of the Sky People saw him.

'Look!' he said. 'Look at that eagle. There are some fine feathers there for a head-dress.' He went to his lodge to get his bow and arrows.

The man with Beaver took him up to the chief's house. That was where the fire was kept. Soon he had almost skinned Beaver and Beaver was afraid. He knew that once his skin was off completely he would never be able to get it back on again.

Outside the house Eagle was frightened, too. A lot of the Sky People were shooting at him now and some of their arrows were coming close. They were getting very excited.

'Come on, everybody!' they shouted. 'Come and shoot this eagle before it flies away.'

'I'll finish this first,' thought the man who was skinning Beaver, 'then I'll go.' But at that moment a big shout went up outside and the man ran out with his knife in his hand to see what was happening.

Beaver jumped up and pulled his skin back on again. He looked round for the fire, took some, and rushed out to the river. Everybody was looking at Eagle flapping about in the top of a cottonwood tree dodging the arrows. Eagle saw Beaver making for the river and flew off as soon as he seemed safe.

'Oh, it's going! It's going!' cried some of the Sky People as Eagle flapped away.

The man who had been skinning Beaver went back into the chief's lodge, then rushed out again.

'The beaver's gone, too,' he shouted. 'And that's not all. He's stolen some of our fire.'

Eagle and Beaver rushed back to the top of the arrow road where the rest of the animal people were gathered waiting for them.

'We've got it!' shouted Eagle. 'Let's get away before the Sky People come!'

'It's no use,' the animals told him. 'The ladder's broken, remember? Grizzly Bear and his bag of food were too heavy for it.'

'Well, birds can fly down,' said Eagle, 'and the small animals can ride on their backs. The rest of you go down the road as far as you can and jump or . . . or find some other way down.'

And so they did, though several of them got some rather nasty bruises.

When they reached earth, the animals had a big gathering.

'Who has the fire?' they asked. They all looked at Eagle.

'*I* don't have the fire,' sang Eagle, spreading his wings wide.

'*We* don't have the fire,' sang Frog and Dog.

'*We* don't have the fire,' sang Magpie and Crow.

They sang and danced and spread their hands wide. Beaver stepped forward. He, too, spread his hands out, wide open, and began to sing and dance.

'I've got what we went for! I've got what we went for!' he sang.

No one could see any fire. They looked between his toes and behind his ears. They looked under his arms and even in his mouth, but they couldn't find any fire.

Beaver began to dance again.

'I'm *holding* what we went for! I'm *holding* what we went for!' he sang.

At last his two daughters caught hold of his hands and found the fire hidden in his double fingernails.

Beaver stored the fire in the trees. It is still there. Fire is in every tree. Whenever we want fire we can get it from the wood where Beaver stored it.

NORTH AMERICA

The Oyster Brothers
and the Shark

Retold by A.W. Reed

The Oyster brothers sat on the beach watching Shark as he rushed backwards and forwards. It was a beautiful day with a cloudless sky and a soft, cool breeze blowing along the beach. They had full bellies and nothing to do but watch Shark chasing the stingrays. Presently he caught one and carried it to the beach, where he left it on the sand and went back to hunt for more.

'It would make a good meal for us when we feel hungry again,' one of the Oyster brothers remarked.

'Yes, much better to eat when someone else has caught it! Let's hide it.'

They carried the stingray to their camp in the scrub on the edge of the beach and covered it with branches and wisps of dried grass.

Shark had no more luck after his one catch. The stingrays had decided that the stretch of open water was no place for them when Shark was on the prowl, and had gone to a bay where they could hide among the rocks.

Shark waded out of the water and looked everywhere for his stingray. He noticed the Oyster brothers who were sitting innocently on the sand. He strode up to them.

'Where is my stingray?' he demanded.

'What stingray?'

'You know very well. I left it here a while ago, and you are the only people on the beach.'

The elder Oyster held out his hands as if to show that they were empty.

'We have been here all day and we haven't seen any stingrays.

21

They don't go walking about on the beach for our benefit, you know.'

Shark made an angry noise and stalked away. As he was leaving he turned and said threateningly, 'If it was you who took it, you will be sorry.'

After giving him plenty of time to get away, elder Oyster stood up and said to his brother, 'Do you feel like a nice feed of stingray?'

'Yes, that would be good, but where can we find one?'

'Who knows?' elder brother chuckled. 'Maybe the good spirits have left one in our camp. Let's go and see.'

'There you are!' big brother Oyster said as he pulled it out from under the leaves and grass. 'It's a pity Shark isn't here. He could have shared it with us.'

Some time later he wiped his mouth and patted his stomach.

'But perhaps it's just as well,' he remarked. 'There was only enough for us.'

They lay down by the fire to sleep; and then it was morning, and Shark was kicking them.

'You have been eating stingray,' he shouted. 'I knew you had stolen mine.'

'How can you be sure?' the elder Oyster asked. 'Ouch! Stop it! That hurt. How do you know it was your stingray? We are able to go fishing just as well as you are.'

Shark towered over him.

'Oysters are too lazy to go fishing for themselves. I know you are the thieves.'

He belaboured young brother Oyster with his spear, and when elder brother Oyster tried to protect him he pushed him aside. He drew back his spear ready to hurl it at him. Oyster struck it aside with his woomera and leaped on to Shark, who grappled with him at once. They fell to the ground, rolling over the ashes of the dead fire. Shark managed to struggle to his feet. He buried his hands in the ashes, smearing them over Oyster's body until he was covered with the white powder. Stung to retaliation, Oyster dug out some hot sand and threw it into Shark's eyes, until he begged for mercy.

The Oyster brothers stood back, but Shark was not finished

with them. Swinging his waddy round his head, he brought it down twice, flattening the bodies of the Oysters. The younger one was so furious with pain that he chased Shark down the beach and into the water, where he flung his boomerang at him. It stuck into his back, projecting above the water as Shark swam out to sea.

None of them forgot that day. Shark's eyes have been small ever since because of the hot sand that was thrown into them, and Oyster's boomerang is still in his back. As for the Oysters, they were so small and flat after their beating, and covered with white ashes, that they crept round to the hiding place of the stingrays and sank down into the water, where they attached themselves to the rocks and waited for someone to come and eat them. And someone always does!

ABORIGINAL AND TORRES STRAIT ISLANDER PEOPLE

The Wren,
the King of
the Birds

Gaelic, retold by Eileen O'Faolain

All the birds of the air came together one time to see which of them could fly furthest up in the air. And as they all gathered together on one hill the little wren was so small that not one of them noticed him, and he was able to hide himself in between two downy feathers in the eagle's back. Then they all rose in the air and went up and up, to see who would fly the highest, and they spent five nights and five days rising straight up into the sky. Only a few of the birds lasted that long, but the eagle was one of them. Then at last when he had gone up as far as he was able to go he said that he had won, for he was the highest. He called out three times that he was the highest up in the sky, and then he began to come down.

When the wren saw that the eagle was not able to go any higher he flew out of his hiding place among the eagle's feathers, and he rose three or four feet up over him.

'You have not won,' said the wren.

'Where were you?' asked the eagle. 'I never saw a bit of you coming up.'

'I was very close to you,' said the wren, 'but I was unseen by you.'

'You have won the day!' said the eagle. 'You are the King of the Birds.'

The wren has been king ever since.

IRELAND

Why the Bat
Flies at Night

Modoc, retold by Robert Scott

In the war between the birds and the beasts, Bat was on the birds' side. 'After all,' he said to himself, 'I've got wings and I can fly so this is the right side for me.'

But in the first battle the birds were badly beaten. As soon as Bat saw that they were losing, he crept away and hid under a log. He stayed there until all the fighting had finished. When the beasts were going back home to celebrate, he slipped out and joined them.

'How is this?' said one of them, looking at Bat very hard. 'You are one of those who fought against us. What are you doing here?'

'Me?' said Bat. 'Oh, no! I am one of you. I don't belong to the bird people. Just look in my mouth. Have you ever seen a bird with teeth like mine? No, I'm one of you people. My teeth are like yours.'

Nothing more was said. Bat stayed with the beasts.

Soon after there was another battle and this time the birds won. When Bat saw that the beasts were getting beaten, he crept away and hid under a log again. When the birds were going home after the battle, Bat slipped in among them.

'What are you doing here?' they said when they saw him. 'You are one of the enemy. We saw you fighting on the other side.'

'Who, me?' said Bat. 'Oh no! I am one of you. I don't belong to the beast people. Just look at me. Have you ever seen a beast with wings like mine? No, I'm one of you people. I'm like you.'

Nothing more was said. Bat stayed with the birds.

And so it went on for as long as the war lasted. Bat joined the winning side at the end of each battle.

But when the war itself was over, the birds and the beasts held a council. One of the things they had to decide was whether Bat belonged to the birds or the beasts.

'Very well,' the chiefs said when all who wished to had spoken. 'Bat has wings and is a bird. Bat has teeth and is a beast. From now on, Bat will fly like the birds but he will do so only at night when beasts are hunting. He will be alone. He will never have any friends, among those who fly or those who walk.'

And so it has been ever since.

NORTH AMERICA

Why Bear has a Stumpy Tail

Norse, retold by Robert Scott

In the beginning, and for a long time after the beginning, Bear had a magnificent tail. Bear had been at the back of the queue when ears were being handed out, so he got only small, stubby ears (though he could hear very well with them). He was so tired with queueing all day that he fell asleep as soon as he had been given his ears. When he woke up, he found that he was at the front of the queue for tails.

Bear chose the best tail there was. It was long and thick and wavy. He could use it to fan himself when he was hot and to keep off flies when they tried to torment him. He could wave it, or lash it, or wag it. He even thought he might, possibly, be able to hold things with it if he tried hard enough.

Fox was very jealous. He was always up early and near the front of the queue when anything useful was being given out. He had been very near the front for ears, of course, and he had hoped to have the choice of tails. As it was, he got a very fine tail – but it was nowhere near as wonderful as Bear's.

One day, in the very depths of the hardest of hard winters, when snow drifted deep in the fields and frost cracked among the treetops, Bear was searching for grubs under a rotten log and thinking it might be a good idea to sleep all winter and eat all summer when Fox suddenly appeared. He was carrying a string of stolen fish in his jaws.

'Where on earth did you get those?' Bear demanded. He loved fish but found it difficult to catch them.

Fox came to a sudden halt, then began to back slowly. He hadn't seen Bear behind the log and now there was a good chance that he would lose his fish.

'Well?' said Bear, moving closer.

'Shlishnig.'

'What?'

'Shlishnig.'

'Put them down and tell me properly,' Bear said.

Fox dropped the fish and placed a paw firmly and possess-ively on top of them.

'Fishing,' he said. 'I caught them. Honest.'

'I wish I could catch fish like that,' said Bear, looking longingly at them. 'I don't suppose —'

'But of course I'll tell you how to do it,' Fox interrupted. 'With a tail like yours you'll catch loads and loads of fish.'

'Tail?' said Bear suspiciously. 'What's my tail got to do with it?'

'Well, I caught all these in a couple of hours and my tail's not nearly as big and bushy as yours. Of course, it smarted a bit and got very cold, but there you are. The longer you stick it, the more you catch. Well, I'll leave you to it, then. See that — Now what's the matter?'

Bear was suddenly very close. He put his face even closer.

'You have not,' he said, 'even *begun* to explain yourself.'

'I haven't?' said Fox. 'Oh, I'm sorry. I thought I had. What didn't you understand?'

'All of it,' said Bear. 'And especially the bits you missed out.'

'Oh. Right. Well, first of all you go down to the river. All right?'

'All right.'

'Or lake.'

'Or lake.'

'Or sea.'

'Or sea.'

'Or —' but Fox caught the look in Bear's eye and decided that it would be wiser to get on with it. 'Or anywhere where there's water with fish in and then, *then*, you cut a hole in it.'

'In the water?'

'In the *ice*! It's winter, remember? You cut a hole in the ice and lower your tail through and wave it about a bit to attract attention. Then you just wait. For as long as you can. Of course, as I said, it stings and smarts a bit, but that's just the fish biting. The longer you wait, the more fish you get. I caught all these in just two hours. Someone with your patience and with a tail like yours – why, I shouldn't be surprised if you couldn't stay out all night and break the record.'

'It sounds easy enough,' said Bear. 'What's the catch?'

'Enough fish to last you for weeks,' said Fox, 'but there is just one thing.'

'Oh?' said Bear suspiciously. 'What's that?'

'Well, there's no point in taking your tail out slowly. If you do, the fish will just drop off. When you've finished you have to give the strongest jerk you can. Pretend you're trying to jump over the moon. Then all the fish come straight out on to the ice and all you have to do is collect them up.'

'Right!' said Bear firmly. 'You just drop by tomorrow and see what I'll have to show you.' And with that he hurried off down the hill to the nearest river.

Fox watched him for a moment, then picked up his fish and trotted off home.

Bear did exactly as he had been told. For the rest of that day and much of the night he sat with his tail dangling through the ice. He sat for so long that it was completely frozen in. Then he gathered his feet beneath him, set his eye firmly on the moon now sinking palely behind the trees, and gave the biggest, strongest leap he had ever made. And his tail snapped off.

Bear rushed home howling to wait for Fox to show up, but he never did.

That is why, today, all bears have short, stumpy tails (and why foxes keep away from them).

NORWAY

The Old Woman's Animals

Angami Naga, retold by John Mercer

There was a time when all the animals were wild, looking after themselves in the forests, around the lakes and up in the mountains. The people hunted the animals if they wanted meat, furs, and skins and, because the animals would not live with them, they had to do without milk and had to carry their loads on their backs.

The old woman who changed all this lived alone but for a daughter. One evening, on the way back from the rice-fields, the old woman felt a pair of hands over her eyes.

It was Zize, a spirit. 'I'll let you go if you'll give me your daughter as a wife,' he said.

The old woman promised and the next day the spirit carried off the girl as she walked some way behind her friends on their way back home from the rice-fields.

A year went by and then the girl came back to see her mother. After a few days, she said to the old woman, 'Please come back with me now, to spend a little while at my new home.'

So the mother and daughter set off to the spirit's house. The old woman took care to mark the way with a trail of rice husks.

When they were almost there, the girl said, 'One important thing; as a gift when you leave, ask for the little basket which hangs in the centre room of our house, to the right as you go in.'

The mother's stay passed quietly. But, when she was about to leave and asked for the basket, Zize tried very hard not to give it to her.

In the end, he said, 'Very well, you can have it, but on three conditions. You mustn't open it on the way home and, when

31

you get there, you must build a fence round the basket before
you do open it, and then, for five days, you must take special
care of what's inside it.'

The old woman said goodbye to her daughter and to Zize.
Following the trail of rice-husks, she walked along with the
little basket under her arm.

'I wonder what's inside it . . .' she said to herself every few
steps.

Her curiosity won. She put down the basket and undid the
string fastening down its lid. As she was about to lift this she
heard growlings, twitterings, and squeakings coming from
inside. She tried to do up the lid again but it was too late – it
was flung back and out poured bears, birds, mice, monkeys . . .
in an endless stream they ran and flew and scampered away
into the forest!

'Oh, dear, look what I've done now!' cried the old woman.
Then with great determination, she threw herself on the basket
and managed to close the lid, though she was not quick enough
to stop a snake slipping out. 'I think there are still a few animals
left inside,' she said to herself. 'I heard a mooing and a grunting
and a barking just before I closed the lid.' She sat on the basket
for a while, to get her breath back.

That night she reached home. The next morning she asked her friends to help her build a fence right around her house. Then she opened the basket . . . and out poured cows and buffaloes and pigs and chickens and several sorts of dogs, all mooing and snorting and squawking and barking at being out in the open again. They tried to run off – since they were still wild animals – but the fence stopped them.

The old woman and her friends cut and collected up food for the animals, took them water and made them shelters. After five days, all the different animals had settled down in their new home.

A year later the old woman's daughter, this time with Zize the spirit, came on another visit. The little house and the ground around it were full of animals.

These are the animals which today live with man. The Nagas say that, if the old woman had not opened the basket while she was coming home, all the animals which are still wild would also be tamed too.

ASSAM

The Sleep Test

Luba, retold by Robert Scott

Kalumba the Creator had given Dog and Goat a job to do and now they were quarrelling about it.

'It doesn't take both of us,' Dog said. 'I'm quite able to do it on my own.'

'If you do it on your own you'll just go chasing off into the forest every time you think you hear something. Then we'll miss them.'

'Of course I won't,' said Dog. 'This is much too important. In any case, you won't be much good. You'll just start eating and wander off, so you might as well stay behind in the first place.'

'I'm not leaving you alone and that's the end of it,' said Goat. 'We'll do it together, as Kalumba said, or you can go back and tell him you're not going to do it.'

'Kalumba gave us the job to do, but he didn't say we had to do it together. He left us to decide how we would do it. Anyway, if you're here they'll know we're waiting for them and go a different route.'

'What's that!' said Goat, who was very sensitive about his smell. 'What do you mean?'

Dog sniffed, and said nothing.

'You'd fall asleep. You're always falling asleep.'

'Don't talk nonsense!' Dog shouted. 'I only go to sleep when there's nothing else to do.'

'You'd fall asleep,' Goat repeated with conviction.

'Rubbish!'

Goat rubbed himself against a tree and looked up the track, chewing quietly.

'Right!' said Dog. 'Here's what we'll do. We'll take turns and

34

change over every morning, then we'll see who falls asleep.'

'All right,' said Goat.

'And I'll take the first turn. That'll show you.'

'If you like,' Goat said. He was feeling rather hungry and was not at all happy with Dog's company. Besides, if he was going to stay awake all night it would be an idea to have a good sleep first. Certainly Dog could have the first turn.

After Goat had left, Dog built up a big fire and sat down by the track.

First Kalumba the Creator had made all the animals. Now he had made the people. He knew that Life and Death would be coming in search of the people he had made so he had told Goat and Dog to guard the track. They were to let Life pass but keep Death away.

Dog was proud of the responsibility he had been given and was determined to show that he could guard Kalumba's people from Death. And as for Goat . . . well, he'd soon learn.

Dog put some more sticks on his fire and watched the track. He was nice and warm. He stretched out and yawned. He put his nose down, and fell asleep.

In the night Death went past.

When Goat appeared next morning, Dog pretended that he had stayed awake all the time. No one, he said, had been along.

Goat kept watch. He stayed awake. When Life came along, Goat caught him.

'You've caught the wrong one!' shouted Dog when he came the next day. They decided to return and ask Kalumba what they should do but when they got back they found that Death was already there.

That is how Death came to the people. If only Dog could have sat by a fire without falling asleep, things would have been different for Kalumba's people.

ZAIRE

2
Tales of
the Early World

The Monkey
and the Crocodile

Retold by Ellen C. Babbitt

A monkey lived in a great tree on a riverbank. In the river there were many crocodiles.

A crocodile watched the monkeys for a long time, and one day she said to her son, 'My son, get one of those monkeys for me. I want the heart of a monkey to eat.'

'How am I to catch a monkey?' asked the little crocodile. 'I do not travel on land, and the monkey does not go into the water.'

'Put your wits to work, and you'll find a way,' said the mother.

And the little crocodile thought and thought.

At last he said to himself, 'I know what I'll do. I'll get that monkey that lives in a big tree on the riverbank. He wishes to go across the river to the island where the fruit is so ripe.'

So the crocodile swam to the tree where the monkey lived. But he was a stupid crocodile.

'Oh, monkey,' he called, 'come with me over to the island where the fruit is so ripe.'

'How can I go with you?' asked the monkey. 'I do not swim.'

'No – but I do. I will take you over on my back,' said the crocodile.

The monkey was greedy, and wanted the ripe fruit, so he jumped down on the crocodile's back.

'Off we go!' said the crocodile.

'This is a fine ride you are giving me!' said the monkey.

'Do you think so? Well, how do you like this?' asked the crocodile, diving.

'Oh, don't!' cried the monkey, as he went under the water. He was afraid to let go, and he did not know what to do under the water.

When the crocodile came up, the monkey sputtered and choked. 'Why did you take me under water, crocodile?' he asked.

'I am going to kill you by keeping you under water,' answered the crocodile. 'My mother wants monkey heart to eat, and I'm going to take yours to her.'

'I wish you had told me you wanted my heart,' said the monkey, 'then I might have brought it with me.'

'How queer!' said the stupid crocodile. 'Do you mean to say that you left your heart back there in the tree?'

'That is what I mean,' said the monkey. 'If you want my heart, we must go back to the tree and get it. But we are so near the island where the ripe fruit is, please take me there first.'

'No, monkey,' said the crocodile, 'I'll take you straight back to your tree. Never mind the ripe fruit. Get your heart and bring it to me at once. Then we'll see about going to the island.'

'Very well,' said the monkey.

But no sooner had he jumped on to the bank of the river than – whisk! he ran into the tree.

From the topmost branches he called down to the crocodile in the water below:

'My heart is way up here! If you want it, come for it, come for it!'

INDIA

Rabbit and
King Lion

Retold by Robert Scott

King Lion ruled the forest and all the other animals lived in fear. Each day he hunted for food and each day the animals fled before him. Finally he called a meeting.

'You run in terror,' he said, 'because I need to eat and you don't want to be my next meal. Yet I kill only one animal a day. It's a bad arrangement and I want to make some changes, so listen to me. I must eat, and that means I must eat you, but there is no need for all of you to run from me whenever I'm about. If one of you comes to me each morning, I won't need to hunt and the rest of you can then go freely about the forest. You decide.'

He put his head on his paws and closed his eyes. The animals went off to talk about King Lion's proposal. They weren't quite as happy with it as Lion himself was, but they recognized that it had its advantages – though not, as Monkey pointed out, for the animal who was going to provide the next breakfast. In the end they agreed to draw lots each evening. The one who lost would present himself to Lion early the following day.

At first all went well. Each morning, one animal crept up to the Lion's den to be eaten and the rest then went about their business without fear of being attacked.

One evening, the lot fell on Rabbit.

'No,' he said.

'You didn't make any objections before,' the others pointed out.

'I'm not going to do it.'

'Everyone else has stuck to the bargain, even King Lion, so why can't you?'

'No.'

'If you don't,' said Monkey, 'Lion will start his hunting again and none of us would like that. Least of all you,' he added.

'I have an idea,' said Rabbit.

'Fine. Just as long as it doesn't stop you from going to Lion's den early tomorrow morning.'

Rabbit's idea didn't come to him until much later but when it did he felt rather better. It might work.

Lion was growling and pacing angrily up and down when Rabbit arrived at his den late the following morning.

'Are you my breakfast?' he snarled.

'Yes, sir, I'm sorry but —'

'You're late.'

'Yes, sir, I know but —'

'Very late.'

'Yes, sir, but —'

'I like an early breakfast.'

Rabbit was silent.

'Well?' snarled Lion, licking his lips. 'You don't expect me to come over there and catch you, do you?'

Rabbit didn't move.

Lion growled again and took a step towards him.

'I don't think the new King would like it if you were to eat me,' said Rabbit quickly.

Lion was suddenly very still.

'Would you mind repeating that?'

'No, sir. I don't think the new King would like it if you were to eat me.'

'That's what I thought you said.'

'Yes, sir. He wants to eat me himself.'

Lion roared and stalked menacingly towards Rabbit. 'I think you'd better explain yourself,' he snarled.

'Yes, sir. It's not my fault, sir. You see, I was coming here ever so early when I was stopped by this other lion and he said he was going to eat me for breakfast and I said he couldn't do that because I was going to be eaten by you, sir, and he became very angry and said he was the King of the Forest and would eat anyone he pleased and I said *you* were King and he must let me pass because you liked your breakfast early and he became even angrier and roared at me and then he said, "Go and tell that miserable little usurper —" sorry, sir — "Go and tell that miserable little usurper that *I* am the true King of the Forest and if he —" that's you, sir — "if he doesn't make himself scarce I'll come and have *him* for breakfast." Sir.'

Lion roared with fury.

'Take me to him!' he cried. 'Take me to him! We'll soon see who's King of the Forest.'

'Yes, sir. He's very big, sir.'

Lion growled again and thought how much he was going to enjoy his breakfast once he had seen to the intruder.

Rabbit led King Lion through as many thickets and as much undergrowth as he could find then, after a long and tiring trek, signalled to him to stop.

'His den's just over there, sir,' he said, pointing to a deep well he had discovered some days before. King Lion snarled savagely and pushed his way forward. He looked over the edge and saw a savage, snarling face glaring up at him. With an angry roar he leapt at his reflection. The battle was short.

Rabbit went back to the other animals and explained that they wouldn't have to draw lots any more.

BURMA

The Big Drought

Retold by Robert Scott

Once there was a big drought over the land. The only water left was in a small pool where the antelopes came to drink. When the leader of the elephants found the pool he drove the antelopes away so that the elephants could have it to themselves.

This can't go on, thought the oldest and wisest of the antelopes. Soon the water will have gone and we shall all die.

So he climbed a hill by the side of the trail and waited for the leader of the elephants to pass.

'O Great King of the Elephants!' he cried as the elephant came into sight. 'I come to you with a message from the Monarch of the Moon.'

'What's that?' cried the elephant. 'Who are you? What do you want?'

'I am the Moon Monarch's special messenger,' intoned the antelope, making sure he was well-hidden, 'and I come to you by his command. You have driven his guardians from his Sacred Pool and he is very angry. Tonight he will descend and punish you.'

'Oh,' said the elephant. 'I'm very sorry. I didn't know. We won't go near the pool again.'

'Repentance comes too late,' said the antelope. 'But if you would escape the Moon Monarch's wrath, if you and your wretched followers would live in peace, you must come alone to the Sacred Pool tonight and seek his forgiveness there.'

That night, the fearful elephant came to the pool. The special messenger ordered him to kneel before the Moon Monarch's reflection.

44

'If you would save your life, beg for it,' he demanded.

'Great King —'

'Mighty Monarch!' interrupted the messenger.

'O Mighty Monarch,' said the elephant in a tiny voice, 'I am very sorry. My offence is great, I know, but I didn't know. That is, I didn't know it was your pool and that those animals were guarding it for you. Grant forgiveness, Great Ki— Mighty Monarch, and I will take my people far away.'

At that moment clouds covered the moon.

'It is a sign,' said the special messenger quickly. 'Go now, before my master changes his mind.'

'And don't come back!' he shouted after the elephant's disappearing tail.

After that the antelopes had the pool to themselves.

INDIA

The Deceitful Heron

Retold by Eleanor Brockett

Once upon a time there was a crafty Heron who lived beside a lake. He used to sit in a tree and watch the fish, thinking how he might catch and eat them one by one without the rest getting suspicious and swimming away.

And as he sat there one day pondering on this wicked plan, a little fish swam up to him and said:

'Good day to you, friend Heron! Why are you looking so serious?'

'I am looking serious,' said the wily Heron, 'because I have a serious matter on my mind.'

'Tell me what it is,' said the little fish kindly. 'Perhaps I can help you to feel more cheerful.'

'There can be no question of that,' said the Heron sadly. 'It is the fate of you and your brothers that is weighing heavily with me.'

'Really?' said the little fish as if he could hardly believe this was true.

'Yes, indeed,' said the Heron weightily. 'Do you know that this lake is going to dry up this summer? It makes me sad when I think of you all high and dry here, with no water!'

'Oh, I don't believe it,' said the little fish. 'This lake has never dried up before.'

'Maybe not,' said the Heron, 'but I have it on the best authority that it's going to dry up this year.'

There was silence for a while. Then the Heron looked hard at the little fish and said:

'I know where there is a beautiful lake that never dries up. You really should come and see it some time.'

'How can I get there?' asked the little fish.

'I could carry you there,' suggested the Heron.

'Oh, but I wouldn't want to go and leave all my family behind here,' said the little fish.

'There's no question of that,' replied the Heron. 'I could take you there just to see it and bring you back again. You could then report to your family and, if you liked it, I could take you all there, one by one, before the summer.'

'That's a splendid idea,' cried the little fish. 'I'll come with you straight away.'

The Heron picked up the little fish and flew with it to another lake near by. This really was a beautiful lake, large and deep, and with many kinds of waterlilies growing upon it.

'See what a lovely lake this is!' said the Heron, putting the fish down for a while.

'Oh yes!' exclaimed the fish excitedly. 'The others will love this. Do bring us all here, friend Heron!'

And the Heron, crafty bird that he was, picked up the fish, carried him back to his family, and awaited events.

The little fish described this other lake in glowing terms and then returned to the Heron to tell him that all the fish were simply longing to move to the other lake, and would the Heron please begin taking them as soon as possible.

This was exactly what that wicked Heron wanted. One by one the fishes were taken from their own lake and flown away in the Heron's mouth. But did the Heron really deliver them to the other lovely lake with the waterlilies? No! He took them to a tree and ate them. And at the foot of the tree there collected a pathetic pile of fish-bones.

The crafty Heron went on doing this until there was not a fish left in the lake. This brought his activities to a halt for a time, but as he was always hungry, he began to think about the possibility of eating the Crab.

'Friend Crab,' he said one day as he stood by the water wondering what he should do next. 'I feel so sorry for you.'

'Sorry for me? Why?' enquired the Crab, who was an independent sort of creature.

'You must be so lonely here now that all the fishes have

gone,' said the Heron. 'Wouldn't you like to be with them in the lovely lake they have gone to?'

'That would be very pleasant,' said the Crab, 'but how do I get there?'

'I will take you, willingly,' said the Heron in his most friendly manner.

'Thank you,' said the Crab rather thoughtfully, 'but I am large and I am slippery, and I don't think you could carry me in your beak as you carried the fishes. I think it would be better if I hung on round your neck.'

The Heron agreed that this might be a sensible idea and so the two set forth.

When the Heron reached his favourite tree with the pile of fish-bones beneath it, he stopped and lighted on a low branch.

'Why are we stopping here?' asked the Crab.

'Because I am going to eat you here,' said the Heron, 'as I ate the fishes. Look down and you will see the bones of the stupid creatures.'

'You are certainly not going to eat me here,' said the Crab. 'You are going to take me to the lake,' and with these words the Crab tightened his grip on the Heron's neck.

'Let go of my neck!' cried the Heron. 'You are choking me.'

'Take me to the lake,' said the Crab firmly, and the Heron did as he was told.

He landed by the water's edge, the claws of the Crab still gripping tightly round his neck.

'Now, please let go,' choked the Heron.

'No!' said the Crab and he dug his strong claws in more tightly still, tighter and tighter until snap! the Heron's head was severed from its body.

So did the Crab avenge the death of these poor fish who had trusted the treacherous Heron and been eaten by him. Then he crawled off into the water.

And to this day Burmese children say a little rhyme about a crafty Heron who deceived the fishes, and a clever Crab who snapped off the wicked Heron's head.

BURMA

Anancy and Commonsense

Retold by Robert Scott

One time Anancy thought to himself, If I can collect up all the commonsense in the world and keep it for myself, I will be really powerful. Then everybody will have to come to me with their worries because I will be the only one with any sense. And I will charge them plenty of money.

Anancy started collecting up and collecting up all the commonsense he could find. He stored it in a big calabash. The time came when he searched and searched and could find no more commonsense, so he grinned to himself and sealed up his calabash. He decided to hide it high at the top of a tall tree where nobody else could reach it.

Anancy tied a rope round the neck of the calabash and looped it round his own neck so that it hung in front of him. Then he started to climb the tree. But he couldn't do it. The calabash got in the way every time. He tried and tried, but he could not climb the tree with the calabash in front of him.

Someone burst out laughing and Anancy looked round.

'You're stupid, man!' cried a little boy who had been watching him. 'Haven't you got any sense? If you want to climb the tree, why don't you hang your calabash over your back?'

Well, that was it. Anancy thought he had gathered up all the commonsense yet here was a big bit of commonsense coming from a little boy who happened to be standing by. He was so angry, he took his calabash and smashed it against the tree. All the commonsense he had collected scattered all over the world. Everybody's got a little bit of it somewhere.

Anancy did it.

JAMAICA

50

The Hyena and the Dead Ass

Retold by René Guillot

The hyena once had the luck to come upon a dead ass. There was enough meat for three whole days. He was busy enjoying his meal when suddenly he saw his children coming. He knew their healthy young teeth and growing appetites, and as he did not want to share the magnificent carcass with them, he said: 'You see that village over there? If you're quick you'll find plenty of asses there, just like this one. Only run.'

The hyena's children rushed towards the village, shouting the news at the tops of their voices. As the tale travelled to all corners of the bush, starving animals crept out – jackals, civet-cats, tiger-cats, all the smaller wild animals – and ran towards the village where the feast of asses' meat was to be found.

The whole morning the hyena watched them go by, singly or in flocks, until in the end he began to be worried.

Well, he said to himself, it looks as if it must be true. That village must be full of dead asses. And leaving the carcass he had had all to himself, he started off to join a band of other animals who were running towards the village.

WEST AFRICA

51

Brer Rabbit and the Tar Baby

Black American, retold by Julius Lester

Early one morning, even before Sister Moon had put on her negligee, Brer Fox was up and moving around. He had a glint in his eye, so you know he was up to no good.

He mixed up a big batch of tar and made it into the shape of a baby. By the time he finished, Brer Sun was yawning himself awake and peeping one eye over the topside of the earth.

Brer Fox took his Tar Baby down to the road, the very road Brer Rabbit walked along every morning. He sat the Tar Baby in the road, put a hat on it, and then hid in a ditch.

He had scarcely gotten comfortable (as comfortable as one can get in a ditch), before Brer Rabbit came strutting along like he owned the world and was collecting rent from everybody in it.

Seeing the Tar Baby, Brer Rabbit tipped his hat. 'Good morning! Nice day, ain't it? Of course, any day I wake up and find I'm still alive is a nice day as far as I'm concerned.' He laughed at his joke, which he thought was pretty good. (Ain't too bad if I say so myself.)

Tar Baby don't say a word. Brer Fox stuck his head up out of the ditch, grinning.

'You deaf?' Brer Rabbit asked the Tar Baby. 'If you are, I can talk louder.' He yelled, '*How you this morning? Nice day, ain't it?*'

Tar Baby still don't say nothing.

Brer Rabbit was getting kinna annoyed. 'I don't know what's wrong with this young generation. Didn't your parents teach you no manners?'

Tar Baby don't say nothing.

'Well, I reckon I'll teach you some!' He hauls off and hits the

Tar Baby. BIP! And his fist was stuck to the side of the Tar Baby's face.

'You let me go!' Brer Rabbit yelled. 'Let me go or I'll really pop you one.' He twisted and turned, but he couldn't get loose. 'All right! I warned you!' And he smacked the Tar Baby on the other side of its head. BIP! His other fist was stuck.

Brer Rabbit was sho' nuf' mad now. 'You turn me loose or I'll make you wish you'd never been born.' THUNK! He kicked the Tar Baby and his foot was caught. He was cussing and carrying on something terrible and kicked the Tar Baby with the other foot and THUNK! That foot was caught. 'You let me go or I'll butt you with my head.' He butted the Tar Baby under the chin and THUNK! His head was stuck.

Brer Fox sauntered out of the ditch just as cool as the sweat on the side of a glass of ice tea. He looked at Brer Rabbit stuck to the Tar Baby and laughed until he was almost sick.

'Well, I got you now,' Brer Fox said when he was able to catch his breath. 'You floppy-eared, pom-pom-tailed good-for-nothing! I guess you know who's having rabbit for dinner this night!'

Brer Rabbit would've turned around and looked at him if he could've unstuck his head. Didn't matter. He heard the drool in Brer Fox's voice and knew he was in a world of trouble.

'You ain't gon' be going around through the community raising commotion any more, Brer Rabbit. And it's your own fault too. Didn't nobody tell you to be so friendly with the Tar Baby. You stuck yourself on that Tar Baby without so much as an invitation. There you are and there you'll be until I get my fire started and my barbecue sauce ready.'

Brer Rabbit always got enough lip for anybody and everybody. He even told God once what He'd done wrong on the third day of Creation. This time, though, Brer Rabbit talked mighty humble. 'Well, Brer Fox. No doubt about it. You got me and no point my saying that I would improve my ways if you spared me.'

'No point at all,' Brer Fox agreed as he started gathering kindling for the fire.

'I guess I'm going to be barbecue this day,' Brer Rabbit

sighed. 'But getting barbecued is a whole lot better than getting thrown in the briar patch.' He sighed again. 'No doubt about it. Getting barbecued is almost a blessing compared to being thrown in that briar patch on the other side of the road. If you got to go, go in a barbecue sauce. That's what I always say. How much lemon juice and brown sugar you put in yours?'

When Brer Fox heard this, he had to do some more thinking, because he wanted the worst death possible for that rabbit. 'Now that I thinks on it, it's too hot to be standing over a hot fire. I think I'll hang you.'

Brer Rabbit shuddered. 'Hanging is a terrible way to die! Just terrible! But I thank you for being so considerate. Hanging is better than being thrown in the briar patch.'

Brer Fox thought that over a minute. 'Come to think of it, I can't hang you, 'cause I didn't bring my rope. I'll drown you in the creek over yonder.'

Brer Rabbit sniffed like he was about to cry. 'No, no, Brer Fox. You know I can't stand water, but I guess drowning, awful as it is, is better than the briar patch.'

'I got it!' Brer Fox exclaimed. 'I don't feel like dragging you all the way down to the creek. I got my knife right here. I'm going to skin you!' He pulled out his knife.

Brer Rabbit's ears shivered. 'That's all right, Brer Fox. It'll

hurt something awful, but go ahead and skin me. Scratch out my eyeballs! Tear out my ears by the roots! Cut off my legs! Do what'nsoever you want to with me, Brer Fox, but please, please, please! don't throw me in that briar patch!'

Brer Fox was convinced now that the worst thing he could do to Brer Rabbit was the very thing Brer Rabbit didn't want him to do. He snatched him off the Tar Baby and wound up his arm like he was trying to throw a fastball past Hank Aaron and chunked that rabbit across the road and smack dab in the middle of the briar patch.

Brer Fox waited. Didn't hear a thing. He waited a little longer. Still no sound. And just about the time he decided he was rid of Brer Rabbit, just about the time a big grin started to spread across his face, he heard a little giggle.

'Tee-hee! Tee-hee!' And the giggles broke into the loudest laughing you've ever heard.

Brer Fox looked up to see Brer Rabbit sitting on top of the hill on the other side of the briar patch.

Brer Rabbit waved. 'I was born and raised in the briar patch, Brer Fox! Born and raised in the briar patch!' And he hopped on over the hill and out of sight.

USA

55

Bear says 'North'

Retold by Robert Scott

Bear had been hunting. Moreover, he had been successful and now had a big, fat grouse in his mouth. He was very pleased with his success and wanted everyone in the forest to know of it so he lumbered up and down the tracks with the grouse flapping its wings in his face.

'Won't they be surprised when they see me,' he thought. 'Won't they just! This'll show them I don't eat berries all the time. I can hunt as well as the best of them.'

Then Fox appeared round a bend. He had not had a good day's hunting so he pretended not to notice Bear or the big, fat grouse flapping in his mouth.

'Unph! Unph!' grunted Bear.

Fox pricked up his ears and looked behind him.

'UNPH!'

'Ah,' said Fox, seeming to notice Bear for the first time. 'I thought I heard someone. Chilly today, isn't it?'

'Unph.'

'Wind seems to have changed all of a sudden. Which way do you think it's blowing now?'

'Unph!' He couldn't answer without opening his mouth and Fox still seemed not to have seen the grouse he had caught.

'South, you say. Is it really?' Fox sniffed the air.

'Unph! UNPH!' Bear was growing impatient.

'Not south? Are you sure?'

'*UNPH!*'

'Well, I wish you'd make up your mind.'

'NORTH!' shouted Bear, forgetting about his grouse. 'The wind's com . . .' Bear's voice faded as he saw his grouse flap

away among the bushes by the side of the track. 'Now see what you've done!'

'Me?' said Fox innocently. 'What have I done?'

'Made me lose my grouse, that's what!'

'What grouse?'

'That grouse!' shouted Bear, waving a paw. 'The grouse I had in my mouth. You kept asking me questions and when I opened my mouth it flew away.'

'But why did you open your mouth if you had a grouse in it?'

'Because you can't say "north" without opening your mouth, can you?' shouted Bear, getting more and more angry.

Fox burst out laughing.

'If I'd had a mouthful of grouse I wouldn't have said "north".'

Bear sniffed the north wind and looked bewildered.

'What would you have said, then?'

Fox laughed louder than ever. Then he looked up at Bear, clenched his teeth together, and said firmly, 'Eeeeast!'

FINLAND

The Tiger, the Elephant, and the Monkey

Retold by Barbara Ker Wilson

Deep in the heart of the green forest, the Elephant and the Tiger came face to face in a narrow pathway.

'Get out of my way, Elephant,' said the Tiger. 'I am the Lord of the Forest.'

The Elephant was angry. 'I acknowledge only the Lion as Lord of the Forest,' he retorted. 'And now I will trample you underfoot for insulting me.'

'Let us hold a trial to see which of us is the mightier,' suggested the Tiger. 'The winner shall eat up the loser.'

The Elephant agreed to this. Then the Tiger opened his mouth and gave a mighty roar that resounded through the forest. It was so loud that a Jackal who was prowling nearby died of fright when he heard it.

'I can do better than that,' boasted the Elephant.

He lifted his long trunk and trumpeted for all he was worth. The trees shook at the noise, but no creature died of fright.

'Aha, Elephant,' said the Tiger triumphantly, 'I am the winner of the contest, and now I am going to eat you up!'

The Elephant could only agree that the Tiger had shown himself to be the mightier animal, and had therefore the right to eat him up, but he begged the Tiger to spare his life for a few days, so that he could say goodbye to his wife and family.

'Very well,' said the Tiger, 'but be sure to return here to me in seven days' time.'

'I shall not forget,' replied the Elephant.

Sadly he went home to his wife and their two little calves, and told them about the unhappy fate that had befallen him. Tenderly he bade his family farewell, and showed them how to find their food when he should no longer be there to look after them. And on the sixth day following his unlucky encounter with the Tiger, he set off through the forest to keep the bargain he had made. On his way he met the Rabbit.

'What is the matter with you, Elephant?' asked the Rabbit. 'You look so sad and miserable.'

'Alas, little Rabbit,' answered the Elephant, 'I have made a bargain with the Tiger, who is going to eat me up.' And he told the Rabbit all about the contest they had held, and how the Jackal had died of fright when he heard the roar of the Tiger.

The Rabbit listened carefully. Then he said: 'If you follow my advice you need not lose your life, Elephant.'

Then the Rabbit called a meeting of all the creatures who lived in the forest – except for the troublesome Monkey (who was always playing tricks on the other animals) and, of course, the Tiger. He asked the assembly to help him to save the Elephant's life.

'Willingly, friend Rabbit, if you will tell us what to do,' said the Bear. And there were murmurs of assent from all around – from the swift-footed Deer, the Hippopotamus, the prickly Porcupine, the yellow Toad, and every other creature.

'This is what you must do,' the Rabbit told them. 'Tomorrow you must run through the forest in great terror, shouting: "The mighty Rabbit has conquered the Elephant, and now he is searching for the Tiger!" '

The animals agreed to do this, for they knew the wisdom of the Rabbit, and guessed he had thought of a good plan to save the Elephant's life.

The next morning was the seventh day since the Elephant had met the Tiger. At sunrise, the Rabbit jumped on to the Elephant's back, holding a bunch of bananas.

'Now, Elephant,' he said, 'take me to the place where you are to meet the Tiger.'

As they went slowly into the heart of the green forest, terror-stricken cries arose on every side: 'The mighty Rabbit has conquered the Elephant, and now he is searching for the Tiger!'

The Tiger was waiting for the Elephant at their appointed meeting place. He heard the terrified cries of the forest animals, and was uneasy.

'How could the little Rabbit possibly harm such mighty creatures as the Elephant and myself?' he scoffed. 'Yet why are the other animals so afraid? I hear the cry of the Bear, the swift-footed Deer, the Hippopotamus, the prickly Porcupine, and the yellow Toad . . . It would be as well to have an ally to stand beside me and fight the Rabbit, if he has really conquered the Elephant and is now searching for me.'

It so happened that the Monkey was sitting on the branch of a tree, above the Tiger's head. 'I will help you fight the Rabbit, Tiger,' he said. And he waited by the Tiger's side.

Still the cries of terror echoed throughout the forest. The Tiger and the Monkey became very worried.

'The Tiger is a treacherous animal,' thought the Monkey. 'For all I know, he may run away from the Rabbit and abandon me to my fate.'

'The Monkey is not to be trusted,' thought the Tiger. 'He may take to his heels as soon as the Rabbit arrives, and leave me to fight it out alone.'

'Friend Tiger,' said the Monkey, 'let us tie our tails together in a knot, so that we shall not be separated when the enemy appears.'

'Friend Monkey,' said the Tiger, 'that is an excellent idea.'

So they tied their two tails together.

Now they heard the plodding steps of the Elephant as he drew near. A moment later they saw him walking towards them, with the Rabbit sitting on his back eating the bananas one by one.

'Ho, Tiger!' called the Rabbit, 'I am eating the brains of the Elephant, and soon I shall eat your brains as well!'

The Tiger was so ignorant that he believed the bananas really were the brains of the Elephant.

'Oh friend Monkey, let us run away!' he cried in fear.

'How stupid you are, Tiger!' retorted the Monkey. 'Those are bananas, not brains. I eat them every day, so I should know!'

Just then the Rabbit looked at the Monkey and said to him, 'What is the meaning of this, Monkey? You boasted that you would bring me a big, fat Tiger to eat. This is only a small, thin Tiger.'

60

At these words, the Tiger turned and fled. 'You wicked creature!' he shouted at the Monkey. 'Now I see why you offered to help me fight the Rabbit, why you suggested we should tie our tails together, and why you said the brains were bananas. You pretended to be my ally, but all the time you were really helping the Rabbit!'

The Monkey had not breath to answer the Tiger's accusations, he was being pulled along at such a rate. 'Stop, stop!' he cried. 'I cannot run so fast as you, friend Tiger!' But the Tiger was too frightened to stop.

At last they each ran either side of a tall tree that stood in their path, and their tails were pulled so hard against the trunk that the knot was broken. Then the Tiger ran off to the hills, and the Monkey found refuge in the tree-tops. As for the Elephant, he went back to his wife and two little calves, thanks to the clever plan of the wise Rabbit.

BURMA

The Wisdom of Crows

Retold by Miloš Malý

Once an old crow settled on a large island where there was enough food for both people and animals. In early spring she laid three speckled eggs, and when three awfully hungry nestlings were born, the old crow was extremely pleased. All around she had a lot to feed them with, and did not have to fly around so much as she would surely have had to anywhere else.

However, she was not to remain content for long. One night a terrible storm broke out and sea waves flooded the whole island. They were mounting higher and higher until they were level with the nest. The crow was aware that if she was to save her young, she would have to take them far out beyond the sea, but just one and no more was all she could carry.

And so without thinking much she just clutched the first of her young that came her way, and soared from the nest.

When they left the island behind, she said to the young chick, 'How will you repay me if I carry you across the sea?'

'I too will carry you about some day, only don't drop me,' replied the young chick.

'You lie!' said the old crow angrily, and she dropped the nestling into the water and returned to the island.

The nest was half flooded already, so she took up her second young and hurried off as fast as her wings would carry her. After a while she asked again, 'How will you repay me if I save you?'

'When I grow up, I will carry you anywhere you will want to go.'

This time, too, the old crow got angry, and dropped the young chick into the sea.

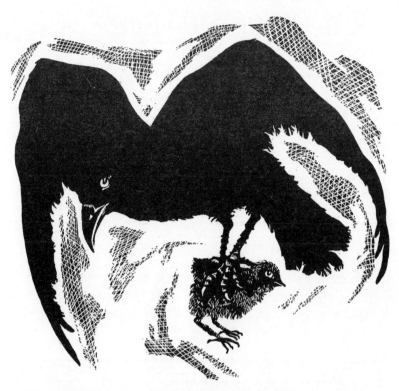

Then she set out on her journey back to the nest.

It was already flooded, there was just the little head of the last young crow sticking out of the water, and the moment the old crow seized it, the nest disappeared altogether.

Then she flew for a day and a night, and only when she saw the shore with birches on it in the distance did she ask for the third time, 'How will you repay me, if I save you from drowning?'

'What can I say? When I grow up, I shall have to carry my own young, if need be,' answered the young chick after a while.

This time the old crow was satisfied. 'You are telling the truth, because birds never look after their parents. Therefore I will carry you as far as the shore, build a new nest, and feed you until you fly out of it by yourself.'

BALTIC

Kitten and Little Rat

Retold by Maria Leach

Once long ago Kitten and Little Rat were friends. They played together. They ran and jumped and tumbled and scrambled around. They ate berries off the bushes. One would hide behind a tree and jump out when the other was looking for him.

Sometimes when they got tired they curled up together on a warm rock and slept till they were ready to begin all over again.

One day when Little Rat got home his mother said, 'Did you have fun today? Whom did you play with?'

'Kitten,' said Little Rat.

'You must not play with Kitten,' said Mother Rat. 'Don't you know that rats are cats' favourite food?'

That same day when Kitten got home, the mother cat said, 'With whom did you play today?'

'Little Rat,' said Kitten. 'We had fun.'

'Silly Kitten!' said the mother cat. 'Don't you know that rats are your favourite food?'

The next day when Kitten and Little Rat met, they just looked at each other.

'Do you want to play?' said Kitten.

'No,' said Little Rat, 'my mother told me.'

'I know,' said Kitten. 'My mother told me, too.'

'Well – goodbye,' said Little Rat.

'I wish they hadn't told us,' said Kitten.

SURINAM

Cat, Lion, and Man

Retold by Georgios A. Megas

There was once a cat who went out for a walk on the mountain. All at once she saw a lion in her path. She moved to one side, and waited to see what the lion would do. The lion went up to her, sniffed at her, and then said to her, 'You seem to be of our kind, but you are very small.'

And the cat answered, 'You'd be, too, if you had to live cheek-by-jowl with Man.'

'How's that?' asked the lion. 'What is Man? Is he so big and fierce? Where is he? I want to see.'

To this the cat said, 'Come with me, and I'll show him to you.'

The lion made no objection; so off they went. As they walked along the mountain path, they beheld a man cutting wood.

The cat said to the lion, 'There he is. That's Man.'

They moved closer. The lion bade the man good day, and said, 'Are you Man?'

'I am,' said he.

'I have heard that you are very strong; so I've come to wrestle.'

'So be it, let's wrestle. But, first, help me split this wood, I've already done half – and then we'll wrestle.'

'That will I do.'

'As you are so obliging, put your paws in here, where it's split, and I will finish it off.'

The lion put in his paws, and the man released first one side of the wood that he had been holding, and then the other side, so that the lion's paws were caught fast in the wood. Then the man picked up a thick stick and began to rain down blows on the lion. 'Take that! And that! And there's one to make you tingle! And one to make you ache!'

He was half dead by the time the man was done.

Then the man pulled the wood apart, and freed the paws of the lion, who lay down like a dog. The man hoisted the wood on his back, picked up his axe, and went off home.

When the man had gone, the cat, who had been hiding, came out, went up to the lion, and asked him if he had recovered.

'And what did you think of Man?'

'Well,' the lion answered, 'if I were in your shoes, I'd make myself smaller still!'

GREECE

3
Serves You Right

Think Before You Jump

Retold by J. Frank Dobie

One time in the middle of summer in a very dry land a coyote's nose brought him to the edge of a deserted well. It was not very deep, but the water stood far too low for lapping. While, quivering with thirst, he panted on the rim, a goat came up. This goat was just as thirsty as the coyote. His thirst made him forget his enemy, and the thirst of the coyote made him forget all hunger. He did not forget his cunning, however.

'Brother Goat,' he said, 'there is no remedy except that we jump in. It is better to die in cool, sweet water than to burn of thirst on the burning ground. The water is not deep, I know. We shall not drown. Perhaps God will help us get out.'

'Y-e-e-s-s,' bleated the goat, 'I will risk my life for a drink of water.'

They both jumped into the well. As the coyote had said, the water was shallow. He lapped and lapped the water with his tongue. The goat sucked and sucked the water down his throat.

After they were full and refreshed, the coyote said, 'Brother Goat, I am thinking of a way to get out of this hole. Do as I say, and all will be well.'

'All right, Brother Coyote,' the goat quavered, 'let us have your idea.'

'That is sensible, Brother Goat,' the coyote complimented his fellow prisoner. 'Now place your front feet up on the wall of the well as high as you can. At the same time, raise your head and throw back your horns. Then I'll jump upon your back, then gather my feet on your hard head, and next leap out. When I am safely out, I can reach down and pull you out after me.'

The goat followed directions and the coyote jumped out of

the well. But when he was safe, he turned with a laugh and said, 'Brother Goat, I'll have to tell you good-bye.'

'You have played me false. You have tricked me.'

'Friend,' retorted the coyote, 'if you had as much astuteness in your brains as you have hairs in your beard, you would have thought how you were going to get out before you jumped in.'

MEXICO

Lion, Goat, and Vulture

Aesop, retold by James Reeves

It was a hot day. Lion and Goat were both thirsty, but the pool was small. Goat bent down his head to drink, when Lion came up beside him and growled fiercely. 'I shall drink first,' he said. 'I am King of All the Animals, and it is my right. Get out of my way!'

'No,' said Goat, '*I* shall drink first. I found the water. You can wait till I've finished.'

'You'll drink it all up,' said Lion. 'There's not very much left, and I am nearly dead with thirst.'

'And I haven't had a drop all day,' answered Goat.

So they quarrelled. Lion chased Goat to the top of a great rock, and, hot as he was, Goat bounded out of the way. Neither of them was able to drink in peace.

Suddenly Lion stopped chasing Goat and looked up into the hot blue sky. Goat looked too. There, circling slowly above them, was Vulture. All the animals knew and feared him. He is the Bird of Death, who waits to pounce on the bodies of dead animals and eat their flesh. Lion and Goat knew, both at once, that if they did not stop fighting, they would die of thirst, and Vulture would pick their bodies to the bone.

'If we go on quarrelling,' said Lion, 'we shall both die of thirst, and that will be the end of us. Go to the water and drink, but don't take it all!'

Goat did as he was told, and the two animals quenched their thirst instead of fighting.

When a common danger threatens, it is best to stop quarrelling.

ANCIENT GREECE

The Wolf and
the Lamb

Aesop, retold by Robert Scott

It so happened that a fat young Lamb had strayed from her mother's side and got lost. She dashed about, bleating and anxious, but couldn't find her way back to the safety of the rest of the flock. At last she stopped by the side of a stream and bent her head to drink. A rumbling growl startled her. There, further up the stream, was a large, grey Wolf.

The Wolf, who had been watching the Lamb for some time, was not only very large; he was very hungry as well. All he needed was a good excuse to satisfy his hunger. He licked his chops, then bent his head to drink. Suddenly he stopped, lifted his head and snarled at the Lamb.

'What do you mean by paddling your muddy little feet in the water when I've come down to drink?'

The Lamb stepped back quickly.

'But please, sir,' she said. 'The water's flowing this way. I haven't made it muddy for you. Look!'

'Whichever way it's flowing, you've been messing it up. *And* you've been drinking it. Drinking in my stream!' he snarled. 'How dare you!'

'No, sir. Please, sir, no, sir. I was just going to drink when I saw you. I haven't touched a drop. Honest.'

'But you were going to!'

'I didn't know it was yours, sir. I thought it belonged to the farmer. And,' added the Lamb bravely, 'I would only be drinking what you left.'

'What's that got to do with it? You're a trouble-maker, you are. I can tell that.'

'Me, sir? Oh, no, sir. I'm just lost.'

'*And* you're a trespasser, too. A self-confessed trespasser caught in the act. I bet it was you who led all those other sheep through my fields last year, wasn't it?'

'No, sir. Oh no. I wasn't born last year so it couldn't have been me.'

'Excuses!' snarled the Wolf, licking his lips. 'Always excuses. You needn't think you're going to escape simply because you can dream up some fancy excuse. Besides, it's getting late and it's past my suppertime.'

With that the Wolf sprang on the Lamb and ate her up.

The tyrant can always find some reason.

ANCIENT GREECE

The Fox
and the Lion
in Partnership

Aesop, retold by Barbara Ker Wilson

Once upon a time it happened that a Lion fell sick. He could no longer stalk his prey across the plains and through the forest. He lay in a cave all day long, and in order to get his food he was forced to resort to cunning. He decided to go into partnership with the red-brown Fox; for what creature is more crafty than the Fox? And on his side, the Fox was glad enough to become the Lion's comrade.

'If you would like to see me recover,' the Lion told his new partner, 'you must use your quick wits and flattering tongue to entice the other animals within reach of my claws.' He licked his lips. 'I should like to get my teeth into the tender flesh of the big Deer that lives in the forest. Go and see if you can persuade him to come here, my dear friend.'

The Fox trotted off into the forest, and presently he came upon the big Deer playing in a sunlit glade. The Fox spoke to the Deer with honeyed words.

'I bring you good news, brother. As you may have heard, our king the Lion is very ill. Alas, he will soon be dead. Before he dies, however, he wants to appoint one of the other animals to reign after him. He has considered each animal in turn – the pig thinks of nothing except filling his belly; the bear is a lazy good-for-nothing; the leopard is bad-tempered; the tiger is vain and boastful. But you, brother Deer, seem well qualified to take the Lion's place. You are tall and stately, you live long, and your antlers are a good defence against your enemies. Yes, the Lion would like you to succeed him as king.'

The Deer listened carefully to the Fox's speech, and his mind became puffed up with pride. He was to be king of all the animals! The Lion had chosen him to rule in his place!

'The Lion has paid me a great honour, brother Fox,' said the Deer. 'And indeed, all that you say about my stately bearing, my strong antlers, and my long life is true. I shall reign well over my fellow creatures. I will be a good king.'

The Fox smiled craftily. 'If you will take my advice, I think you should come back with me now to the Lion's cave. He is waiting to know whether you will agree to accept the nomination.'

The Deer followed the Fox through the forest back to the Lion's cave, without any suspicion of what lay in wait for him. Sure enough, there the sick Lion lay, his great head resting on his paws. When he saw the red-brown Fox returning with the Deer, his eyes glinted with pleasure. As soon as the Deer came within reach, he pounced upon him eagerly – but he only succeeded in tearing his ears. The Deer escaped from the Lion's grasp, and fled back to the forest.

The Fox beat his paws together in disappointment, and the Lion growled and groaned. He begged the Fox to try to entice the Deer to the cave again.

'And this time he shall not escape me!' the Lion promised. 'Oh, how hungry I am!'

The Fox waved his bushy tail. 'It will be a difficult task to perform, dear friend. But for your sake I will attempt it.'

So he set off once more. It was easy enough to follow the tracks of the Deer, for they were spotted with blood from the wound the Lion had inflicted on him. Before long the Fox found the Deer resting beneath a tall tree.

The Deer was furious when he saw the Fox. 'I wonder how you dare to show your face again!' he said angrily. 'You can't trick me a second time. You'd better go and spin your story to some other creature who would like to be king. Be off with you – or I'll charge you with my antlers!'

The Fox looked at the Deer slyly. 'How suspicious you are, brother Deer. And how nervously you behaved in the presence of the Lion. I assure you that he is filled with benevolence towards you. He wishes you nothing but good. When he caught hold of your ears, he only meant to whisper some secrets of kingship. If he gave you a little scratch by mistake – why, that was only because he does not realize his own strength.'

The Deer considered the Fox's words. Could what he said be true? Perhaps he had acted foolishly in the presence of the Lion.

'If you really do want to be king,' the Fox continued, pressing his advantage, 'I advise you to return with me to the Lion's cave at once, and tell him how sorry you are that you behaved so badly. He is very angry about it, and is talking of choosing the Wolf to reign after him instead. Make haste! Follow me, and go up to him without fear. He won't hurt you, I swear it!'

Once more the Deer was persuaded. Meekly he followed the Fox back to the cave.

The Lion was overjoyed when he saw the Fox returning with the Deer a second time.

'How wise of me to form a partnership with such a crafty creature!' he thought.

As soon as the Deer entered the cave, the Lion fell upon him and swallowed his flesh and bones. The Fox looked on, as pleased as the Lion at the success of his mission. As the Lion ate his meal, the Fox seized upon the brains and gulped them down, for he was hungry too. The Lion noticed they were missing and began looking for them among the left-overs.

'You might as well stop looking,' the Fox told him. 'The simple truth is that the Deer had no brains. Well – I ask you – would you expect a creature with any brains at all to come twice into a Lion's den?'

ANCIENT GREECE

76

The Fox, the Wolf, and the Mule

translated by Eilís Dillon

The Fox was taking a walk in a wood one day when he saw a Mule, and never in his life had he seen the like before. He was greatly frightened, and his first thought was to fly for his life. As he galloped along, who should he see but the Wolf, and told him that he had seen a new beast whose name he did not know. The Wolf said at once: 'Let's go. I'm all for seeing this beast.'

They found the Mule, and the Wolf was astonished: he had never seen such a beast either.

The Wolf swaggered up and asked the Mule his name. The Mule answered: 'I'm afraid I just can't remember it at this moment. But if you are able to read, you'll find it written on one of my hind hoofs.'

'That's too bad,' said the Fox. 'If I knew how to read, I'd find out your name in two shakes.'

'Let me have a look,' said the Wolf. 'I'm well able to read.'

The Mule lifted up his hoof so that the underside showed, and the nails looked exactly like letters.

'I can't see it properly,' said the Wolf.

'Come a little nearer,' said the Mule. 'The letters are very small.'

Trustingly the Wolf came closer, until he was right underneath the Mule's hoof, gazing up at it. The Mule made a swipe with his hoof and kicked the Wolf on the head, killing him stone dead.

The Fox cleared off, saying to himself: *'Not everyone who can read is wise.'*

ITALY

The Fox,
the Duck,
and the Lion

Ambrose Bierce

A Fox and a Duck having quarrelled about the ownership of a frog, referred the matter to a Lion. After hearing a deal of argument the Lion opened his mouth to deliver judgement.

'I know what your decision is,' said the Duck, interrupting. 'It is that by our own showing the frog belongs to neither of us, and you will eat him yourself. Permit me to say that this is unjust, as I shall prove.'

'To me,' said the Fox, 'it is clear that you will give the frog to the Duck and the Duck to me and take me yourself. I am not without experience of the law.'

'I was about to explain,' said the Lion, yawning, 'that during the arguments in this case the property in dispute has hopped away. Perhaps you can procure another frog.'

USA

Hare and Tortoise

Aesop, retold by James Reeves

When Tortoise was very little, his mother said to him, 'You will never be able to go very fast. We Tortoises are a slow-moving family, but we get there in the end. Don't try to run. Remember, "steady and slow" does it.' Tortoise remembered these words.

One day when he was grown up, he was walking quietly round in a field minding his own business; and Hare thought he would have some fun, so he ran round Tortoise in quick circles, just to annoy him. Hare was proud of himself because everyone knew he was one of the swiftest of animals. But Tortoise took no notice, so Hare stopped in front of him and laughed.

'Can't you move faster than *that*?' said Hare. 'You'll *never* get anywhere at that rate! You should take a few lessons from *me*.'

Tortoise lifted his head slowly and said:

'I don't want to get anywhere, thank you. I've no need to go dashing about all over the place. You see, my thick shell protects me from my enemies.'

'But how *dull* life must be for you!' Hare went on. 'Why, it takes you half an hour to cross one field, while I can be away out of sight in half a minute. Besides, you really do look silly, you know! You ought to be ashamed of yourself.'

Well, at this Tortoise was rather annoyed. Hare was really very provoking.

'Look here,' said Tortoise, 'if you want a race, I'll give you one; and I don't need any start either.'

Hare laughed till the tears ran down his furry face, and his sides shook so much that he rolled over backwards. Tortoise just waited till Hare had finished, then he said:

'Well, what about it? I'm not joking.'

Several other animals had gathered round, and they all said: 'Go on, Hare. It's a challenge. You'll have to race him.'

'Certainly,' said Hare, 'if you want to make a fool of yourself. Where shall we race to?'

Tortoise shaded his eyes with one foot and said:

'See that old windmill on the top of the hill yonder? We'll race to that. We can start from this tree-stump here. Come on, and may the best animal win!'

So as soon as they were both standing beside the tree-stump, Chanticleer the Cock shouted 'Ready – steady – go!' and Tortoise began to crawl towards the far-off windmill. The other animals had hurried on ahead so as to see the finish.

Hare stood beside the tree-stump watching Tortoise waddle away across the field. The day was hot, and just beside the tree-stump was a pleasant, shady place, so he sat down and waited.

He guessed it would take him about two and a half minutes to reach the windmill, even without trying very hard, so there was no hurry – no hurry at all. Presently he began to drop off to sleep.

Two or three minutes passed, and Hare opened one eye lazily. Tortoise had scarcely crossed the first field. 'Steady and slow,' he said to himself under his breath. 'Steady and slow. That's what mother said.' And he kept on towards the far-off windmill.

'At that rate,' said Hare to himself sleepily, 'it'll take him just about two hours to get there – if he doesn't drop dead on the way.'

He closed his eye again and fell into a deep sleep.

After a while Tortoise had crossed the first field, and was making his way slowly over the second.

'Steady and slow does it,' he muttered to himself.

The sun began to go down, and at last Hare woke up, feeling chilly.

'Where am I?' he thought. 'What's happened? Oh yes, I remember.'

He got to his feet and looked towards the windmill. But where was Tortoise? He was nowhere to be seen. Hare jumped on to the tree-stump and strained his eyes to gaze into the distance. There, half-way across the very last field before the windmill, was a tiny black dot. Tortoise!

'This won't do,' said Hare. 'I must have overslept. I'd better be moving.'

So he sprang from the stump and darted across the first field, then the second, then the third. It was really much further than he had thought.

At the windmill the other animals were waiting to see the finish. At last Tortoise arrived, rather out of breath and wobbling a little on his legs.

'Come on, Tortoise!' they shouted.

Then Hare appeared at the far side of the last field, streaking along like the wind. How he ran! Not even Stag, when he was being hunted, could go faster. Even Swallow could scarcely fly faster through the blue sky.

'Steady and slow,' said Tortoise to himself, but no one could hear him, for he had very, very little breath left to talk with.

'Come on, Tortoise!' cried some animals, and a few cried, 'Come on, Hare! He's beating you!'

Hare put on extra speed and ran faster than he had ever run before. But it was no good. He had given Tortoise too much start, and he was still twenty yards behind when Tortoise crawled over the last foot of ground and tumbled up against the windmill. He had won the race!

All the animals cheered, and after that Hare never laughed at Tortoise again.

Slow and steady wins the race.

ANCIENT GREECE

The Tortoise
and the Hare

James Thurber

There was once a wise young tortoise who read in an ancient book about a tortoise who had beaten a hare in a race. He read all the other books he could find but in none of them was there any record of a hare who had beaten a tortoise. The wise young tortoise came to the natural conclusion that he could outrun a hare, so he set forth in search of one. In his wanderings he met many animals who were willing to race him: weasels, stoats, dachshunds, badger-boars, short-tailed field mice, and ground squirrels. But when the tortoise asked if they could outrun a hare, they all said no, they couldn't (with the exception of a dachshund named Freddy, and nobody paid any attention to him). 'Well, I can,' said the tortoise, 'so there's no use wasting my time on you.' And he continued his search.

After many days, the tortoise finally encountered a hare and challenged him to a race.

'What are you going to use for legs?' asked the hare.

'Never mind that,' said the tortoise. 'Read this.'

He showed the hare the story in the ancient book, complete with moral about the swift not always being so terribly fast.

'Tosh,' said the hare. 'You couldn't go fifty feet in an hour and a half, whereas I can go fifty feet in one and a fifth seconds.'

'Posh,' said the tortoise. 'You probably won't even finish second.'

'We'll see about that,' said the hare.

So they marked off a course fifty feet long. All the other animals gathered around. A bullfrog set them on their marks, a gun dog fired a pistol, and they were off.

When the hare crossed the finish line, the tortoise had gone approximately eight and three-quarter inches.

Moral: a new broom may sweep clean, but never trust an old saw.

USA

84

The Turtle
and the Swans

Panchatantra, retold by Robert Scott

The turtle lived in a great lake with a lot of other creatures. He made particular friends with a pair of swans. They had a lot of interests in common and each evening they would settle down together for a pleasant chat. The swans would tell about the many different places they had visited and the turtle would reveal some of the interesting things he had discovered while exploring the bed of the lake.

Then one year the rains failed and the lake began to dry up. Soon it was little more than dry, cracked mud.

'It's no use,' the swans said to the turtle one evening, 'we shall have to leave here. We're sorry to say goodbye when we've been such good friends, but there's nothing else for it. How will you manage?'

The turtle shook his head sadly. 'I've no idea,' he said. 'You can fly off somewhere else, but I'm stuck here. Not only that. I *need* the water. I can't live without it. It isn't quite so serious for you.'

The swans looked uncomfortable. 'I don't see how we can help,' one of them said. 'If only you could fly. We'll try to think of something.'

'Perhaps you could carry me,' said the turtle when they met again the next day.

'You'd be too heavy,' said one of the swans.

'You'd fall off,' said the other. 'Nothing to hold on to.'

'I can grip very tight,' said the turtle, clamping his mouth round a stick to prove his point.

'I'm sure you can,' said the first swan, 'but it's my neck you'd be holding on to.'

'But that's the answer!' the other exclaimed. 'He can hold on to the stick and we'll carry him that way.'

They began to work out the details. They would find a suitable stick, the turtle would grip the middle firmly in his mouth and the swans would hold the ends. That way they could all go to a lake the swans knew of that never dried up.

'But no talking!' the swans said. 'We must all grip the stick tightly and not open our beaks. Or mouth,' he added, turning a beady eye on their friend. 'If you do, you'll fall off.'

'Of course not!' snapped the turtle. 'I can keep my mouth shut when I have to. Let's get started.'

So they carried out their plan and the swans were soon flying strongly out towards their new home.

As they were passing over a small town someone happened to notice them.

'Hey, look up there!' he shouted in admiration. 'Look at that! There's a turtle being carried along on a stick by a couple of swans. Isn't that clever of it.'

The three friends looked down but said nothing. 'They're right, though,' thought the turtle. 'It's very clever to hold on and be carried like this.'

The swans' powerful wings carried them out into the country across parched fields and hills until once more they were flying over a town. Again they were seen.

'Look at that!'

'What? Where?'

'Up there. Those two swans are carrying a turtle on a stick.'

'So they are. That's very clever of them.'

'I'll say! Very clever birds, swans.'

The turtle, hearing all this, was becoming more and more irritated. 'Stupid fools!' he thought. 'Don't they realize that I'm the one that's being clever. The swans are just flying like they always do but you don't see a flying turtle every day. Really!' Then he forgot where he was.

'Hey! You down there! Don't you —' but as soon as he opened his mouth to speak he began to fall. He never did finish what he wanted to say, but was dashed to pieces on the ground below.

That night the people had turtle soup for dinner.

Keep your mind on the job in hand.

INDIA

The Snapping Turtle
and the
Wisteria Vine

William March

Of all the creatures of the forest, the snapping turtle was the most tenacious: once he seized an enemy in his jaws, he wouldn't turn loose until his adversary admitted he was beaten or until it thundered. One day he was crawling through the underbrush when a big snake, hanging down from a tree, swung forward and struck him between his near-sighted eyes. The turtle stopped in his tracks, wondering if the affront were intentional or not; then deciding it was not, he continued on his way, saying over his shoulder, 'Do that again and I'll bite you; and if I bite you, I'll hold on until you admit you've had enough or until it thunders. I have great strength of character, as anybody will tell you.'

He'd hardly finished before the snake swung back, this time catching the turtle in the rear. The turtle, furious at the insult, seized the tail of the snake in his jaws – and instantly he knew his poor eyesight had betrayed him again. It wasn't a snake at all; it was only the dangling end of an old wisteria vine.

For a time the turtle hung on, knowing he had made a mistake but unwilling to act contrary to the traditions of his kind, and after a while the other animals gathered to watch the spectacle of a live turtle fighting a dead wisteria vine. 'It's nothing but a vine,' they said. 'The vine can't admit it's beaten, so why don't you turn loose and go home to supper?'

'I'll turn loose when it thunders, and not before,' said the turtle. He glanced upwards, but there was not a cloud in the sky, and it looked as though it would stay fair for a long time. And so things went, with the friends of the turtle urging him to turn loose and with him shaking his head stubbornly. 'When it thunders,' he said. 'Not until it thunders.'

Nobody was surprised when, towards the end of the week, the turtle died and fell to the ground. His friends gathered about him and said, 'Sometimes it's hard to tell the difference between strength of character and plain stupidity.'

USA

4
In the Wild

Encounter

James Pollard

Iga, the old-man kangaroo, rested in the shade of a redgum-tree. About the roots of this tree countless kangaroos had during many years scraped a number of shallow holes in the loose red soil. Iga, scraping in his turn, moved away the sun-warmed topsoil and couched in the cooler earth uncovered. From time to time during the day he exchanged one hollow for another, always scraping anew.

Towards evening he rose and sat half erect, looking through the forest, which was now patterned with long lights and shadows. Listening, he heard only the voices of birds and the sounds of wind and tree.

He crawled a few paces, setting his paws to ground and gliding his long legs pace by pace beside them. He nibbled the herbage. A wagtail dropped down to chatter and to wag about his nose, on the alert for any insects that his browsing lips might disturb. Once the bird danced into the air in pursuit of a frantic cricket and, having caught it, floated down to perch on Iga's shoulder.

Iga turned back an ear to listen to the fantail's chattered commentary, then stood up and, as the bird spread its wings, moved off, slowly hopping through the timber.

He halted beside a clump of wattle-trees and remained for some moments still, watching, listening. Unalarmed, he passed between the trees and lowered his muzzle to a shadowed pool, lapping the water.

The sun dipping below the earth's rim briefly gilded the forest roof, and a magpie carolled there. Through the under-shrubs ran twitterings of tom-tits and silver-eyes as the birds lingered over their choice of perch for the night.

From the pool Iga proceeded through open forest, hopping leisurely but without pause until, approaching a road that crossed his path, he observed a bulky object. He stopped abruptly, sitting erect on the long pads of his hind feet, and gazed at a motor-car deserted on the road.

For several minutes Iga watched the car. Then with a few short hops he approached nearer to it and again stood watching, listening, obviously curious; yet as obviously ready to depart if his senses should warn him of danger. He sniffed the wind, but it carried only the familiar scents of the forest. He was reassured, and moved and stood again. Having the car now clearly in view, with its smooth surface and its windows reflecting the sunset hues, he stooped, then made the rest of the way on all fours, gliding quietly over the shadowed ground.

So he came to the road and to the side of the car, where he again raised himself and stood for some moments looking now at the vehicle and now through the forest. He was not alarmed. When he eyed the car he appeared puzzled; and when he looked away he appeared to enquire of the world about, sniffing the evening air, twitching his ears, casting glances near and far.

Presently he pawed his muzzle with one hand, lifted both paws to rub over his ears, then again surveyed the machine.

A rabbit loped across the road. Iga saw it begin to feed, unconcerned. A bat flitted across the sky and swooped to a moth close above the kangaroo. Wind and trees quietly sighed.

Iga stooped and crawled to the near front wheel of the car. In his nostrils were the mingled scents of oil and rubber. He reared above the mudguard, eyed the bonnet and the windscreen, and again pawed the muzzle. He turned and crawled along the side of the vehicle, stood at its rear, stooped again and crawled along the other side until an open door brought him erect. After a brief wary stand he sniffed at the edge of a cushion. Perhaps he recognized man-scent there, for he achieved a quaint backstep and stood watching the car intently, his ears stiffly forward. After a few moments he dropped his hands again, glided on, and so completed the circuit.

Half-crouched, he spent a minute or two on a toilet, muzzling the fur about his flanks, pawing an ear, rubbing his nose. Then, looking along the road, he failed to observe or to hear the rabbit that had been feeding there, yet instantly glimpsed the shadowy movement of a man approaching along the dusky track.

For a moment yet he remained crouched, and observed the dim figure in the distance, then turned quietly on his toes, into the darkening timber. He did not hasten. He had not lost interest in the car. After half a dozen hops he rested beside an anthill, looking back over his shoulder; but soon he squared himself and looked directly down the road.

Footsteps echoed to him along the ground. He watched the man stride to the car. On the further side of the machine the man was for a moment or two invisible. Then he appeared, making a slow round of the vehicle, studying the ground. Beside the near front wheel he stood to glance up and about, and because he was a man of the forest his glance, sweeping the anthill and the kangaroo, separated them. For perhaps half a minute he stared at Iga, who returned his stare. Then he entered the car and drove away.

Iga watched the vehicle merge with the gloom, listened until its throbbing had murmured away, then moved and stooped to feed.

Dusk deepened into night and the stars looked down. The wind strengthened, and the trees rustled – but intermittently, stilling at times as though to listen. During one lull there reached Iga from far through the timber the mourn of a wild dog. He crouched, listening until he heard it again, then turned and went quietly away from the sound. When he halted he listened for some time before he fed.

An hour later that eerie dingo-howl was borne again on the wind to within range of Iga's hearing. But at the time the old-man's ears were filled with another sound. He had wandered again to a roadside and, crossing, had paused on the bitumen to look one way and then the other. A glimmer of light had caught and held his glance and a tremor of sound his ears.

The glimmer became the beam from the headlights of a motor-car, the tremor the hum of its engine. Iga might have gone from the sound, but from the light he could not, for its glare first dazzled and then blinded him. He stooped as though to avoid the light, but failed to look away. He stood up again and stared into the light.

The man at the wheel saw Iga brilliantly illuminated, with eyes like jewels. He drove so near that he realized the kangaroo would not move. On impulse he applied the brakes and stopped his machine, flooding Iga with light, not twenty yards in front.

For a few seconds the man sat observing the kangaroo, and once fingered a rifle at his side. But he shook his head, relaxed, and waited for Iga to move, interesting himself meantime in the kangaroo's startled, almost stupefied, yet defensive, pose – standing erect.

He was about to drive on round the animal when Iga shook his head, stooped, released his eyes from the light and, pivoting, dissolved into the darkness. The man heard the kangaroo crash through bushes and its leaping fall silent, then went his way.

Iga regained his senses and once more began to feed.

While he had been thus enthralled by the car, the mourn of dingoes carried on the wind. Now, far back along the road, two wild dogs crossed and circled and came upon Iga's trail. They sniffed silently about where he had foraged, nosed the tracks he had made going towards the road, but lost the scent where on the roadway it had been doused by the stronger scent of burnt gas.

Yet only once did they cast for the lost trail, then picked it up where Iga had stumbled blindly through the scrub. Thereafter they followed unerringly until they heard the kangaroo leaping in the dark before them.

Iga caught a faint sound from the night wind, sat up and looked to where the dogs cast for his trail. Though he could not see them, he recognized the menace and turned, leaping away.

The dingoes began the pursuit. Soon they closed on the kangaroo sufficiently to discern his dark bulk as it rose and fell before them. For a time they did not approach closely, though he in turn did not run fast.

Iga was old, and he could not for long have maintained his top speed. Nor was he easily terrified. He would go away from danger, not in panic, but wanting only peace. If danger pressed he would sooner turn at bay than continue running.

For a mile or more through the dark forest he led those dingoes at a steady pace, turning occasionally from open timber to pass through a belt of thicket or to circle a clump of eucalypt-scrub. Once or twice he halted and listened, only to leap on as he realized that the hunters were hard on his trail.

The dogs followed without difficulty. If briefly they lost sight of him they could always register his footfalls. If he turned from the wind they did not need his scent to guide them but only the sounds he made thudding the earth, disturbing dry leaves and sticks or brushing the shrubs.

At last Iga pulled up to stand, facing about, going high on his toes and the tip of his tail. So he challenged the hunters.

They loomed close at a fast trot, seeking; but at sight of him they sank to ground, to wait. And presently Iga went on a little way.

Again he halted and reared. Again the dogs closed, and this time squatted on their haunches.

Once more Iga moved on and stopped. And now the dogs approached, slinking, and circled one on either side of him. One darted in to nip at his buttocks. As Iga moved to retaliate with thrusting toe, the other leapt in on the far side, and bit, and darted away.

They held off, watching. In a minute more Iga turned, going

away. But after a leap or two he stood again. Now there was a tree at his back, and before him an open road.

The dingoes approached, slinking as before, and repeated their tactic of attacking from either side. They drew blood from his side and crouched, wanting him to run again. Thus they might harry him until he became too tired to resist strongly.

But Iga now wanted to fight. From his throat issued hoarse rumblings as he felt with his paws for the dog that again went into attack. If he could hold the enemy for an instant it would be enough – there would be one dog rent almost in twain, howling its last there in the roadway.

He failed to get that hold. The dingo dropped to lie on its belly on the road, watching its fellow's following attempt.

Then from around a turn in the road came a sudden beam of light flooding the trio before the tree. And Iga was helpless again, blinded by the headlights of a motor-car.

The dog attacking blundered in the glare and shouldered the old-man's hips. Iga lurched, then struck, and by chance drove home.

The death-howl of the dog was drowned by the roar of an engine as the man of the forest, taking in the situation, stepped on his accelerator and ran down the dog, illumined and staring and crouched on the road.

Iga gathered his wits as the car zoomed flashing by. And in the darkness behind, he once more pivoted and went crashing free into the forest.

In the Deep of the Grass

Charles G. D. Roberts

Misty grey green, washed with tints of the palest violet, spotted with red clover blooms, white oxeyes, and hot orange Canada lilies, the deep-grassed levels basked under the July sun. A drowsy hum of bees and flies seemed to distil, with warm aromatic scents, from the sun-steeped blooms and grass-tops. The broad, blooming, tranquil expanse, shimmering and softly radiant in the heat, seemed the very epitome of summer. Now and again a small cloud-shadow sailed across it. Now and again a little wind, swooping down upon it gently, bent the grass-tops all one way, and spread a sudden silvery pallor. Save for the droning bees and flies there seemed to be but one live creature astir between the grass and the blue. A solitary marsh-hawk, far over by the rail fence, was winnowing slowly, slowly hither and thither, lazily hunting.

All this was in the world above the grass-tops. But below the grass-tops was a very different world – a dense, tangled world of dim green shade, shot with piercing shafts of sun, and populous with small, furtive life. Here, among the brown and white roots, the crowded green stems and the mottled stalks, the little earth kindreds went busily about their affairs and their desires, giving scant thought to the aerial world above them. All that made life significant to them was here in the warm, green gloom; and when anything chanced to part the grass to its depths they would scurry away in unanimous indignation.

On a small stone, over which the green closed so thickly that, when he chanced to look upwards, he caught but the scantiest shreds of sky, sat a half-grown field-mouse, washing his whiskers with his dainty claws. His tiny, bead-like eyes kept

100

ceaseless watch, peering through the shadowy tangle for whatever might come near in the shape of foe or prey. Presently two or three stems above his head were beaten down, and a big green grasshopper, alighting clumsily from one of his blind leaps, fell sprawling on the stone. Before he could struggle to his long legs and climb back to the safer region of the grass-tops, the little mouse was upon him. Sharp, white teeth pierced his green mail, his legs kicked convulsively twice or thrice, and the faint iridescence faded out of his big, blank, foolish eyes. The mouse made his meal with relish, daintily discarding the dry legs and wing-cases. Then, amid the green debris scattered upon the stone, he sat up, and once more went through his fastidious toilet.

But life for the little mouse in his grass-world was not quite all watching and hunting. When his toilet was complete, and he had amiably let a large black cricket crawl by unmolested, he suddenly began to whirl round and round on the stone, chasing his own tail. As he was amusing himself with this foolish play, another mouse, about the same size as himself, and probably of the same litter, jumped upon the stone, and knocked him off. He promptly retorted in kind; and for several minutes, as if the game were a well-understood one, the two kept it up, squeaking soft merriment, and apparently forgetful of all peril. The grass-tops above this play rocked and rustled in a way that would certainly have attracted attention had there been any eyes to see. But the marsh-hawk was still hunting lazily at the other side of the field, and no tragedy followed the childishness.

Both seemed to tire of the sport at the same instant; for suddenly they stopped, and hurried away through the grass on opposite sides of the stone, as if remembered business had just called to them. Whatever the business was, the first mouse seemed to forget it very speedily, for in half a minute he was back upon the stone again, combing his fine whiskers and scratching his ears. This done to his satisfaction, he dropped like a flash from his seat, and disappeared into a small hollow beneath it. As he did so, a hairy black spider darted out, and ran away among the roots.

A minute or two after the disappearance of the mouse, a creature came along which appeared gigantic in the diminutive world of the grass folk. It was nearly three feet long, and of the thickness of a man's finger. Of a steely grey black, striped and reticulated in a mysterious pattern with a clear whitish yellow, it was an ominous shape indeed, as it glided smoothly and swiftly, in graceful curves, through the close green tangle. The cool shadows and thin lights touched it flickeringly as it went, and never a grass-top stirred to mark its sinister approach. Without a sound of warning it came straight up to the stone, and darted its narrow, cruel head into the hole.

There was a sharp squeak, and instantly the narrow head came out again, ejected by the force of the mouse's agonized spring. But the snake's teeth were fastened in the little animal's neck. The doom of the green world had come upon him while he slept.

But doomed though he was, the mouse was game. He knew there was no poison in those fangs that gripped him, and he struggled desperately to break free. His powerful hind legs kicked the ground with a force which the snake, hampered at first by the fact of its length being partly trailed out through the tangle, was unable to quite control. With unerring instinct – though this was the first snake he had ever encountered – the mouse strove to reach its enemy's back and sever the bone with the fine chisels of his teeth. But it was just this that the snake was watchful to prevent. Three times in his convulsive leaps the mouse succeeded in touching the snake's body – but with his feet only, never once with those destructive little teeth. The snake held him inexorably, with a steady, elastic pressure which yielded just so far, and never quite far enough. And in a minute or two the mouse's brave struggles grew more feeble.

All this, however – the lashing and the wriggling and the jumping – had not gone on without much disturbance to the grass-tops. Timothy head and clover bloom, oxeye and feathery plume-grass, they had bowed and swayed and shivered till the commotion, very conspicuous to one looking down upon the tranquil, flowery sea of green, caught the attention of the marsh-hawk, which at that moment chanced to be perching on

a high fence stake. The lean-headed, fierce-eyed, trim-feathered bird shot from his perch, and sailed on long wings over the grass to see what was happening. As the swift shadow hovered over the grass-tops, the snake looked up. Well he understood the significance of that sudden shade. Jerking back his fangs with difficulty from the mouse's neck, he started to glide off under the thickest matting of the roots. But lightning quick though he was, he was not quite quick enough. Just as his narrow head darted under the roots, the hawk, with wings held straight up, and talons reaching down, dropped upon him, and clutched the middle of his back in a grip of steel. The next moment he was jerked into the air, writhing and coiling, and striking in vain frenzy at his captor's mail of hard feathers. The hawk flew off with him over the sea of green to the top of the fence stake, there to devour him at leisure. The mouse, sore wounded but not past recovery, dragged himself back to the hollow under the stone. And over the stone the grass-tops, once more still, hummed with flies, and breathed warm perfumes in the distilling heat.

The Parachutist

D'Arcy Niland

The hurricane came down from Capricorn, and for two days and a night it rained.

In the darkness of the second night, softening away to dawn, there was silence. There was only the gurgle and drip of the wet world, and the creatures that lived on the earth began to appear, freed from the tyranny of the elements.

The hawk, ruffled in misery, brooding in ferocity, came forth in hunger and hate. It struck off into the abyss of space, scouring the earth for some booty of the storm – the sheep lying like a heap of wet kapok in the sodden paddocks, the bullock like a dark bladder carried down on the swollen stream and washing against a tree on the river flats, the rabbit, driven from its flooded warren and squeezed dead against a log.

With practised eye it scrutinized the floating islands of rubble and the wracks of twigs lying askew on the banks for sign of lizard or snake, dead or alive. But there was nothing. Once, in the time before, there had been a rooster, daggled, forlorn derelict riding a raft of flotsam: too weak to fight and too sick to care about dying or the way it died.

The hawk rested on a crag of the gorge and conned the terrain with a fierce and frowning eye. The lice worried its body with the sting of nettles. Savagely it plucked with its beak under the fold of its wings, first on one side, then on the other. It rasped its bill on the jagged stone, and dropped over the lip. It climbed in a gliding circle, widening its field of vision.

The earth was yellow and green. On the flats were chains of lagoons as if the sky had broken and fallen in sheets of blue glass. The sun was hot and the air heavy and humid.

Swinging south, the hawk dropped over a vast graveyard of dead timber. The hurricane had ravaged the gaunt trees, splitting them, felling them, tearing off their naked arms and strewing the ground with pieces, like a battlefield of bones, grey with exposure and decay.

A rabbit sprang twenty yards like a bobbing wheel, and the sight drew the hawk like a plummet, but the rabbit vanished in a hollow log, and stayed there, and there was no other life.

Desperate, weak, the hawk alighted on a bleak limb and glared in hate. The sun was a fire on its famished body. Logs smoked with steam and the brightness of water on the earth reflected like mirrors. The telescopic eye inched over the ground – crawled infallibly over the ground, and stopped. And then suddenly the hawk swooped to the ground and tore at the body of a dead field mouse – its belly bloated and a thin vapour drifting from the grey, plastered pelt.

The hawk did not sup as it supped on the hot running blood of the rabbit in the trap – squealing in eyeless terror; it did not feast in stealthy leisure as it did on the sheep paralysed in the drought, tearing out bit by bit its steaming entrails. Voraciously it ripped at the mouse, swallowing fast and finishing the meal in a few seconds.

But the food was only a tantalization, serving to make the hawk's appetite more fierce, more lusty. It flew into a tree, rapaciously scanning the countryside. It swerved into space and climbed higher and higher in a vigilant circle, searching the vast expanse below, even to its uttermost limits.

Hard to the west something moved on the earth, a speck: and the hawk watched it: and the speck came up to a walnut, and up to a plum, and up to a ball striped with white and grey.

The hawk did not strike at once. Obedient to instinct, it continued to circle, peering down at the farmhouse and the outbuildings, suspicious; seeing the draught horses in the yard and the fowls in the hen coop, the pigs in the sty, and the windmill twirling, and watching for human life in their precincts.

Away from them all, a hundred yards or more, down on the margin of the fallowed field, the kitten played, leaping and running and tumbling, pawing at a feather and rolling on its back biting at the feather between its forepaws.

Frenzied with hunger, yet ever cautious, the hawk came down in a spiral, set itself, and swooped. The kitten propped and froze with its head cocked on one side, unaware of danger but startled by this new and untried sport. It was no more than if a piece of paper had blown past it in a giant brustle of sound. But in the next moment the hawk fastened its talons in the fur and the fat belly of the kitten, and the kitten spat and twisted, struggling against the power that was lifting it.

Its great wings beating, paddling with the rhythm of oars, the hawk went up a slope of space with its cargo, and the kitten, airborne for the first time in its life, the earth running under it in a blur, wailed in shrill terror. It squirmed frantically as the world fell away in the distance, but the hawk's talons were like the grabs of an iceman.

The air poured like water into the kitten's eyes and broke against its triangular face, streaming back against its rippling furry sides. It howled in infinite fear, and gave a sudden desperate twist, so that the hawk was jolted in its course and dropped to another level, a few feet below the first.

Riding higher and higher on the wind, the hawk went west by the dam like a button of silver far below. The kitten cried now with a new note. Its stomach was wambling. The air gushing into its mouth and nostrils set up a humming in its ears and an aching dizziness in its head. As the hawk turned on its soundless orbit, the sun blazed like flame in the kitten's eyes, leaving its sight to emerge from a blinding greyness.

The kitten knew that it had no place here in the heart of space, and its terrified instincts told it that its only contact with solidity and safety was the thing that held it.

Then the hawk was ready to drop its prey. It was well practised. Down had gone the rabbit, a whistle in space, to crash in a quiver of death on the ruthless earth. And the hawk had followed to its gluttonous repast.

Now there at two thousand feet the bird hovered. The kitten was alarmingly aware of the change, blinking at the pulsations of beaten air as the wings flapped, hearing only that sound.

Unexpectedly, it stopped, and the wings were still – out-stretched, but rigid, tilting slightly with the poised body, only the fanned tail lifting and lowering with the flow of the currents.

The kitten felt the talons relax slightly, and that was its warning. The talons opened, but in the first flashing shock of the movement the kitten completed its twist and slashed at the hawk's legs and buried its claws in the flesh like fish-hooks. In the next fraction of a second the kitten had consolidated its position, securing its hold, jabbing in every claw except those on one foot which thrust out in space, pushing against insupportable air. And then the claws on this foot were dug in the breast of the hawk.

With a cry of pain and alarm the bird swooped crazily, losing a hundred feet like a dropping stone. And then it righted itself, flying in a drunken sway that diminished as it circled.

Blood from its breast beaded and trickled down the paw of the kitten and spilled into one eye. The kitten blinked, but the blood came and congealed, warm and sticky. The kitten could not turn its head. It was frightened to risk a change of position. The blood slowly built over its eye a blinding pellicle.

The hawk felt a spasm of weakness, and out of it came an accentuation of its hunger and a lust to kill at all costs the victim it had claimed and carried to this place of execution. Lent an access of power by its ferocity, it started to climb again, desperately trying to dislodge the kitten. But the weight was too much and it could not ascend. A great tiredness came in its dragging body; an ache all along the frames of its wings. The kitten clung tenaciously, staring down at the winding earth and mewling in terror.

For ten minutes the hawk gyrated on a level, defeated and bewildered. All it wanted to do now was to get rid of the burden fastened to its legs and body. It craved respite, a spell on the tallest trees, but it only flew high over these trees, knowing it was unable to perch. Its beak gaped under the harsh ruptures of its breath. It descended three hundred feet. The kitten, with the wisdom of instinct, never altered its position, but rode down like some fantastic parachutist.

In one mighty burst the hawk with striking beak and a

terrible flapping of its wings tried finally to cast off its passenger – and nearly succeeded. The kitten miauled in a frenzy of fear at the violence of the sound and the agitation. Its back legs dangled in space, treading air, and like that it went around on the curves of the flight for two minutes. Then it secured a foothold again, even firmer than the first.

In a hysterical rage, the hawk tried once more to lift itself, and almost instantly began to sweep down in great, slow, gliding eddies that became narrower and narrower.

The kitten was the pilot now and the hawk no longer the assassin of the void, the lord of the sky, and the master of the wind. The ache coiled and throbbed in its breast. It fought against the erratic disposition of its wings and the terror of its waning strength. Its heart bursting with the strain, its eyes dilated wild and yellow, it came down until the earth skimmed under it; and the kitten cried at the silver glare of the roofs not far off, and the expanding earth, and the brush of the grass.

The hawk lobbed and flung over, and the kitten rolled with it. And the hawk lay spraddled in exhaustion, its eyes fiercely, cravenly aware of the danger of its forced and alien position.

The kitten staggered giddily, unhurt, towards the silver roofs, wailing loudly as if in answer to the voice of a child.

The Seal

Liam O'Flaherty

The seal had his head raised high above the water as he intently watched a row boat from which a net was being cast, a short distance to the east. There were four men in the boat. One of them stood in the stern paying out the net. The other three kept rowing gently, in order to keep the boat steady against the strong current. The man in the bow noticed the seal when the net was almost cast. He cursed and shipped his oars at once. Then he picked up a gun that lay behind him in the bow, took aim at the seal's head and fired.

The seal submerged just as the shot was about to leave the muzzle of the gun. He had barely disappeared when the pellets of lead tore the surface of the sea at the exact spot where his head had been. He sank tail first for a few fathoms. Then he stretched out flat and swam at full speed under water to the base of a steep dark cliff. He surfaced there and stood in the water with his back to the rock. Now he was safe from observation. His dun body was exactly the same colour as the stone. He again began to watch the boat intently.

The men rowed away to the east after having cast their net. They soon passed out of sight behind a sandy promontory. The sound of their rowing, however, remained loud for some time. The deep rumble of the oar glambs turning round the thole pins was distinct from the swish of the blades through the water.

When the last faint echo of these sounds had died in the caverns overhead, the seal thrust forward from the rock. He swam warily towards the small inflated buoy of tarred sheepskin that the men had left floating at the end of a rope, above their net. He submerged when he came abreast of the buoy.

111

There lay the net before him, like a wall of black lace, swaying idly back and forth on the current. He greedily inspected the meshes. They were all empty.

Then a large salmon shot past him at great speed and struck the middle of the net, which bulged deeply before the impact. The head of the hapless fish went through one of the meshes as far as the gills. He shook himself fiercely and began to struggle. His beautiful body sent rays of light streaming through the dark water as he leaped in his wild efforts to escape. His violence merely made his prison more secure. Soon his tail also was enmeshed and forced up against his belly. He continued to writhe within a circle that grew even smaller. In the end he was caparisoned from snout to tail by the meshes and so firmly held that he could struggle no longer. He swayed without resistance with the net, back and forth on the current, gasping spasmodically for breath.

The seal waited until the leaping of the imprisoned fish had ceased. Then he came forward to secure his prey. He took the salmon's head between his jaws and crushed it at one bite. Having released the carcass by cutting the meshes all round, he took it in his teeth and swam towards the surface. He was halfway when he himself was attacked by a conger eel of giant size.

The eel had come whirling straight up from the depths at lightning speed, like an enormous black screw. He threw himself at the base of the seal's neck, which he enveloped several times in the folds of his seven-foot body. While he hugged with all his strength, he drew back his head and snapped at the seal's sleek fur with his vast semi-circular jaws. His keen teeth drew blood at several points.

Stunned by the sudden attack, the seal continued slowly towards the surface for a little way. Then he began to choke within the ever-tightening embrace of his enemy. He released the salmon and turned to defend himself. The conger eel did not wait to receive the counter-attack. He released his hold, as soon as he saw that his ruse had succeeded. He pursued the dead salmon, which had continued towards the surface on being released. Then he in turn grabbed the carcass and made off with it towards the depths. At the moment he did so, however, he found himself gripped securely by the navel in the seal's jaws.

The seal came swiftly to the surface. He raised his head high above the water and began to swing his pinioned enemy from side to side, in the way a dog shakes a rat. The conger eel clung to the salmon at first, as he curved and dangled like a dancing rope about the seal's head. Then he dropped the carcass. The salmon floated away slowly on the current, with a ring of torn meshes still clinging to the centre of his body.

The seal hurled his enemy into the air after having thoroughly shaken him. The conger eel's body curved in a graceful arc as it reached the highest point in its ascent. Then it came down head first. The seal was poised to receive it. He cut the head clean from the body at one snap of his jaws.

The headless body plunged straight down through the sea several fathoms, whirling almost as swiftly as when it had been whole. Then it lost direction and momentum. Belching blood from its great wound, it began to wander aimlessly in wide arcs. The detached head remained on the surface. It continued to snap its jaws convulsively for a while as it floated with the current.

Tiny streams of blood flowed from the seal's wounds as he went after the dead salmon. He bellowed in triumph as he came up with it. He took it in his jaws and swam at full speed to his cave within the bowels of the cliff.

The Sea Beast
and the *Queen*
of Heaven

Juanita Casey

The porpoises were lazing in the summer sea a fathom deep off the rocks of Barra, idle with content and two pups already in the herd, when the big grey mother rose slowly to the world of air and rested quietly near the pale surface. The small shining body was born into a world of shifting lights and gentle water, a lapping green cradle of water; and he was one with the sea from the moment of his birth. By the side of his wise grey mother the young Barra came to understand the ways of water, and the momentary brightness and strangeness of the world above; of the suddenness of sun's heat by day, and the glittering eyes of night. He learned of the black depths of the sea, and of the great rush of joy when he leaped in a boil of silver into the world of winds, his body curving like the rainbow. He learned how to root out the foolish sole from shallow sands, to hunt the soft-mouthed mullet from the harbour mud, and fling headlong after shoals of herring, hungry for the cold red blood.

Soon he left his mother's side and rolled with the herd, sleek and rounded and with a smiling eye.

Their leader was the old grey-headed Arran, wise and heavy-browed, scarred with the wounds of many battles, careful of his happy herd.

But as the years passed he grew slower, and the greyness spread over his body; he found he could no longer be the father of his herd, and the young bulls ranged relentlessly at his flanks. One day Phoca, the strongest among them, challenged him and took his place, and Arran fell away from the herd, making his slow way alone through the seas to die. And Barra his son ran close to the new leader, awaiting his season.

114

Rolling down the sea lanes the herd gambolled past the Welsh headlands and rounded the islands of the west. Heading in from the Bishop Light they ran close to the outer isles, surprising Grypus, the grey seal, on his throne of rock. Grypus beat his flipper angrily and barked a warning to his wives, who shuffled higher up the ledges to their pups, rolling and huffing in their haste to escape from the water and the hunting porpoise pack. Turning eastward, the herd was some miles off the Wolf when Barra became aware of a vast unease, a taste, a smell of something acute and dangerous in the waters behind. The singing of the water had ceased, something was rising like thunder from the depths; something that cut the seas away like a knife, and came black and headlong in a roar of water.

Barra's fear tainted the sea around him, and several of the herd dived sharply with him, away from Phoca, and fled downwards into darkness, their fear twittering like birds. They were not with the main herd when Orca the black killer smashed into them.

They splintered under the impact, and the dreaded Orca chopped among them like a vast black hound, his little eye insane with double lust; with the savagery of the world of beasts and of the world of fish beneath the water; the savagery of the killer-whale. He ripped and tore until he swam through red water, and Phoca, bitten through the spine, sank bubbling numbly into the depths, whining as he slowly drowned in his own blood. When they came together again it was a pitiful small herd that limped on up-Channel, some with great wounds that looked as though cut out by spades, some with hanging tattered flesh and one old female with her flipper torn away. And Barra passed to their head and became their leader; the father of the little herd, nursing them on their painful way, careful of the pups and females, fierce towards the upstart bulls; a wise ruler in his small water-world. They followed the fine ships of those days, the tall windships, the exulting clippers, who raced the sun around the world. Foaming up-Channel with every stitch singing, the fighters of Cape Horn returned to their home ports, and beside them rolled the porpoises, the travellers of the sea.

It was on a cold March morning, when the wind blew hard from the west in a flurry of ice-blue sky and shouting blue water, that the *Queen of Heaven* entered the Channel approaches, and running rails under she creamed past the Lizard, thundering to her press of sail. The loveliest of her line and generation, she was so beautiful that old sailors told of her in later years with the dreaming eyes of lovers; and where some carried devils in their hearts, and some cried out with unquiet spirits, and some killed their master and half their crew before they killed themselves, the *Queen of Heaven* was a sweet ship – a great ship.

On that shouting March day Barra and his herd ran close to her up the Channel, and her crew came into the bows to watch them as they played.

As the great forefoot dipped and rose Barra would let her touch his tail for a moment before effortlessly increasing his pace. He dived beneath her and came up to windward, seeing the clean and lovely lines of her hull surging above him, cutting through green water and leaving a hissing silver trail smoking like a comet.

Over the years Barra and his herd greeted the *Queen of Heaven* as she entered English waters after her long flight from the ends of the world, and the sailors came to look for their approach as a sign of homecoming.

Sometimes she would roll in greasy calms off Start Point and remain idle for the day, until an evening wind breathed again; then joyfully she would begin to move, whispering over the water, and lean into the night for a quiet run home, the porpoise pack rolling with her. And sometimes she would come glorious, carrying all sail to a strong sou'westerly, storming past the Lizard in a burst of white water, her jib boom singing a strange song of wandering horizons, of her flight around the Horn, of her long-awaited landfall.

Such a ship was the *Queen of Heaven*: a perfect union of man's craftsmanship with wind and water – but her soul, her ship's soul, her own until her ending.

And Barra grew slowly grey with years, and one day he left the pack and went on his way alone. He was tired with the efforts of piloting his large herd, of the constant vigilance and the unrelenting challenge of the younger bulls.

And as he grew old the ships of sail became fewer, and the pump and bellow of engines and the blackness of smoke heralded a future age: an age of clanging iron and thrashing propellers. The new iron ships thrust aside the wind and fouled the seas with soot and rainbow-oils, and Barra fled from their presence.

He could now accompany the few remaining windships for only a little while; but their crews still looked for him as they entered the Channel reaches and became fond of the 'white-headed porpoise' who travelled alone.

His speed was gone and he could no longer keep up his effortless run by the flying forefoot. He grew faint for air when pressed, and one day he left the sweetness of the sea to rest in muddy harbours. And one by one the windships went from the sea.

Lying under the sodden branches of half-submerged oaks, Barra waited for straying mullet or a sickly salmon, and ignobly hustled to a grimy kill in the brown waters of shallow creeks.

He rubbed his itching back on the keels of boats at anchor, listlessly scratching like a farmer's pig to rid his body of the harbour lice.

One day a great toothed whale, old and desperate with sickness, crept into the little harbour and rolled despairing beside the quay to a slow and monstrous death; such a vastness, such an enormity of death that dismayed the people watching on the quayside, and filled their hearts with pity for the stricken giant.

And Barra felt a great need to go from the unhealthy waters of the harbour, for he felt the spirit leaving him, and he wished his ending to be in the clearness of the sea, in the truth of green water, in his beginning. He lay on the outgoing tide and, slipping past the last rocks of the land, he reached out to sea as a traveller eagerly approaches home.

Through a night of running cloud, with a sprinkling of rain flighting down in the wind-gusts, Barra drifted quiet in his loved sea lanes.

Dawn came yellow-bellied, with a streak of livid green where the sun should be, and the wind swung south-east and whined uneasily. All through the morning the sea rose and the wind harrowed the crests and roared in to savage the land, and under the lash of the wind the sea smoked. Barra swam slowly below the storm, only rising into the troubled surface waters to blow. The shrieking wind and flying spray bewildered him, and he found difficulty in breathing through the whip of water. The smaller ships had run for safety, and by evening the storm was at its height.

Two ships only could be seen from the Lizard station – one an ocean tug, the other all that remained of the *Queen of Heaven*.

Ploughing and veering behind her small jailer, chained like a dog, the *Queen of Heaven* floundered on her last journey to a knacker's end in a breaking-yard. Stripped of her pride, she heaved and plunged, forced unwillingly against the wind which had exalted her in all her former victories.

The small tug laboured against tide and wind, shaken by the erratic plunging of her great prisoner as a rabbit is shaken by a hound. To the watchers at the Lizard her task became unbearable, and with relief they saw her cast off all lines and steer out to sea, to the safety of deep water, leaving the great hulk to drive ashore. As Barra forced himself up to gasp into the gale, the *Queen of Heaven* roared down upon him, and his old eyes were too dim to see her ravaged superstructure. He saw only the lovely waterlines of her hull as she swept by; and suddenly his heart leaped with a great shaft of happiness like sunlight, and he took his accustomed place by her side as she raced towards the land. Intent as a hawk for the kill she flew at the raging rocks, and to the watchers on shore it was as though a terrible voice cried from her – the cry of a ship that has lost her soul . . .

In the calm of morning they found her.

All that could be called ship had vanished. Only a great mass of broken wood lay on the beach of the little cove, and broken wood washed gently in the weary tide.

And they found, cast high up on the beach and lying across the shattered golden figurehead of the *Queen of Heaven*, the body of an old white-headed porpoise.

Look at him, they said. He must have followed the old ship home. Look at the way he's smiling – it's almost human, they said. And as they turned away up the beach the sun rode out from behind the clouds and a crow dropped heavily to the water's edge, and strutting along the sands began to peer and prod amongst the wreckage.

The Last Husky

Farley Mowat

The people built the little igloo and departed into the wastelands. They went from the place singing the laments for the dying, and they left nothing behind them except the old man. They even took Arnuk, the dog, for that was the old man's wish, and Arnuk was the most precious gift that an old man could make to his son and to his people.

It had been a bitter season, the long, hungry weeks before the spring, and in the camp of the people there had been the cries of children who were too young to know that starvation must be faced in silence. There had been death in the camp; not of men, but of those who were almost as important to the continuance of human life. For the dogs had died, one by one, and as each was stilled so did man's hopes for the future shrink. For in the stark plains country of the Barren Lands the lives of men and dogs are one in their need for each other.

Yet though it had been a bitter time, there had been no word spoken against the folly of feeding one old and useless human body. Maktuk, the son, had shared his own meagre rations equally between his aged father and his starving child, who also bore the name that linked the three together. No word was said, but one dark day in early May the old man raised himself slowly from the sleeping ledge and gazed for a little while at his grandchild, and out of the depths of a great love and greater courage, old Maktuk spoke these words.

'I have it in my heart,' he said, 'that the deer await you at the Western Lakes. Go when morning comes, and I will stay. And you shall take Arnuk with you, so that in the years ahead you will remember me and leave the spirit gifts upon my grave.'

There had been no discussion, for even an old man has his rights, and this is his final one. In the morning the people were gone, and behind young Maktuk's sled the dog, Arnuk, tugged convulsively at her tether and turned her head backwards to a small white igloo, rising shadowless against the endless snows.

Arnuk had been born in the preceding spring, in the lean times that always grip the land before the deer return. She was the seventh pup of the litter, and there was no food for her. And if an old man had not taken it upon himself to feed and care for her, she would have died before her life began. Yet she saw summer come and knew the pleasures of long days spent romping with the other young dogs by the side of the great river where the summer camp was pitched. When she grew tired, she would come to the skin tent and push against the old man's knees until he opened his aged eyes and smiled at her.

And so she grew through the good summer months, and the people in the camp gazed at her almost with awe, for she became beautiful and of a size and strength surpassing that of any other dog. Maktuk, the elder, gave her the name she bore: Arnuk – The Woman – for she was wife and mother to him in the last winter of his years.

Because there can be no death while there is birth, old Maktuk insisted that his dog be mated in the April days, when the moon stands still and the white wolves howl their passion to the flickering northern lights. So it was arranged, for Arnuk bore within her the promise of a strength that would be the people's strength in years to come. And when Maktuk, the elder, felt the throb of new life in the womb of The Woman, he was content.

The spring hunger had already begun before Arnuk was mated, and the famine grew with the passing days. The older dogs died first, yet near the end even Arnuk's litter mates lay silent in the snows. But Arnuk's strength was great, and when there was some scrap of bone or skin that the people could spare, she received it, for in her womb lay the hopes of the future.

This was the way of things when the people turned from the lonely igloo and, dragging the sleds with their own failing muscles, set their faces to the west.

The ties that bind man and his dog can be of many strengths, but the ties which bound Arnuk to old Maktuk were beyond human power to break. Arnuk went with the people, but resisting fiercely. And on the third day of the journey she gnawed through the rawhide tether, and before dawn she had vanished into the swirling ground drift. In the morning, Maktuk, the son, held the frayed tether in his hand and his face was filled with the sorrow of foreboding. Yet when he spoke to his family, it was with these words:

'What must be, surely cannot be denied. The Woman has gone to my father, and she will be with him when the Snow Walker comes. But my father's spirit will know of our need, and perhaps the day will dawn when he will return The Woman to us, for if she does not come, the years ahead are dark.'

As for Arnuk, she reached the little igloo before daybreak, and when the old man opened his eyes to see if it was the Snow Walker at last, he saw the dog instead. And he smiled and laid his bony hand upon her head, and once more he slept.

The Snow Walker was late in coming, but on the seventh day he came, unseen, and when he passed from the place the bond was broken. Yet it was not broken, for Arnuk lingered with her dead three days, and then it was the wind, perhaps, that whispered the unspoken order: 'Go to the people; go.'

When she emerged from the igloo she found her world had been obliterated beneath a heavy blizzard. For a while she stood in the pale sun, her golden coat gleaming against the purple shadows; then she turned her face with its broad ruff and wide-spaced amber eyes towards the west, for that way lay her path. And within her, the voices of the unborn generations echoed the voice of the wind, but with a greater urgency. 'Go to the tents of men,' they told her. 'Go.'

She did not halt even when darkness swept the bleak plains into obscurity. At midnight she came to the place where she had chewed her way free of young Maktuk's sled. She knew it was the place only by an inner sense, for the snow had levelled all signs and had drifted in all trails. She circled among the hard drifts, whining miserably, for terrible doubts had begun to seize upon her. She climbed a rock ridge to test the night air for some sign that men were near. Scents came to her. The acrid odour of an arctic fox that had fled into invisibility at her approach. But there was no scent of man.

Her whines rose to a crescendo, a wild pleading in the darkness, but there was no answer except the rising moan of the wind. And at length, worn into a stupor by the weight of her hunger and by her loneliness, she curled up in the shelter of a drift and lost herself in dreams.

So the dog slept in the heart of the unfathomable wilderness. But as she dozed uneasily, a profound change was taking place in the secret places of her body. A strange alchemy was at work. She lay with her nose outstretched on her broad forepaws and her muscles twitched with erratic impulses. Saliva flowed to her mouth, and in it was the taste of blood. In her mind's eye she laid her stride to that of the swift deer, and her teeth met in the living flesh, and she knew the savage ecstacy of the last quiver in a dying prey.

From somewhere out of time, the ageless instincts that lie in all living cells were being reborn so that the dog, and the new life within her, would not perish. And when Arnuk raised her head to the dawn light, the thing was done, the change complete.

The dawn was clear, and Arnuk, her perceptions keenly sharpened by the chemistry of change, tested the wind. When she found the warm smell of living flesh, she rose to seek it out.

Not far distant, a snowy owl, dead white and shadowless in the predawn, had earlier swept across the plains with great eyes staring. The owl had seen and fallen so swiftly on a hare that the beast had known nothing until the inch-long talons clutched his life and took it from him. It was a good kill, and the owl felt pleasure as it perched above the corpse. The great bird savoured the weight of its own hunger, and while it sat complacent, crouched above the hare, it did not see the flow of motion on a nearby drift.

Arnuk was a weasel creeping up upon a mouse; a snake slithering upon a sparrow. Skills she had never known, skills that had come to her in all completeness from forgotten half beasts lost in the dimmest aeons, were hers now. Her belly dragged on the hard snows and she inched forward. When she was a dozen feet away, the owl raised its head and the yellow eyes of the bird stared with expressionless intensity full into Arnuk's face. Arnuk was the stillness of death, yet every muscle vibrated in the grip of a passion such as she had never known before. And when the owl turned back to its prey, Arnuk leaped. The owl saw the beginning of the leap and threw itself backwards into its own element with a smooth thrust of mighty wings. But those wings were a fraction slow and the hurtling form of the dog, leaping six feet into the air, struck flesh beneath the feathers. It was a brief battle. Three times the talons of the bird drew blood, and then they stiffened and relaxed in death.

Arnuk slept afterwards while white feathers blew into the bleak distance, and tufts of white fur moved like furtive living things in the grip of the wind. And when she woke again, the agony of her hunger was at an end and the savage drive of her new instincts was momentarily dulled. Once more she was man's beast, and lost.

She woke and, without a glance at the red snow beside her, set out again into the west, unconscious, yet directly driven.

The people whom she sought were wanderers on the face of a plain so vast that it seemed limitless. The dog could not conceive of the odds against her finding them, but in her memory was the image of the summer camp by the wide river where she had spent her youth, and with an unerring perseverance she set her course for that far-distant place.

The days passed, and after each the sun stood a little higher in the sky. Space lengthened under the dog's feet until the explosion of spring disturbed the world. The snows grew soft and the Barrens rivers, freed from their chains, thundered angrily across the plains. In a white and glaring sky, flights of ravens hung like eddies of burned leaves, and on the opening ponds geese mingled with the flocks of raucous gulls.

The awakening of life was in the deep moss where the lemmings tunnelled, and it was on the stony ridges where cock ptarmigan swaggered before their mates. It was in all living things and in all places, and it was within the womb of the dog, Arnuk. Her journey had been long, and her broad paws were crusted with the dried blood of a hundred stone cuts. Her magnificent coat was matted now, and lustreless under the spring sun. Nevertheless, she drew upon unknown strengths and upon her own indomitable will, and she went forward into the western plains.

Gaunt, hot-eyed and terribly exhausted, she brought her quest to an end on a day in early June. Breasting a long ridge, she saw before her the brilliant light of sun on roaring water, and she recognized the river. She had come home.

Whining with excitement, she ran clumsily down the slope, for her body had grown awkward in these last days. And soon she was among the rings of weathered boulders where, in the summer that was past, men's tents had stood.

The tents were gone. There was no living man to welcome the return of the lost one. Only on the nearby ridges the motionless piles of rocks that the Inuit call *Inukok*, Men of Stone, were there to see the coming of Arnuk. They and the hidden piles of bones under rock cairns near the river, the old graves of forgotten people. Arnuk understood that the place was empty of living men, yet for an hour she refused to believe it. Pathetically she ran from old tent ring to old meat cache, sniffing each with a despairing hope, and finding nothing to give her heart; and when realization became inescapable, the dog curled herself in a hollow beside the place where old Maktuk had once held her at his knees, and she gave herself up to her great weariness and to her bitter disappointment.

Yet the old camp was not quite so empty as it looked. While Arnuk made her fruitless search she had been too preoccupied to know that she was being watched. Had she glanced up the riverbank she might have seen a lithe shape that followed her every move with eyes that held in them a hunger not born of the belly. She would have seen and recognized a wolf, and her hackles would have risen and her teeth been bared. For the dogs of man and the dogs of the wilderness walk apart, theirs being the ancient hatred of brothers who have denied their common blood.

This wolf was young. Born the preceding season, he had stayed with his family until, in the early spring of this year, the urge to wander had come over him and he had forsaken his ancestral territory. Many adventures had befallen him, and most had been bitter ones, for he had learned, at the cost of torn flanks and bleeding shoulders, that each wolf family guards its own land with savage jealousy and there is no room for a stranger. His offers of friendship had been met with bared teeth in the lands of three wolf clans before, at last, he came to the river and found a place where no wolves were.

It was a good place. Not far from the empty Inuit camp the river flared angrily over a shallow stretch of rounded boulders to lose itself in the beginning of an immense lake, and at the shallow place the caribou had made a ford in their spring and midsummer migrations. They crossed the river here in untold thousands, and not all escaped the river's anger. The drowned bodies of dead deer lay among the rocks at the river mouth, and so there was ample food for a great population of arctic foxes, ravens, and white gulls. But the wolves of the country did not visit the place, for it belonged to man, and that which man claims to himself is forbidden to the great wild dogs.

Knowing nothing of this prohibition, the young male wolf, the outcast, had taken up his home by the river, and here he nursed his loneliness. Perhaps even more than dogs, wolves are social animals. Companionship in the hunt and in the games that are played after a hunt are vital to the happiness of the big white beasts. Isolation from their own kind is purgatory for them, and they can know a loneliness that eats away the heart.

It had been so with the young wolf, and when he saw and smelled the dog, Arnuk, he was filled with conflicting emotions. He had seen no dog before, yet he sensed that the golden-coated beast below him was not quite of his blood. The smell was strange, and yet it was familiar. The shape and colour were strange, and yet they roused in him a warmth of memory and desire.

He had been rebuffed so many times before that he was cautious now, and when Arnuk woke from her sleep of exhaustion, she did not at first see the stranger, but her nostrils told her at once of the nearness of deer meat. Her hunger was savage and overpowering. Without caution, she leaped to her feet and flung herself upon a ragged haunch of caribou that had been dragged to within a few

yards of her. Only when she had satisfied her first desperate hunger did she glance up and meet the still gaze of the young wolf.

The wolf sat motionless a hundred feet from the dog, nor did he so much as twitch an ear as Arnuk's hackles lifted and the threat took form deep in her throat. He remained sitting, yet tense to spring away, and after a long minute, Arnuk again dropped her head to the meat, satisfied that the wolf meant her no harm. This was the way of their first meeting. And this is what came of it.

With the mockery of this second deserted camp before her, Arnuk gave up her search for men. She could no longer fight against the insistent demands of her heavy body, and there was no more time for searching. Now once again, in her hour of despair, the hidden force within her took command. Before that first day was out, her mood had changed magically from deep dejection to a businesslike alertness.

Ignoring the wolf, which still kept its distance, Arnuk made a tour of the familiar ground. She carefully examined the carcasses of five drowned deer, and from each of these she chased the screaming gulls, for this meat was hers now by right of greater strength. Then, satisfied with the abundant food supply, Arnuk

left the river and trotted inland to where a rock outcrop had opened its flanks to form a shallow cave. Here, as a pup, Arnuk had played with the other dogs of the camp. Now, as a full-grown female, she examined the cave with more serious intent. The place was dry and protected from the winds. There was only one thing wrong, and that was the smell. The rock cleft was pervaded with a potent and unpleasant stench that caused Arnuk to draw back her lips in distaste – for no animal upon the arctic plains has any love for the ugly and murderous wolverine. And a wolverine had clearly used the cave during the winter months.

Arnuk's nose told her that the wolverine had been gone for several weeks, and there was little likelihood that he would return until the winter winds forced him to seek shelter. Arnuk scratched earth and sand over the unclean floor; then set about dragging moss into the deepest recess. And here at last she hid herself and made surrender to her hour.

Arnuk's pups were born on the third day she spent in the cave, on a morning when the cries of the white geese were loud in the spring air. It was the time of birth, and the five squirming things that lay warm against the dog's fur were not alone in their first day of life. On the sand ridges beyond the river a female ground squirrel suckled the naked motes of flesh that were hers, and in a den by a ridge a mile distant an arctic fox thrust his alert face above the ground while the feeble whimpers of the pups his mate was nursing warned him of the tasks ahead. All living things in the land by the river moved to the rhythm of the demands of life newborn or soon to be born. All things moved to this rhythm except the outcast wolf.

For the three days that Arnuk remained hidden, the young wolf knew a torment that gave him no peace. Restless, yearning for things he had never known, he haunted the vicinity of the cave. He did not dare go too close, but each day he dragged a piece of deer meat within a few yards of the cave mouth and then drew back to wait with pathetic patience for his gift to be accepted.

On the third day, as he lay near the cave, snapping at the flies which hung about his head, his keen ears felt the faintest tremors of a new sound. He was on his feet instantly, head out-thrust and his body trembling with attention. It came again, so faint that it was felt rather than heard – a tiny whimper that called to him across the ages and across all barriers. And in that instant his great unease was at an end. He shook himself sharply and, with one quick, proprietary glance at the cave mouth, trotted out across the plain – no longer a solitary outcast, but a male beginning the evening hunt that would feed his mate and pups. So, simply and out of his deep need, the young wolf filled the void that had surrounded him through the torturing weeks of spring.

Arnuk did not easily accept the wolf in the role he had chosen to play. For several days she kept him at bay with bared teeth, although she ate the food offerings he left at the cave mouth. But before a week was out she had come to expect the fresh meat – the tender ground squirrels, the arctic hares and plump ptarmigan. And from this it was not really a long step to complete acceptance of the wolf.

Arnuk sealed the compact with him in the second week after the pups were born. Coming to the den mouth one morning, she found the carcass of a freshly killed hare lying ready for her, and only a few feet away, the sleeping form of the young wolf.

It had been a long, hard hunt that night, and the wolf had covered most of the hundred square miles of territory that he had staked out for his adopted family, and so, exhausted by his efforts, he had not bothered to retire the usual discreet distance from the den.

For a long minute Arnuk stared at the sleeping beast, and then, with the motion of one who stalks an enemy, she moved towards the wolf. But there was no real menace in her action, and when she reached the wolf's side her great plumed tail went up into its husky curl and her lips spread as if in laughter.

The wolf woke, raised his head, saw her standing over him, and knew that here at last was the end to loneliness. The morning light blazed over the den ridge as the two great beasts stood shoulder to shoulder, gazing out over the awakening plains.

In the days that followed, life was good by the banks of the river. For Arnuk there were no fears and no empty places in her heart. And for the wolf there was the swelling pride with which he lay in the sun outside the den while the pups tussled with his fur and chewed at his patient feet.

So time passed until the pups were in their seventh week. Midsummer was in the Barrens, and the herds of deer were drifting southwards once again in the July migration that precedes the final autumn trek to timberline. The crossing place was once more thronged with caribou, and the young calves grunted beside their ragged mothers, while the old bucks, their velvet-covered antlers reaching to the skies, moved aloofly in the van.

And then one evening a desire for the long chase came over Arnuk, and in the secret ways that men know nothing of, she made her desire apparent to the wolf. When the late summer dusk fell, Arnuk went out alone into the darkening plains, secure in the knowledge that the wolf would remain to guard the pups until her return, though she be gone a year.

She did not intend a long absence – only a few hours at the most – but near the outskirts of the territory she came on a band of young buck deer. They were fine beasts, and fat, which at this time of the year was a mouth-watering oddity. Tired of too much lean meat, Arnuk knew a sudden surge of appetite, and she circled the resting herd, filled with an ardent hunger.

A change of the uncertain breeze betrayed her, and the startled deer sprang to their feet and fled. Arnuk was hungry, and the night was a hunter's night. She took up the long chase.

So the hours drove the brief darkness from the land, and when the hard early winds of dawn rose in the north the young wolf roused himself from his vigil at the cave mouth. A sense of dim foreboding made him turn to the den and thrust his head and shoulders into the entrance. All was well, and the pups were rolled together in a compact ball, jerking their stubby legs in sleep. Yet the feeling of uneasiness persisted in the wolf's mind, and he turned towards the river, where the grey light picked out the roll of distant ridges.

Perhaps he was worried by the long absence of the dog, perhaps he had been warned by senses that remain unknown to us. His uneasiness grew, and at last he trotted away from the den, sniffing at the cold trail of Arnuk, hoping to see her golden form approaching from inland.

He had gone no more than half a mile when the vague sense of something evil took concrete form. A vagrant eddy brought the north breeze to his nostrils and instantly he knew what had disturbed him when he woke. He turned back towards the cave with startling speed.

As he breasted the slope beside the den, the stink of wolverine rose like a foul miasma in his nostrils, and the young wolf was transformed in the instant into a savage thing, distrait with the most elemental rage. He came down the slope in half a dozen gigantic leaps, his ears flat to his skull and his great throat rumbling with incoherent hate.

Several hours earlier, the wolverine had winded the young pups in his old winter lair. He had not had any intention of revisiting the foul winter den as he made his way slowly upriver, but the smell of the pups had tempted him. Perhaps he would have ignored even that temptation, for though he feared no living thing he had no particular desire to meet the fury of a female wolf defending her young. But the night had been empty for him, and his cavernous belly rumbled with hunger. His temper, always vile, was edged by hunger, and so, in the grey dawn light, he turned from the river and circled cautiously upwind until he found a rock out-thrust that gave him cover, and from which he could observe the den. Here he waited with a terrible patience until he saw the young wolf trot from the den mouth towards the inland plains.

Still cautiously, the wolverine left his cover and moved in upon the den, pausing for long moments to reassure himself that the pups were really undefended. His squat, massive body hugged the rough ground as he drew closer, and now fully certain of success, he could already taste the pleasure of the killing and the salt warmth of blood.

There was blood enough for him to taste that dawn. But it was not the blood of Arnuk's pups.

The young wolf's savage rush was so swift that the wolverine had only sufficient time to slew about and take the weight of the attack upon his side. It was enough to save him, for the wolf's white teeth sank deep through the tough skin, but missed their promised hold upon the throat, and met

instead in the sinews of the killer's shoulder. On any other beast it would have been a good hold, leading to victory, but on the wolverine it was not good enough. The wolverine knows neither fear nor pain, and its squat body is possessed of a strength equal to any beast three times its size. A weasel by blood, with all the weasel's maniac ferocity, the wolverine has the body of a bear, and such is its vitality that life remains in it until that body has been literally torn apart.

So it was with the old beast at the cave mouth. He did not feel his injury, but instead was aflame with an insane anger. He swung his fifty pounds of bone and gristle into a savage counterthrust.

134

Had the wolf been older and more experienced, he might have sidestepped that lunge, but he was young, and blinded by the allegiance that he had so freely given to the pups that he had never sired. He held his grip and did not slacken it as the wolverine's teeth raked his unprotected flank.

They fought in silence from that moment. The sun, red on the eastern rim, was pallid beside the glare of blood upon the rocks. The pups, drawn to the cave mouth by the first onslaught, watched the terrible duel for an instant, and then, appalled by the fury of the struggle, slunk into the dark earth and lay in trembling fear.

It was the gulls that warned Arnuk. From afar off, as she came wearily homeward in the warmth of the morning, she saw them circling and heard their strident screams. They eddied above the rocks where the den lay, and weary as she was, a great anxiety gave her new strength and she came on at full pace. And so she found the murderer, torn to bloody fragments before the murder was begun. And so she found the wolf, his throat ripped raggedly across and his still body stiffening beneath the rising sun.

The bodies still lay near the cave when, a week later, the voices of men echoed once more along the shores of the river. And they still lay by the cave a little later on, when the young man called Maktuk bent down to the dark opening and very gently thrust his hand under the timid pups, while Arnuk, half wild with old emotions, stood trembling by his side. Maktuk was a man of the plains, and he could read much that cannot ever be written, so that he knew all there was to know of what had taken place beneath those shattered rocks.

It was because he knew, that, on an evening in late summer, he took his son to the bank of the river and placed the boy's hand on the head of the golden dog and spoke these words:

'Maktuk, my son. In a little time you shall be a man and a hunter, and all the wide plains will know your name and skill. In those days you will have certain friends to help you in the hunt, and of these the greatest you shall always call Arnuk, and then my father will know that we have received his gift and he will be at ease. And in those times to come, all beasts shall fall to your spear and bow, save one alone. For never while you live shall your hand be raised against the white one, against Amarok, the wolf – and so shall the people pay their debt to him.'

5
The Hunter and the Hunted

The Rockfish

Liam O'Flaherty

Flop. The cone-shaped bar of lead tied to the end of the fishing-line dropped into the sea without causing a ripple. It sank rapidly through the long seaweed that grew on the face of the rock. It sank twenty-five feet and then struck the bottom. It tumbled around and then lay on its side in a niche at the top of a round pool. The man on top of the rock hauled in his line until it was taut. The bar of lead bobbed up and down twice. Then it rested straight on its end in the niche. Three short plaits of stiff horsehair extended crookedly like tentacles from the line above the leaden weight at regular intervals. At the end of each plait was a hook baited all over with shelled periwinkle. A small crab, transfixed through the belly, wriggled on the lowest hook. The two upper hooks had a covering of crushed crab tied by thin strings around the periwinkles. The three baited hooks swung round and round, glistening white through the red strands of broad seaweed that hung lazily from their stems in the rock face. Dark caverns at the base of the rock cast long shadows out over the bottom of the sea about the hooks. Little bulbous things growing in groups on the bottom spluttered methodically as they stirred.

The man sitting above on the top of the rock spat into the sea. Resting his fishing-rod in the crutch of his right arm, he began to fill his pipe, yawning.

A little rockfish came rushing out from a cavern under the rock. He whisked his tail and stopped dead behind a huge blade of seaweed when he saw the glistening baits. His red scaly body was the colour of the weed. It tapered from the middle to the narrow tail and to the triangular-shaped head. He stared at the baits for a long time without moving his body. His gills rose and fell steadily. Then he flapped his tail and glided to the upper hook. He touched it with his snout. He nibbled at it timorously three times. Then he snatched at the top of it and darted away back into the cavern with a piece of periwinkle in his mouth. The man on the rock sat up excitedly, threw his pipe on the rock, and seized the rod with both hands, breathing through his nose.

Several rockfish gathered around the little fellow in the cavern. They tried to snatch the piece of periwinkle from his mouth. But he dived under a ledge of rock and bolted it hurriedly. Then, all the rockfish darted out to the hooks. The little ones scurried around hither and thither. Three middle-sized ones stood by the two upper hooks, sniffing at them. Then they began to nibble carefully. One little rockfish stood on his head over the bottom hook and sniffed at it. But the crab wriggled one leg and the rockfish darted away at a terrific speed. All the rockfish darted away after it into the cavern. Then one of the middle-sized ones came back again alone. He went up to the highest hook and grabbed at it immediately. He took the whole bait from it. The hook grazed his lower lip as it slipped from his mouth. The rockfish dropped the bait, turned a somersault, and dived into the cavern.

The man on the rock swung his rod back over his head, and dropped it forward again with an oath when he found the line coming slack. 'Missed,' he said. Then the leaden weight slipped back again into the niche. A crowd of rockfish quarrelled over the pieces of periwinkle fallen from the middle-sized fellow's mouth. The pieces, too light to sink, kept floating about. Then they disappeared one by one into the fishes' mouths.

A huge rockfish prowled in from the deep. He stood by the corner of a rock watching the little ones quarrel over the pieces of fallen bait. He was as big as all the others together. He must have been three feet long and his middle was as thick as a bull-dog's chest. The scales on his back were all the colours of the rainbow. His belly was a dun colour. He stood still for a time, watching like an old bull, his gills showing large red cavities in his throat as they opened. Then he swooped in among the little ones.

They dived away from him into the cavern. He gobbled the remaining pieces of bait. Then he turned around slowly twice and swam close to the bottom towards the hooks. He saw the crab wriggling on the lowest hook. With a rush he swallowed the crab and the hook, turned about and rushed away with it, out towards his lair in the deep. The leaden weight rushed along the bottom with him. The line went taut with a snap over his back. The fishing-rod was almost wrenched from the hands of the man on the rock. Its tip touched the water. Then the man heaved the rod over his head and grasped the line. The hook was wrenched back out of the rockfish's gullet and its point tore through the side of his mouth.

141

The rockfish was whirled about by the wrench and dragged backwards headlong. With a swishing sound he heaved straight through the water towards the cavern. Then the line went taut again as the man hauled in. The rockfish was tugged up along the face of the rock. He jumped twice and heaved. He tore a strip of the soft thick skin in which the hook was embedded from his jaw at one end. Hanging to the hook by this strip, he came up gasping through the hanging weeds. The man groaned as he heaved.

Then the bared top hook got caught in a broad blade of seaweed. It combed its way through to the hard stem and then got stuck. The man heaved and could draw it no further. The rockfish hung exhausted from the bottom hook. The man stuck his right foot against a ledge and leaning back with the line held in his two hands across his stomach he pulled with all his might. The top hook broke. The line jerked up. The rockfish reached the surface. He tried to breathe with wide open mouth. Then he hurled himself into the air and dived headlong downwards. The hanging strip of skin parted from his jaw. He was free.

The Sea Devil

Arthur Gordon

The man came out of the house and stood quite still, listening. Behind him, the lights glowed in the cheerful room, the books were neat and orderly in their cases, the radio talked importantly to itself. In front of him, the bay stretched dark and silent, one of the countless lagoons that border the coast where Florida thrusts its great green thumb deep into the tropics.

It was late in September. The night was breathless; summer's dead hand still lay heavy on the land. The man moved forward six paces and stood on the sea wall. He dropped his cigarette and noted where the tiny spark hissed and went out. The tide was beginning to ebb.

Somewhere out in the blackness a mullet jumped and fell back with a sullen splash. Heavy with roe, they were jumping less often now. They would not take a hook, but a practised eye could see the swirls they made in the glassy water. In the dark of the moon, a skilled man with a cast net might take half a dozen in an hour's work. And a big mullet makes a meal for a family.

The man turned abruptly and went into the garage, where his cast net hung. He was in his late twenties, wide-shouldered and strong. He did not have to fish for a living, or even for food. He was a man who worked with his head, not with his hands. But he liked to go casting alone at night.

He liked the loneliness and the labour of it. He liked the clean taste of salt when he gripped the edge of the net with his teeth as a cast netter must. He liked the arching flight of sixteen pounds of lead and linen against the starlight, and the weltering crash of the net into the unsuspecting water. He liked the harsh

143

tug of the retrieving rope around his wrist, and the way the net came alive when the cast was true, and the thud of captured fish on the floor boards of the skiff.

He liked all that because he found in it a reality that seemed to be missing from his twentieth-century job and from his daily life. He liked being the hunter, skilled and solitary and elemental. There was no conscious cruelty in the way he felt. It was the way things had been in the beginning.

The man lifted the net down carefully and lowered it into a bucket. He put a paddle beside the bucket. Then he went into the house. When he came out, he was wearing swimming trunks and a pair of old tennis shoes. Nothing else.

The skiff, flat-bottomed, was moored off the sea wall. He would not go far, he told himself. Just to the tumbledown dock half a mile away. Mullet had a way of feeding around old pilings after dark. If he moved quietly, he might pick up two or three in one cast close to the dock. And maybe a couple of others on the way down or back.

He shoved off and stood motionless for a moment, letting his eyes grow accustomed to the dark. Somewhere out in the

channel a porpoise blew with a sound like steam escaping. The man smiled a little; porpoises were his friends. Once, fishing in the Gulf, he had seen the charter-boat captain reach overside and gaff a baby porpoise through the sinewy part of the tail. He had hoisted it aboard, had dropped it into the bait well, where it thrashed around, puzzled and unhappy. And the mother had swum alongside the boat and under the boat and around the boat, nudging the stout planking with her back, slapping it with her tail, until the man felt sorry for her and made the captain let the baby porpoise go.

He took the net from the bucket, slipped the noose in the retrieving rope over his wrist, pulled the slipknot tight. It was an old net, but still serviceable; he had rewoven the rents made by underwater snags. He coiled the thirty-foot rope carefully, making sure there were no kinks. A tangled rope, he knew, would spoil any cast.

The basic design of the net had not changed in three thousand years. It was a mesh circle with a diameter of fourteen feet. It measured close to fifteen yards around the circumference and could, if thrown perfectly, blanket a hundred and fifty square feet of sea water. In the centre of this radial trap was a small iron collar where the retrieving rope met the twenty-three separate drawstrings leading to the outer rim of the net. Along this rim, spaced an inch and a half apart, were the heavy lead sinkers.

The man raised the iron collar until it was a foot above his head. The net hung soft and pliant and deadly. He shook it gently, making sure that the drawstrings were not tangled, that the sinkers were hanging true. Then he eased it down and picked up the paddle.

The night was black as a witch's cat; the stars looked fuzzy and dim. Down to the southward, the lights of a causeway made a yellow necklace across the sky. To the man's left were the tangled roots of a mangrove swamp; to his right, the open waters of the bay. Most of it was fairly shallow, but there were channels eight feet deep. The man could not see the old dock, but he knew where it was. He pulled the paddle quietly through the water, and the phosphorescence glowed and died.

For five minutes he paddled. Then, twenty feet ahead of the skiff, a mullet jumped. A big fish, close to three pounds. For a moment it hung in the still air, gleaming dully. Then it vanished. But the ripples marked the spot, and where there was one there were often others.

The man stood up quickly. He picked up the coiled rope, and with the same hand grasped the net at a point four feet below the iron collar. He raised the skirt to his mouth, gripped it strongly with his teeth. He slid his free hand as far as it would go down the circumference of the net so that he had three points of contact with the mass of cordage and metal. He made sure his feet were planted solidly. Then he waited, feeling the tension that is older than the human race, the fierce exhilaration of the hunter at the moment of ambush, the atavistic desire to capture and kill and ultimately consume.

A mullet swirled, ahead and to the left. The man swung the heavy net back, twisting his body and bending his knees so as to get more upward thrust. He shot it forward, letting go simultaneously with rope hand and with teeth, holding a fraction of a second longer with the other hand so as to give the net the necessary spin, impart the centrifugal force that would make it flare into a circle. The skiff ducked sideways, but he kept his balance. The net fell with a splash.

The man waited for five seconds. Then he began to retrieve it, pulling in a series of jerks so the drawstrings would gather the net inward, like a giant fist closing on this segment of the teeming sea. He felt the net quiver, and knew it was not empty. He swung it over the gunwale, saw the silver side of the mullet quivering, saw too the gleam of a smaller fish. He looked to make sure no sting ray was hidden in the mesh, then raised the iron collar and shook the net out. The mullet fell with a thud and flapped wildly. The other victim was an angel fish, beautifully marked, but too small to keep. The man picked it up gently and dropped it overboard. He coiled the rope, took up the paddle. He would cast no more until he came to the dock.

The skiff moved on. At last, ten feet apart, a pair of stakes rose up gauntly. Barnacle encrusted, they once had marked the approach from the main channel. The man guided the skiff between them, then put the paddle down softly. He stood up, reached for the net, tightened the noose around his wrist. From here he could drift down upon the dock. He could see it now, a ruined skeleton in the starshine. Beyond it a mullet jumped and fell back with a flat, liquid sound. The man raised the edge of the net, put it between his teeth. He would not cast at a single swirl, he decided; he would wait until he saw two or three close together. The skiff was barely moving. He felt his muscles tense themselves, awaiting the signal from the brain.

Behind him in the channel he heard the porpoise blow again, nearer now. He frowned in the darkness. If the porpoise chose to fish this area, the mullet would scatter and vanish. There was no time to lose.

A school of sardines surfaced suddenly, skittering along the drops of mercury. Something, perhaps the shadow of the skiff, had frightened them. The old dock loomed very close. A mullet broke water just too far away; then another, nearer. The man marked the spreading ripples and decided to wait no longer.

He swung back the net, heavier now that it was wet. He had to turn his head, but out of the corner of his eye he saw two swirls in the black water just off the starboard bow. They were about eight feet apart, and they had the sluggish oily look that marks the presence of something big just below the surface. His conscious mind had no time to function, but instinct told him that the net was wide enough to cover both swirls if he could alter the direction of his cast. He could not halt the swing, but he shifted his feet slightly and made the cast off balance. He saw the net shoot forward, flare into an oval, and drop just where he wanted it.

Then the sea exploded in his face. In a frenzy of spray, a great horned thing shot like a huge bat out of the water. The man saw the mesh of his net etched against the mottled blackness of its body and he knew, in the split second in which thought was still possible, that those twin swirls had been made not by two mullet, but by the wing tips of the giant ray of the Gulf Coast, *Manta birostris*, also known as clam cracker, devil ray, sea devil.

The man gave a hoarse cry. He tried to claw the slipknot off his wrist, but there was no time. The quarter-inch line snapped taut. He shot over the side of the skiff as if he had roped a

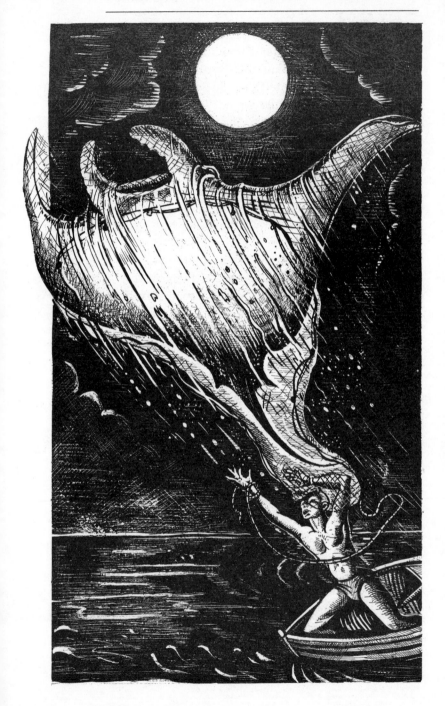

runaway locomotive. He hit the water head first and seemed to bounce once. He ploughed a blinding furrow for perhaps ten yards. Then the line went slack as the sea devil jumped again. It was not the full-grown manta of the deep Gulf, but it was close to nine feet from tip to tip, and it weighed over a thousand pounds. Up into the air it went, pearl-coloured underbelly gleaming as it twisted in a frantic effort to dislodge the clinging thing that had fallen upon it. Up into the starlight, a monstrous survival from the dawn of time.

The water was less than four feet deep. Sobbing and choking, the man struggled for a foothold on the slimy bottom. Sucking in great gulps of air, he fought to free himself from the rope. But the slipknot was jammed deep into his wrist; he might as well have tried to loosen a circle of steel.

The ray came down with a thunderous splash and drove forward again. The flexible net followed every movement, impeding it hardly at all. The man weighed a hundred and seventy-five pounds, and he was braced for the shock, and he had the desperate strength that comes from looking into the blank eyes of death. It was useless. His arm straightened out with a jerk that seemed to dislocate his shoulder; his feet shot out from under him; his head went under again. Now at last he knew how the fish must feel when the line tightens and drags him towards the alien element that is his doom. Now he knew.

Desperately he dug the fingers of his free hand into the ooze, felt them dredge a futile channel through broken shells and the ribbonlike sea grasses. He tried to raise his head, but could not get it clear. Torrents of spray choked him as the ray plunged towards deep water.

His eyes were of no use to him in the foam-streaked blackness. He closed them tight, and at once an insane sequence of pictures flashed through his mind. He saw his wife sitting in their living room, reading, waiting calmly for his return. He saw the mullet he had just caught, gasping its life away on the floor boards of the skiff. He saw the cigarette he had flung from the sea wall touch the water and expire with a tiny hiss. He saw all these things and many others simultaneously in his mind as his body fought silently and tenaciously for its existence. His hand touched something hard and closed on it in a death grip, but it was only the sharp-edged helmet of a horseshoe crab, and after an instant he let it go.

He had been under water perhaps fifteen seconds now, and something in his brain told him quite calmly that he could last another forty or fifty and then the red flashes behind his eyes would merge into darkness, and the water would pour into his lungs in one sharp painful shock, and he would be finished.

This thought spurred him to a desperate effort. He reached up and caught his pinioned wrist with his free hand. He doubled up his knees to create more drag. He thrashed his body madly, like a fighting fish, from side to side. This did not disturb the ray, but now one of the great wings tore through the mesh, and the net slipped lower over the fins projecting like horns from below the nightmare head, and the sea devil jumped again.

And once more the man was able to get his feet on the bottom and his head above water, and he saw ahead of him the pair of ancient stakes that marked the approach to the channel. He knew that if he was dragged much beyond those stakes he would be in eight feet of water, and the ray would go down to hug the bottom as rays always do, and then no power on earth could save him. So in the moment of respite that was granted him, he flung himself towards them.

For a moment he thought his captor yielded a bit. Then the ray moved off again, but more slowly now, and for a few yards the man was able to keep his feet on the bottom. Twice he hurled himself back against the rope with all his strength, hoping that something would break. But nothing broke. The mesh of the net was ripped and torn, but the draw lines were strong, and the stout perimeter cord threaded through the sinkers was even stronger.

The man could feel nothing now in his trapped hand, it was numb; but the ray could feel the powerful lunges of the unknown thing that was trying to restrain it. It drove its great wings against the unyielding water and forged ahead, dragging the man and pushing a sullen wave in front of it.

The man had swung as far as he could towards the stakes. He

plunged towards one and missed it by inches. His feet slipped and he went down on his knees. Then the ray swerved sharply and the second stake came right at him. He reached out with his free hand and caught it.

He caught it just above the surface, six or eight inches below high-water mark. He felt the razor-sharp barnacles bite into his hand, collapse under the pressure, drive their tiny slime-covered shell splinters deep into his flesh. He felt the pain, and he welcomed it, and he made his fingers into an iron claw that would hold until the tendons were severed or the skin was shredded from the bone. The ray felt the pressure increase with a jerk that stopped it dead in the water. For a moment all was still as the tremendous forces came into equilibrium.

Then the net slipped again, and the perimeter cord came down over the sea devil's eyes, blinding it momentarily. The great ray settled to the bottom and braced its wings against the mud and hurled itself forward and upward.

The stake was only a four-by-four of creosoted pine, and it was old. Ten thousand tides had swirled around it. Worms had bored; parasites had clung. Under the crust of barnacles it still had some heart left, but not enough. The man's grip was five feet above the floor of the bay; the leverage was too great. The stake snapped off at its base.

The ray lunged upward, dragging the man and the useless timber. The man had his lungs full of air, but when the stake snapped he thought of expelling the air and inhaling the water so as to have it finished quickly. He thought of this, but he did not do it. And then, just at the channel's edge, the ray met the porpoise, coming in.

The porpoise had fed well this night and was in no hurry, but it was a methodical creature and it intended to make a sweep around the old dock before the tide dropped too low. It had no quarrel with any ray, but it feared no fish in the sea, and when the great black shadow came rushing blindly and unavoidably, it rolled fast and struck once with its massive horizontal tail.

The blow descended on the ray's flat body with a sound like a pistol shot. It would have broken a buffalo's back, and even the sea devil was half stunned. It veered wildly and turned back towards shallow water. It passed within ten feet of the man, face down in the water. It slowed and almost stopped, wing tips moving faintly, gathering strength for another rush.

The man had heard the tremendous slap of the great mammal's tail and the snorting gasp as it plunged away. He felt the line go slack again, and he raised his dripping face, and he reached for the bottom with his feet. He found it, but now the water was up to his neck. He plucked at the noose once more with his lacerated hand, but there was no strength in his fingers. He felt the tension come back into the line as the ray began to move again, and for half a second he was tempted to throw himself backwards and fight as he had been doing, pitting his strength against the vastly superior strength of the brute.

But the acceptance of imminent death had done something to his brain. It had driven out the fear, and with the fear had gone the panic. He could think now, and he knew with absolute certainty that if he was to make any use of this last chance that had been given him, it would have to be based on the one faculty that had carried man to his pre-eminence above all beasts, the faculty of reason. Only by using his brain could he possibly survive, and he called on his brain for a solution, and his brain responded. It offered him one.

He did not know whether his body still had the strength to carry out the brain's commands, but he began to swim forward, towards the ray that was still moving hesitantly away from the channel. He swam forward, feeling the rope go slack as he gained on the creature.

Ahead of him he saw the one remaining stake, and he made himself swim faster until he was parallel with the ray and the rope trailed behind both of them in a deep U. He swam with a surge of desperate energy so that he was slightly in the lead as they came to the stake. He passed on one side of it; the ray was on the other.

Then the man took one last deep breath, and he went down under the black water until he was sitting on the bottom of the bay. He put one foot over the line so that it passed under his bent knee. He drove both his heels into the mud, and he clutched the slimy grass with his bleeding hand, and he waited for the tension to come again.

The ray passed on the other side of the stake, moving faster now. The rope grew taut again, and it began to drag the man back towards the stake. He held his prisoned wrist close to the bottom, under his knee, and he prayed that the stake would not break. He felt the rope vibrate as the barnacles bit into it. He did not know whether the rope would crush the barnacles, or whether the barnacles would cut the rope. All he knew was that in five seconds or less he would be dragged into the stake and cut to ribbons if he tried to hold on; or drowned if he didn't.

He felt himself sliding slowly, and then faster, and suddenly the ray made a great leap forward, and the rope burned around the base of the stake, and the man's foot hit it hard. He kicked himself backwards with his remaining strength, and the rope parted, and he was free.

He came slowly to the surface. Thirty feet away the sea devil made one tremendous leap and disappeared into the darkness. The man raised his wrist and looked at the frayed length of rope dangling from it. Twenty inches, perhaps. He lifted his other hand and felt the hot blood start instantly, but he didn't care. He put this hand on the stake above the barnacles and held on to the good rough honest wood. He heard a strange noise, and realized that it was himself, sobbing.

High above, there was a droning sound, and looking up he saw the nightly plane from New Orleans inbound for Tampa. Calm and serene, it sailed, symbol of man's proud mastery over nature. Its lights winked red and green for a moment; then it was gone.

Slowly, painfully, the man began to move through the placid water. He came to the skiff at last and climbed into it. The mullet, still alive, slapped convulsively with its tail. The man reached down with his torn hand, picked up the mullet, let it go.

He began to work on the slipknot doggedly with his teeth. His mind was almost a blank, but not quite. He knew one thing. He knew he would do no more casting alone at night. Not in the dark of the moon. No, not he.

The Turtle

George Vukelich

They were driving up to fish the White Creek for German Browns and the false dawn was purpling the Wisconsin countryside when they spotted the huge humpbacked object in the middle of the sand road and Jimmy coasted the station wagon to a stop.

'Pa,' he said. 'Turtle. Lousy snapper.'

Old Tony sat up. 'Is he dead?'

'Not yet,' Jimmy said. 'Not yet he isn't.' He shifted into neutral and pulled the handbrake. The snapper lay large and dark green in the headlight beams, and they got out and went around to look at it closely. The turtle moved a little and left razorlike claw marks in the wet sand, and it waited.

'Probably heading for the creek,' Jimmy said. 'They kill trout like crazy.'

They stood staring down.

'I'd run the wagon over him,' Jimmy said. 'Only he's too big.'

He looked around and walked to the ditchway, and came back with a long finger-thick pine branch. He jabbed it into the turtle's face and the snakehead lashed out and struck like spring steel and the branch snapped like a stick of macaroni, and it all happened fast as a match flare.

'Looka that!' Tony whistled.

'You bet, Pa. I bet he goes sixty pounds. Seventy maybe.'

The turtle was darting its head around now in long stretching movements.

'I think he got some branch stuck in his craw,' Jimmy said. He got out a cigarette and lit it, and flipped the match at the rock-green shell.

154

'I wish now I'd brought the twenty-two,' he said. 'The pistol.'

'You going to kill him?'

'Why not?' Jimmy asked. 'They kill trout, don't they?'

They stood there smoking and not talking, and looking down at the unmoving shell.

'I could use the lug wrench on him,' Jimmy said. 'Only I don't think it's long enough. I don't want my hands near him.'

Tony didn't say anything.

'You watch him,' Jimmy said. 'I'll go find something in the wagon.'

Slowly Tony squatted down on to his haunches and smoked and stared at the turtle. Poor Old One, he thought. You had the misfortune to be caught in the middle of a sand road, and you are very vulnerable on the sand roads, and now you are going to get the holy life beaten out of you.

The turtle stopped its stretching movements and was still. Tony looked at the full webbed feet and the nail claws and he knew the truth.

'It would be different in the water, turtle,' he said. 'In the water you could cut down anybody.'

He thought about this snapper in the water and how it would move like a torpedo and bring down trout, and nobody would monkey with it in the water – and here it was in the middle of a sand road, vulnerable as a baby and waiting to get its brains beaten out.

He finished his cigarette and field-stripped it, and got to his feet and walked to the wagon and reached into the glove compartment for the Thermos of coffee. What was he getting all worked up about a turtle for? He was an old man and he was acting like a kid, and they were going up to the White for German Browns, and he was getting worked up about a God-forsaken turtle in the middle of a God-forsaken sand road. *God-forsaken*. He walked back to the turtle and hunched down and sipped at the strong black coffee and watched the old snapper watching him.

Jimmy came up to him holding the bumper jack.

'I want to play it safe,' he said. 'I don't think the lug wrench is long enough.' He squatted beside Tony. 'What do you think?'

'He waits,' Tony said. 'What difference what I think?'

Jimmy squinted at him.

'I can tell something's eating you. What are you thinking, Pa?'

'I am thinking this is not a brave thing.'

'What?'

'This turtle – he does not have a chance.'

Jimmy lit a cigarette and hefted the bumper jack. The turtle moved ever so slightly.

'You talk like an old woman. An old tired woman.'

'I can understand this turtle's position.'

'He doesn't have a chance?'

'That's right.'

'And that bothers you?'

Tony looked into Jimmy's face.

'That is right,' he said. 'That bothers me.'

'Well of all the dumb stupid things,' Jimmy said. 'What do you want me to do? Get down on all fours and fight with him?'

'No,' Tony said. 'Not on all fours. Not on all fours.' He looked at Jimmy. 'In the water. Fight this turtle in the water. That would be a brave thing, my son.'

Jimmy put down the bumper jack and reached for the Thermos jug and didn't say anything. He drank his coffee and smoked his cigarette, and he stared at the turtle and didn't say anything.

'You're crazy,' he said finally.

'It is a thought, my son. A thought. This helpless plodding old one like a little baby in this sand road, eh? But in the water, his home . . .' Tony snapped his fingers with the suddenness of a switch blade. 'In the water he could cut down anyone, anything . . . any man. Fight him in the water, Jimmy. Use your bumper jack in the water . . .'

'I think you're nuts,' Jimmy said. 'I think you're honest to goodness nuts.'

Tony shrugged. 'This does not seem fair for you, eh? To be in the water with this one.' He motioned at the turtle. 'This seems nuts to you. Crazy to you. Because in the water you are not a match.'

'What are you trying to prove, Pa?'

'Jimmy. This turtle is putting up his life. In the road here you are putting up nothing. You have nothing to lose at all. Not a finger or a hand or your life. Nothing. You smash him with a long steel bumper jack and he cannot get to you. He has as much chance as a ripe watermelon.'

'So?'

'So I want you to put up something also. You should have something to lose or it is no match.'

Jimmy looked at the old man and then at the turtle.

'Any fool can smash a watermelon,' Tony said. 'It does not take a brave man.'

'Pa. It's only a turtle. You're making a federal case.'

Old Tony looked at his son. 'All right,' he said. 'Finish your coffee now and do what you are going to do. I say nothing more. Only for the next five minutes put yourself into this turtle's place. Put yourself into his shell and watch through his eyes. And try to think what he is thinking when he sees a coward coming to kill him with a long steel bumper jack.'

Jimmy got to his feet and ground out his cigarette.

'All right, Pa,' he said. 'All right. You win.'

Tony rose slowly from his crouch.

'No,' he said. 'Not me. You. You win.'

'But, Pa, they do kill trout.'

'So,' Tony said. 'They kill trout. Nature put them here, and they kill trout. To survive. The trout are not extinct, eh? We kill trout also, we men. To survive? No, for sport. This old one, he takes what he needs. I do not kill him for being in nature's plan. I do not play God.'

Jimmy walked to the rear of the wagon then and flung down the bumper jack and closed up the door and came back.

'Pa,' he said. 'Honest to goodness you got the nuttiest ideas I ever heard.'

Old Tony walked around behind the snapper and gently prodded it with his boot toe, and the turtle went waddling forward across the road and toppled over the sand shoulder and disappeared in the brushy growth of the creek bank. Tony and his son climbed into the wagon and sat looking at each other. The sun was coming up strong now and the sky was cracking open like a shell and spilling reds and golds and blues, and Jimmy started the engine.

Tony put the Thermos away and got out his cigarettes and stuck one in his son's mouth.

'So?' he said.

They sat smoking for a full minute watching each other, and then Jimmy released the emergency and they rolled slowly along the drying sand road and down past the huge cleansing dawn coming, and the pine forests growing tall in the rising mists, and the quickly quiet waters of the eternal creek.

Drinker of the
Bitter Water

Jack Cope

The Lion turned to glare over its shoulder. At the same time there came the Slam! Slam! of guns and up ahead in the burning red sand-dune spurts of dust like sudden tufts of dead grass where the bullets hit. At the lion's side the wounded lioness dragged herself. Her jaw was open and blood on the teeth and tongue, blood in a streak down her side below the shoulder-blade. There was a blue-grey thing, a truck. They were firing from the truck, afraid to dismount. The lion was afraid too but also enraged.

They had killed one lioness and two half-grown cubs and wounded the second lioness. Now they were after it and after the lion especially; they fired from the moving truck which was cruising across the flat and the aim was not sure.

The wounded lioness and the male at her side got over the knife-rim of the dune and started to go down the heavy hot sand that stood their weight a moment as if congealed and then suddenly flowed under their pads, a thick shining red liquid. The truck was now out of sight and making a whining noise trying to rush the wind-slope of the dune. In front of the lions was the wide ash-grey floor and beyond it another great hump of a red dune running out of sight both ways to the dancing shimmer of the horizon, dune behind endless sand-dune to the furthermost edge of the desert. No trees – the stunted hummocks of dwarf camel-thorn and blue-bush and sparse shining-hair grass – ash and silver and blue under the lowering sun. And in the middle of that flat pale floor a single great blotch of fierce deceptive green – a trassies-bush, dense, defensively low, almost impossible to penetrate.

The lions made for the bush, the one patch of cover visible anywhere but for the shapes that rose like shade-trees in the mirage. The female dragged her weight without feeling into the clawing tangle of the trassies-bush. Hooked thorns ripped at her hide, tore out tufts of hair. Behind her the male pushed heavily, put his face down and let the thorns comb and crackle through his heavy mane. Deep in the tangle the lioness burst into a dry hole of ant-eaten branches and fell on her side. The lion lay near and began to lick at her wound.

The truck came down over the dune and the men saw their

quarry had found shelter in the only cover for miles. It was too dangerous to try flushing a wounded lion out of a trassies-bush. They were afraid to get down and uneasy about the game patrols and the daylight running out. They cruised round the clump of fierce green bush. One man stood up on the roof of the cab and tried to peer into the thicket, but he could see nothing. Each time the truck stopped moving he lifted the Winchester repeating rifle to his shoulder and slapped bullets at quick fire into the bush. There was no movement and no sound from inside. The lion went on licking its mate, which was now dead.

The men in the truck could afford no more time. The sun was far over westwards. They left off trying to get at the two animals, turned the vehicle and sped away south at first along the floor between the dunes. Then they swung left and began to switchback over the red ribs of the desert to get out eastwards and across the border into Botswana, rushing at the lower slopes with the four-wheel-drive; a sick lurch at the top and a glide down the far side. They had the bodies of the one lioness and two half-grown cubs in the back of the truck. There was no time to stop and skin them; that could be done in the night or early morning and the carcasses thrown to the hyenas or buried in a sandpit. The lioness's skin was worth $100 for sale to tourists and the smaller ones, say $60 each. The big male would have made a lot more. It was a very large animal, a prize, larger than they had ever seen, and the Kalahari lions were the greatest in Africa.

The lion licked his mate during the night and nudged her soft flank with his nose, waiting for her to rise up. They prowled mostly by night and he would not go without her. They were on the move. What made the droves of springbok at one moment lower their heads and begin like a slow swell of the blood to trek out? The lesser and the greater antelopes, the ostriches and the winged birds, blue wildebeest and giraffe all knew when the time had come to start a trail, and its only destination was life – life against the hunger of the desert. The lions also knew. The big lion, its two mates and growing young had been trekking a long time, out of the wilderness, over parched sand, through scrub and across the dunes. There had been more of them at first, but the others had fallen to the guns of raiders along the trail until now only the male was left.

The lioness had become stiff and already the small rustling things were gathering towards the body; the flies smelt death in the night and were drifting like sparks in the moonlight and settling round the black hump of the trassies-bush. The lion got up and with head lowered made the dark coughing rumbles that are the voice of desolation. It pushed out through the thorns and from the edge of the bush it looked about. A greybuck flew like a small arrow into the night leaving a trail of smoky dust in the moonlight. Clouds like the side of a fish were catching the first glimmer of dawn and the Morning Star floated large and near in the calm sky. The lion turned its back against the east and continued its trail alone.

At sunrise a green game patrol truck came up between two red lines of dunes and then crossed over into the next floor. A Bushman leaning over the side slammed his hand on the steel panel and the truck stopped. He jumped down and the others followed him, two suntanned rangers in khaki and soft felt hats with a green badge. They looked at the trail and the Bushman traced it some way and came back.

'How old are the marks, Henrik?' the older man asked.

'Yesterday —' he pointed west to the sun's position at the time he meant.

They followed the trail for half an hour and found where the truck had turned to make for the open border. It had too long a start and so they doubled back to see what had brought it. Henrik tracked the wheel-marks up to the trassies-bush, and then he picked up the lion's fresh spoor.

'*Kgam'ma!*' he shouted – Lion!

They came and looked in silence.

'This is the lord of all the lions,' Henrik said at last in Afrikaans.

'Do you know him?'

He shook his head and laughing he spanned his small hand over the great footprints. '*Kgam'ma, oubass van die leeus!*' he repeated – Lord of the lions.

They found the smaller and older spoor of the lioness and the gouts of her blood, and Henrik smelt her dead body inside the trassies-bush. He wormed his way into the thicket with a towing rope and they hauled out the dead body. The bullet had gone through the lung and upper thorax and they found it under the skin of the right shoulder. Barnabas, the younger of the game rangers, cut it out with his knife and it was only slightly flattened.

'Pa, it's a Winchester 309,' he said to Simeon, his father, giving him the bullet. 'I guess I know who did this, the bastard.'

Henrik picked up the spoor of Kgam'ma and tracked it. He had stripped himself of his khaki tunic and boots and loped along at a quick swaying trot. The truck came behind, whining and slithering up the steep wind-slope and over the red dunes. Mile after mile the Bushman ran on without pause. The sun struck on his copper-gold skin and on the sparse ridges of his hair. They came into a dry river-bed, shallow, filled with centuries of wind-drift and marked by a few silvery thorn trees and raisin bushes and the blue-bush growing perceptibly higher. Henrik stopped and climbed in the truck. 'He is near,' he said.

'Well, we can leave him,' Simeon said. 'He's come in from the Botswana side of the border with a lot of animals on this thirst-trek and looks to me he's heading for the Nossob waterholes.'

'I'd like to see him,' his son said.

'We'll see him in time, I don't doubt.'

They cruised about for a while but did not see Kgam'ma that day. No one saw him. The desert was wide and he had merged back into its trackless distances hidden from the sun and living alone under the white fire of the nights, the dust and electric storms. A black man from Ramahoela who had lost his way in an insane attempt to cross the desert on foot slept one night with his head on the roots of a camel-thorn and woke to see a lion under the same tree. He thought he was delirious or already a spirit and closed his eyes to shut out the sight. The Bushman found him there and convinced him that what he had seen was true. The lion had killed and eaten part of an oryx and the remains of the big buck, worried by hyenas and jackal, lay scattered over fifty yards. The lion had gone but, by its spoor, Henrik declared 'it was most likely Kgam'ma himself.'

Three weeks later Simeon took Henrik with him alone on a routine patrol. They had worked together a long time – since the Nossob river had last flowed which was nearly thirty years ago. Simeon had two enemies, the thieves and raiders and slaughterers from outside, and the drought. He ruled his territory, which was a corner of the desert no larger than a small country like Ireland, with the hand of equality. All things had the value of life, the great antelopes, oryx and eland, the little greybuck, the martial eagle and the colony weaver, tortoise and whipsnake and lizard, hyenas or lion. To the wild, man was the destroyer. The animals looked with large strange eyes at the shapes of truck and car, but when man stepped out of them in his own separateness, clothed with his own smell of death, they recognized him.

As the two men left the patrol car the oryx flung back the long sabres of their horns and with full black tails flowing like banners on the hot wind they burnt white trails across the flats. The ostriches leaned in giant strides over stilt legs and vultures waiting like filthy beggars for their last turn at the waterhole stumbled into the air. Simeon walked to the outlet pipe and tasted the water being heaved up by the creaking windmill. It was brack and bitter, almost undrinkable for man, but lifegiving to the wild. The tank was well filled.

Then the two men set out in different directions to read things for themselves. Simeon had left his rifle in the car, as he always did, and the Bushman also went unarmed. Above the river-bed was a ridge of limestone deeply hollowed where the wild black bees made their hives, hyenas slept through the day, and leopards had their lairs. The two men climbed the ridge at different places and commanded a long view over the grey-blue scrub and the ripple of sand-dunes going away like the wave-crests of a red shoreless ocean. They walked on, noting things: the state of the grazing and the tracks in the sand. Tufts of wiry grass nibbled, prickly bitter cucumbers, the tough tree-thorn scrub, almost leafless but nutritious. The presence of birds, spiders, beetles under the furnace of the sun.

Henrik made a sudden call and the ranger stopped. He was being signalled back. Without turning he began to shift away and towards Henrik. Then he saw the cause . . . carefully hidden by blue-bush and a spreading camel-thorn were the lions. They were more than two hundred yards away; lions were inert in the heat of the day, but Henrik was backing out as fast as he could. Now the men kept low, moving cautiously until the animals were out of sight. Then they ran in the hollow and worked back over the stony ridge at a different point.

'What's the matter?' Simeon asked.

'*Kgam'ma* . . .' the way Henrik said it left no doubt which lion he meant. Even though they caught only a glimpse through the bush, they had seen the great lion himself. Simeon fetched binoculars from the patrol car and climbed again for a careful reconnoitre from the ridge. Where they had first seen the animals there were two lionesses but the male had moved forward and was crouching among dwarf bush. It was watching them.

'He's stalking us,' Simeon said.

'Hai!'

'He could reach here in seconds – let's go.' He raised his hat in his hand and saw the lion duck its head. Then they pulled down below the ridge and ran for the car. The Bushman said nothing on the way back; they had both seen enough to understand the danger in Kgam'ma. He had found himself two new mates and he meant to protect them. He seemed to have come to stay.

A small flock of Persian sheep kept to supply meat to the camp and to the Bushman families was taken to graze in a defined area of the desert across the dry river. Every two days they were brought back to water by the shepherd. On the nights he spent in the desert he found a camel-thorn tree, made his fire under it to scare off wild animals and watched his flock. In the heat of the day he slept while the sheep stood with heads under each other's bellies for shade. A week after Kgam'ma had been seen the shepherd fell asleep long enough at night to let his fire die. A lion came among the sheep and scattered them. The shepherd made a calculated leap into the tree and from there he heard the fearful roaring and the crunch of bones and the pattering of hooves away into the distance. In the dawn he ran back to the camp for help.

Simeon went out with trackers. The flock had been harassed over a distance of eight miles and seventy-three sheep, nearly a third of their number, killed; only one was eaten. Henrik tracked beyond the last dead sheep, scaring up vultures, and then came back to Simeon in the truck.

'Well?'

He shook his head. 'It was a big lion.'

'The same one?'

'It is like the same one, *oubaas*, but this one is lame in one foot.'

Simeon did not know what to do. Such a slaughter of domestic stock was something he had never heard of before. He had his feeling about Kgam'ma but could not be sure that he was the killer, and he discussed it with his son, Barnabas.

'Are you thinking of going out to shoot the lion, Pa?' Barnabas asked.

'No, I'm not thinking of that; I haven't shot one in thirty years. Only this animal is different – be careful. I mean, if it's the same one.'

'I'd like to see him, Pa.'

The older man only screwed up his sharp blue eyes against the light and took out his pipe and lit it. 'You'll see him.'

The lion bit and licked and gnawed at the thorn in the central pad of his forepaw. The long white thorn had gone in deep and broken off and he could not get at it with his teeth. Already the paw was swollen with the poison and he could not put it down on the ground. When he walked it was with a heavy limp on three legs. He had driven away other males for the two new mates and now he was at a disadvantage should it come to a fight – he was old too and the poisoned paw made him sick. Each day the lionesses killed, a blue wildebeest or a big heavy oryx, and he ate, though not to his fill. On a night when the pain grew and strung at his whole leg he began to move again. He left the bitter waterhole and drove the two lionesses with him, limping and snarling ferociously, and they went along at his side. They snarled back but were too subdued to do anything. They were his mates so long as he could hold them. The three travelled away from the dry river and towards the dawn, towards life. It was night and the moon shining and no wind; a wind would smother their spoor.

They slept the day and then went on. The lionesses looked for prey, but they were far out across the red sand and there were no big antelope. They killed a springbok and drank its blood, but there was not much blood for Kgam'ma and he was thirsty. The third night there was no kill, and the fourth. The three animals lay together in the sparse burning shade of a blue-grey thorntree and kept their heads down and their ears back, waiting. The wind had risen one night, blowing a great red duststorm over the desert that rolled with a terrible reverberation against the thunderclouds. Then for two nights the lions left a clear trail across the dunes and hollows, Kgam'ma limping badly and losing his strength. Always he drove them on towards the sunrise and the three big animals lay now in the heat in a great extremity.

Kgam'ma raised his head and the females were alert too. They heard a faint long sound and their six yellow slitted eyes turned in the direction it came from. Over the red dune in the searing light they saw the little upright figure appear, stop and suddenly run back. Kgam'ma lowered his head and crouched his hind-legs under him. The lionesses got up and began to trot away. As the noise grew, a big shape came over the crest of the dune where the man had been and jolted straight towards them. They turned for a moment to stare; the lionesses were the first to break into a run, and then Kgam'ma ran too. Weakened and lame on one leg, his power had not left him and he bounded through the tree-thorn scrub and over the first dune. From the top he looked for cover and there was none. Above him in the sky a chanting goshawk rained down its trumpet cry – a thing of air, silver breast, and silver and black wings, it was free above the world; it rolled and dived in the water of the sky.

The two lionesses were loping fast through the next hollow and Kgam'ma trailed behind. The truck came after them. It was screaming and lurching at the windslopes and through the ashen floors, gaining on the lions every minute. Kgam'ma turned away from the line of flight and the truck followed him. Twist and double, it clung to the chase, wearing him down.

Simeon drove the truck and Barnabas stood at the back of the cab with the Bushman trackers. With one hand he clung to the rail and in the other he held the cross-bow wound up and loaded with the short sharp bolt. The truck overtook the lion, running to one side, sixty, forty, thirty yards range – then slowed and gave Barnabas his chance. He raised the cross-bow to his shoulder for a flash aim and pressed the trigger. The bolt with its anaesthetic charge hit the lion high on the shoulder and stuck there.

Then Simeon swung hard off the line of the chase and raced the engine at full speed. Kgam'ma had turned on his pursuers for a final charge. His speed closed the distance and he roared for the kill. In his path the trackers threw down sacks of grass. He fell on one and ripped it apart, growling and rolling in the dust. Just twelve seconds after the strike the great lion-body slackened and the hot brain was released into oblivion.

They left Kgam'ma where he lay and went after the two females and captured them as well.

Kgam'ma was stretched on the floor of the truck and it seemed that the glare in his eyes was fixed on them even in unconsciousness with a total and eternal enmity. They measured him from nose to the end of his brush, they looked in his jaws and treated his ears for bushticks. Barnabas lanced the suppurating fore-pad, drew out the thorn and drained the wound, and into the quivering muscle of the lion's huge haunch he injected a veterinary charge of penicillin. He also branded with an iron on his rump the identity number 17.

Eleven hours later on the dry Auob river the three lions came back to consciousness. Two springbok had been shot and left for them. Kgam'ma steadied himself and slowly he licked with a rasp tongue the healing wound in his paw.

He stayed, not moving far from the sweet waterhole with the two lionesses. And he waited. Each of the females in turn had three cubs. Daily they killed an oryx or a blue wildebeest. The rangers spotted Kgam'ma once only at long range through binoculars and the trackers sometimes picked up his spoor. Then the lion moved by night, unseen and unknown, to another waterhole in the bitter Nossob river, taking his group with him.

Simeon walked with his son at his side. They were talking about something and laughed so that Simeon's blue eyes retreated into small twinkling chips. He was unarmed as his habit was, but Barnabas carried a quickfiring Winchester rifle over the crook of his arm. Henrik walked a little behind and to the left of them. The pale raisin-bushes were flecked with yellow and red berries. It had rained weeks before and there were patches of red-dark gemsbokgrass in full seed like blood blots against the ash-grey dust.

Henrik clicked his tongue and at the same time the two others saw the ears of a lion above a patch of scrub near a fallen thorn branch. It was not twenty yards off.

'All right, back out,' Simeon said. 'I'll watch it. It won't attack.'

'*Oubaas*, it is Kgam'ma,' the Bushman said.

'He's not going to attack. Back away.'

Henrik and Barnabas began stepping slowly backwards. Barnabas had his gun ready, watching the lion and glancing for a flash at his father. They had saved the lion from death, yet he was deeply afraid of it.

'I'd better kill it, Pa,' he said in a low voice.

'No, keep going. It's not stirring.'

Simeon took off his hat so the lion would get that first if it attacked. He kept his stare without blinking on the animal's yellow eyes and it stared back. The other two were moving off silently in the dust.

The lion turned away its head suddenly, rose to its feet and walked sinuously off. Simeon watched it go. He took out a handkerchief and wiped his face and put his hat on again. The lion went on thirty paces or so to a further bush and disappeared behind it.

'All right, get away quick,' Simeon turned to the others. When he looked back an instant later he saw Kgam'ma rise and bound forward. He was making a charge.

'Here he comes, Barnabas!' He braced himself for a side-spring. The lion's jaw dropped to roll out its terrifying roar of the kill.

Barnabas fired at the same instant past his father's shoulder. He shot twice in quick succession and the lion spun to the left and rolled, kicking like a great spring. Then it lay on one side with its flank and haunch quivering and the brand-mark 17 clearly visible on the dusty hide.

None of them said anything. Henrik waited until the

quivering stopped and he went up cautiously to the dead body. He squatted at arm's length from it, touched the ear. He pulled a few hairs from the long, tawny mane and wound them round one finger. 'Hai, you drinker at the bitter waterhole,' he said.

The Meal

Henry Williamson

Walking over the winter stubble to the small gravel pit in a corner of the field, the boots of the two young men took on four clogs of clay. One man carried a sack and crowbar; the other carried a pickaxe and a spade. They were going to dig out a fox whose earth was in the gravel-pit, put it into a sack, and present it to the pack with which they hunted.

The gravel pit was disused. Three small thorns grew among the dead grasses that covered the slight hollow, with brown spires of sorrel, with sapless thistles and the hollow, fragile skeleton of wild carrot and cow-parsley. Withered creepers of goose-grass were tangled with the thorns; and a ruinous bird's-nest in one held rotting berries – the deserted storehouse of a field mouse.

Some of the deeper depressions in the pit were filled with water. Several rabbit runs led through the dead grasses, but there were no buries. The only hole in the gravel sides was larger than that made by rabbits. It was between eight and nine inches across, and some fresh gravel was before it with an appearance of having been pressed down. One of the men knelt before the hole, examining the ground. He looked for half a minute, and beckoned his companion to kneel beside him. There was a smell like hops being dried in an oast-house, tainting the air. The kneeling men again looked at the prick of claws and the mark of pads leading one way – into the earth. They went to a dyke to cut a long willow wand.

The earth had two tunnels, the right one being short, and the left being long. At the end of the long tunnel a fox was lying, curled up, throat resting on his soft brush. He was stiff and tired, having run many miles the day before across ploughlands and dykes, along lanes and down hedges, with hound-music ever following. He was an old fox, and had been run many times before, but this time scent had lain thickly, and he had known it. Often he had flopped down in a furrow to ease his thudding heart, but always the hounds had pursued him.

Then another fox got up in the middle of a ploughed field as he ran past, and the fresh dog laid a scent stronger than that of the exhausted animal, who came to the gravel pit in the stubble field and listened. He knew that the pack was running the new line, and although several riders galloped across the field fifty yards from the pit, he did not worry. That night he crept from the pit and fed upon mice which he snapped in hedge-ditches, worms, and a rabbit taken from a gin. He slunk home at dawn, dug for a while, and crept into the earth, which he had extended several feet.

Reynard awoke and with cocked ears listened to the noises of human voices coming down the tunnel. They ceased, and he lay still. Shortly afterwards something came towards him, scraping the gravel, rapidly. He bared his fangs, and pressed his body tightly against the sand of the dug cavern. It came to him and touched him, but he did not snap at it, knowing that it was a stick. The stick was jerked backwards and forwards many times, but the point never touched the fox. It was withdrawn, and the earth thumped again and again while gravel fell into the tunnel and the dim light of day went out.

After three hours the noises of digging ceased, and the fox waited. He waited for a long time before creeping forward. He came to the loose gravel, and sniffed. He scraped with his claws, and listened. There was no sound except the mournful wailing of the dwarf owl which just before dark came out from a pollard oak in the hedge. The cry was dulled and faint.

All night the fox scraped sand and pebbles, making a new tunnel to the air. The way to the old exit had been blocked by a stout sack filled with gravel and dumped over the hole. A tiny air space allowed just enough air to enter where with broken claws he scraped, and with sweaty jaws he tore at hard flints and pebbles. Often he ceased, and lay panting in the tunnel; and thus the long night passed away. He was hungry and thirsty, but ceased work when daylight came.

In the afternoon the two young men returned, heaved away the sack, and examined the hole. One of them said that the fox had been trying to dig his way out; the other expressed the opinion that everything was as they had left it. He agreed that a smell of fox came up as he kneeled by the entrance, but he declared that scent would lie for days and weeks in a confined space, especially if it were gravel. But he helped his friend with pick, spade, and shovel, and after some hours' work they had excavated three more feet of the tunnel.

The red sun was sinking below the level Essex ploughlands when they ceased work, thirsty and tired. Again the willow wand was pushed down, and the stop of the tunnel prodded and touched. All the while the fox pressed himself against the further wall of the cavern, watching with wide eyes the stick, as though in terror lest it touch him. It was withdrawn, and outside the men examined the end. Of course, no fox was there, declared the doubting one, because no tawny hair was stuck to the damp sand on the stick.

But the other persisted that Reynard was at home. How about the prints of his pads, he asked, that were so clearly leading inwards, when first they had examined the earth. How about the strong scent that had come from the tunnel? He believed that the fox was there; and he had promised the huntsman to bag a fox for him.

He had shot a rabbit that afternoon as they were walking to the gravel pit. He suggested that they should place it inside the tunnel, and leave the filled sack over the hole. Then if it were eaten on the following morning, or disturbed in any way, they would know that a fox was within.

He skinned the rabbit, to make it the more tempting to a starving fox, and, having blocked the hole, they went away, while the dwarf owl on the oak made in the dusk its plaintive cry.

They went hunting the next day, so did not go near the earth. That night there was a frost, and when they returned later the following afternoon the filled sack, in shadow all day, was white with rime. The shallow greenish water in the depression was covered with a thin film of ice. They cracked it with their boots, enjoying the sharp brittle noises of splitting. Nothing had been to the pit; everything was the same. There was the skin of the rabbit, flung on a thorn; the willow wand, the untrodden heap of gravel, the stubs of their cigarettes. They pulled away the sack, and the rabbit was seen, just as it had been left. They drew it out. There was not a mark on it.

They did no more digging, but sat on the edge of the pit, making occasional remarks. They agreed that the untouched rabbit was absolutely conclusive evidence that no living fox was within. He could not have escaped, since there was but one entrance or exit to the earth, and that had been blocked. The prints had led far down and inwards, and certainly no fox would come out of his earth backwards, and expose himself to a possible enemy. Therefore, they argued logically, a dead fox was within. He had either been suffocated, or had starved to death before the rabbit had been left for him – a period of two days and a night. They felt remorse and shame, and decided to tell no one that they had tortured a poor brute of a fox by leaving it without water, air, or food.

They emptied the sack of gravel, slung the dead rabbit into the pool of greenish water, put tools on shoulders and walked away. Over the furrowed field of heavy clay the red winter sun was casting a purple tinge, and the dwarf owl started its petulant hooting.

Their feet in the stubble made a faint flipping sound as they walked across the next field. The dwarf owl wailed for some minutes, then flew to his hunting. Partridges roosting circlewise in the middle of the stubble-field ceased to call *cher-wick, cher-wick*. Through the wands of the willows shone the new moon, like an ancient hunting horn of gold hung on mouldered tapestry of ploughland mist. Night came to the earth.

In slow succession several sounds were made in the pit. Wheezy breathing, a pebble rolled against another. The dry trickle of gravel. Water being lapped. An animal shaking itself. The crunching and cracking of bones.

The curved silver moon wavered in the pool, by the shadow of a lean fox eating the rabbit with the eagerness of an animal that had been hungry four days and three nights.

The Death-Leap

H. Mortimer Batten

Fireflank, the fox cub, sat under the silent stars in the big white world and listened. He had come far and fast, and he was hungry, yet upon him rested the fear of the unknown, for this country was new to him.

Eight days ago Fireflank had left the green fields and pine-woods of his native land, had left his father and mother and sisters and brothers, to seek fortune on his own. He had turned his steps northwards towards the blue hills, loping, loping, mile after mile, sneaking into cover where and when the dawn found him. He had eaten little during this late autumn migration, for he was afraid, horribly afraid of the foxhounds that had chased his sister and him, and had finally pulled his sister down – though he did not know it – within sight of their nursery home. So Fireflank, alone, homeless, had fled into the heart of the mountains, where this peaceful winter evening found him; and here, among the loose rocks of the Garolgome Wood, he had already half decided to make his home.

He sat under the silent stars, I say, at his den mouth, his big ears acock, daring himself to sneak down into the valley towards that white-walled homestead across the river. An hour ago he had heard the honking of geese and the cackling of poultry from away over there, and also the barking of a dog. Fireflank was very young, or he would have waited till after midnight; but now his hunger led him on, and down towards the noisy river he stole, sneaking in and out among the hazels till he reached the bank. The thunder of heavy waters filled the air, the trees at the river edge were all bearded and caked with frozen spray, but, leaping from rock to rock, where a false step

might have meant disaster, Fireflank gained the other side. The idea of having the river between the region of his nightly raids and the place that he already called his home appealed to his native instincts.

There was a light in the farm window, but also there was wafted on the still air a delicious whiff of poultry. Fireflank kept his eyes upon the light. It seemed to draw him. When far out in the centre of the field he saw the farmer and his family seated over their supper. The fox cub snarled a silent snarl, then, making a detour, he got to the back of the farm buildings whence came the scent of fowl and sneaked in under the orchard gate. All was white and silent, and there – oh delight! – sat five plump roosters, huddled together on the branch of a plum tree not twelve feet from the ground!

Fireflank drifted under the branch and looked up with shining golden eyes. The fowls moved uneasily, and their movements seemed to excite him. He yapped twice, two sharp, metallic 'yaps', and the foolish roosters, instead of sitting tight, began to edge out towards the end of the already overstrained branch. 'Yap-yap!' said Fireflank, louder now, for in his excitement he had forgotten the farmer and his dog. 'Yap – Yap – Yap!'

One of the roosters fluttered, began to lose its balance, and then, flapping weakly, slowly subsided backwards till it swung head down, in the most absurd manner imaginable, still hanging on frantically by its feet. Fireflank fairly yelled with glee, making desperate little jumps, though he knew it was only a matter of time ere the rooster fell to meet him.

At that instant the farmer rose from his supper. 'Whist-ye!' he muttered, threatening to cuff one of his boys; then he held up his hand in a gesture for silence. All of them listened. The dog, basking before the peat fire, pricked his ears and assumed an attitude of intentness. 'Yap – Yap! Yap –Yap – Yap!'

'Thond's a fox!' said the farmer in an excited whisper. He snatched his gun from under a rafter, his dog was at his side, and as he opened the door he whispered, 'Fix him, Nell!' Nell shot silently forth, for she knew as well as anyone what was amiss. The word 'fox' was associated in her mind with many a breathless chase in the spring of the year, when she and her master slept out on the hills to guard the newly-born lambs, and Nell knew the ways of mountain foxes. So she stole silently out, swift as an arrow, intending to take the thief by surprise.

'Yap – Yap!' yelled Fireflank, and at that moment the branch on which the fowls sat gave an ominous creak and broke. Down came a veritable avalanche of chickens, each so dead with terror that it fell like a stone, and Fireflank found himself the centre of a hailstorm of descending riches. They landed in his face, on his neck, on his back, and like a little cyclone he whirled this way and that, sending up a cloud of powdery snow, and dealing death at every snap.

Over the high boundary wall appeared a shadow, and had not Fireflank been too busily occupied he would have seen a vision of bristling hair and naked fangs bearing pell-mell upon him. As it was, he did not see Nell till she collided with him, rolling him over and over amidst a maelstrom of chickens, cutting his shoulder with her fangs. But Nell overshot and was too slow in turning. In an instant Fireflank was up, darting like a streak of light for the gate through which he had come. He wriggled under it, and Nell, at his very heels, collided heavily with the bars, for the space was too small for her to follow. She lost two priceless seconds in attempting it, then lost two more in scrambling over the wall. Away went Fireflank, floating easily over the snow, keeping to the shadow of the wall, and heading back towards the river, while the farmer strove in vain with his rusty muzzle-loader to get a line on the drifting shadow.

The sheep-dog was fast, and at the very river margin, as Fireflank was about to cross, she turned him – oh fruitless triumph! – forcing him to run downstream. Fireflank knew he could throw her off among the loose rocks of Garolgome Wood, so cross the river he must at all hazards.

His chance came, and he took it. At the very brink of the fall where the entire waters of that wonderful river topple over a cliff fifty feet in depth, there is a single pointed boulder protruding above the angry flood, and tonight the surface of that boulder was sparkling with ice, affording scarcely sufficient foothold for a fly. It was a tremendous leap for a young fox, but for Fireflank it was neck or nothing. He floated out across the angry flood, seemed scarcely to pat the boulder with his dainty paws, then floated on and up, up into the shadows of the friendly Garolgome.

Nell also leapt, but the boulder was pointed and coated with ice, as I say. Immediately below was the whirlpool, into which whole trees sometimes vanished to come up as splintered drift-wood.

High up in the wood, at the mouth of a crevice among the rocks, all draped and festooned with masses of moss and the dead fronds of ferns, Fireflank sat with lolling tongue and listened. His pursuer was gone! Some minutes later the fox cub stole down to the water's edge and looked. She was not there! He chased his tail a round or two, crossed the river higher up, stole into the orchard and picked up the plumpest of his kill, while two fields away he could hear the farmer calling for his dog!

It was late that night when the man returned, silent and heavy-hearted. Something at the mistle door attracted his attention; it was Nell's food-bowl, filled with dirt scratched up from under the snow and scattered broadcast. The man knew the sign as that of a fox's uttermost contempt, and as he swore heavily under his breath there sounded across the distance Fireflank's 'Yap – Yap' of mockery.

Sweepingly triumphant though his first raid had been, Fireflank had sense enough not to visit the farm a second time. It was too near his home in Garolgome Wood, and during the nights that followed he made several similar raids on other farms, far distant from his own home and located on the ranges of other foxes. In this manner he came to know the gaps in the walls, the gates with the narrowest bars, the drains and the swamps, all of which were endlessly useful to him in the way of baffling the clumsy sheep-dogs.

One day, when all was very quiet, Fireflank stole from his subterranean dwelling, and fell to amusing himself by tearing the bark from a dead tree, in order to nose out the insects hibernating beneath it. Presently a movement near by attracted his notice, and looking up he saw another young fox standing quite near with ears acock, eyeing him enquiringly. Fireflank uttered a rumbling growl and his mane stood on end, but the newcomer did not stir. Fireflank moved to the windward side to get the caller's body scent. Both seemed satisfied, and they approached in attitudes of armed neutrality to sniff each other's noses. Thus introduced, they considered themselves on terms of discussion, and half an hour later, strange to relate, the two solitary little dog foxes were curled up together in Fireflank's den, sharing each other's warmth.

Whence Goldeye had come I do not know, but he proved to be the most warm-hearted, silly-good-natured little fox cub that ever poked his muzzle into a cold mouse hole. The two young foxes now took to hunting together, and ere their strange partnership was a week old it all but culminated in a tragedy for one or both of them. It happened thus.

With intermittent breaks the Frost King still held the country in his iron grip, and Fireflank and Goldeye, hard pressed for food, one night stole through the high boundary wall and out on to the moors above Garolgome. Here the snow lay in deep drifts among the crags. There were blue mountain hares and red grouse in the heather, but the foxes were after nobler game. They paused on a ridge and sniffed the icy wind. It bore to them a strange scent, like the scent of sheep, only more potent. It was the scent of the half-wild goat herd that dwells to this day among the crags of the Redstone Rigg.

Goldeye showered his kisses on Fireflank's nose to indicate his eagerness, then silently up-wind they stole, keeping to the hollows, never showing themselves against the sky-line. There were the goats, gathered in a space among the crags, twenty or thirty strong, comprising mothers with their kids and one enormous billy who possessed towering, upsweeping horns.

Hidden in a hollow, the two foxes decided upon their plan of campaign. Goldeye was to dash right in – which was just his mark – looking as big and terrible as possible, and thus, having scattered the herd, Fireflank would single out one old nanny and keep her occupied, while Goldeye drove her kid down the slope away from the rest and thus made sure of it.

Goldeye carried out his instructions to a nicety. He stole up unseen to within a few paces, then dashed out towards the goats, bristling and snarling. They, for their part, should now have scattered like chaff before a cyclone, but they did nothing of the sort. Every nursing mother of the clan calmly got up and sniffed her kid. It was the most perfectly orderly scene imaginable. The billy also got up, shaking his noble head, stamping his forehoofs, and glaring at the fox. Then, in a most unperturbed manner, without panic, even without haste, the whole herd, led by a disreputable old nanny, trickled out along a narrow shelf running across the face of the precipice to the north. The billy held the way till all were gone, then with dignity he followed.

Once on the shelf the goats began to move, running in single file – drifting like a string of ghosts along the black face of the crags, while the rumble of hoofs filled the air. 'Chase them!' yapped Fireflank, and suiting the action to the words he bounded out along the shelf in hot pursuit, Goldeye, yapping wildly, at his heels.

The shelf was scarcely two feet in width, and below them was a black fall through space almost sheer to the valley. Pell-mell along the perilous path the two young foxes ran, till they reached a point at which the mountainside jutted out, the trail beyond it invisible, and here, just round the corner, that fearless old billy was awaiting them. Fireflank was face to face with him in the twinkling of an eye. Down went those sweeping horns, and with a snort the old warrior dashed to the fray.

Another second and Fireflank would have been swept to his doom, but in that narrow interval of time he saw a protruding boulder jutting out from the face of the cliff twelve feet below. He made a desperate leap for it, and, as he left the shelf, the battering-ram of bone and muscle hurtled past him, filling his eyes with dust. Goldeye had already turned back and was fleeing for his life, so, glaring and shaking his head at Fireflank, now secure below, the billy plunged on into the night after his harem.

Fireflank glanced about him. Only a young and foolish fox would have found himself in such a predicament, for there he was, perched dizzily on a pinnacle protruding from the sheer face of the precipice, gloomy space beneath him, night on every side, and positively no way up or down. He saw immediately that he was a fixture, and remain here he must, until, pressed by hunger, perhaps, he might nerve himself to making this risky and wellnigh impossible leap back to the shelf. He began to whine pitifully, at which Goldeye came back and peered down at him, seeming to think his predicament an immense joke. He yapped in mockery, while Fireflank growled thunder, and eventually Goldeye sauntered off, leaving him to his fate.

But with the first streak of dawn Goldeye was back. All ridicule had left him now; he whined anxiously, and had there been a way down he would doubtless have descended to Fireflank's side, which was the sort of silly thing he would do. When daylight came he sneaked off into the heather near, overlooking the imprisoned Fireflank, and curled himself up there.

Some hours later two peregrines spied the stranded fox and came hurtling down from the clouds, screaming savagely, and apparently intent on driving Fireflank over the edge with their lashing wings; but Goldeye dashed out along the shelf and stood above his friend, fangs gleaming, mane on end, and the peregrines planed and looped and corkscrewed back into the clouds.

The wretched day passed, night came with cold, driving sleet, and the noble little Goldeye, himself lean with hunger, appeared on the shelf above, carrying a blue mountain hare. He dropped it to his mate and Fireflank caught it, feasting hungrily.

Again the cold grey dawn stole across the valley, and then, from away down the corrie at the foot of the crag, there sounded the barking of dogs. There was silence, then the dogs appeared at the foot of the crag, coming in this direction, and with them a man with a gun – a game warden. Foxes are not protected in these wild hills; in fact they are shot and trapped whenever possible.

Fireflank crouched low in terror now, while Goldeye watched anxiously from his outlook near. To them the appearance of the man and dogs could mean but one thing – that the imprisoned Fireflank was seen, and they were coming to destroy him. Steadily the three approached, the man constantly pausing to peer up the face of the crags – looking for the peregrines really, though the foxes did not know this. They knew only that it was a time of mortal peril, and it was then that Goldeye did a very noble thing, which many a fox has done to save its cubs, but few have done to save one of their own kind who was merely a friend. He stole cautiously out to meet the man and his dogs, to lead them off in pursuit of himself and so save Fireflank.

Thus the keeper was suddenly surprised to see a little red fox loping across the open space just ahead of him in full view of the dogs; but alas that Goldeye had never learnt the exact range of firearms! The keeper carried a long-barrelled ten-bore gun, charged with number three, and in an instant little Goldeye was aware of stinging pains all over his body, as though a swarm of hornets had attacked him. He yelped and doubled his pace, not mortally wounded though he was peppered all over, and behind him came those two iron-limbed missiles of death, schooled in all the lore of mountain foxes, and nursing a bitter feud against their kind.

Fireflank, on the pinnacle above, watched the opening of the chase – saw the two hounds closing, while Goldeye, limping as he ran, and leaving little spots of blood upon the whiteness of the snow, headed for a sheep-hole in the wall and vanished. Did Fireflank understand? Did he realize his friend was gambling with death on his behalf? Be that as it may, the sight of the chase excited him, seemed to make him desperate, and he forgot even his terror of the man.

Thus the keeper, looking up the face of the cliff, saw what looked like a sheet of brown paper caught by the wind and beating against a shelf, till he realized that there was no wind. Then he heard a yelp and realized that what he saw was a fox, leaping desperately to gain the goat-track, leaping and falling back again and again, in mortal peril of sliding to its doom. The range was too great, and the keeper stumbled towards a nearer point; but as he went he saw the fox gain a hold with its forepaws on the extreme edge of the shelf, and writhing, struggling madly, haul itself up till its hindpaws gained a hold, and so on to safety. In a moment it was gone, racing along the shelf and into the heather, and the keeper swore softly.

Yet he knew he had seen a noble thing. He had seen a fox risk everything to save its mate, crag-bound on the shelf above.

Goldeye, in the meantime, hard pressed by the dogs, was making desperate efforts to regain Garolgome Wood, but each time he headed in that direction one of the dogs headed him off. His tongue was lolling now, his steps lacked their buoyancy, and every here and there more crimson spots on the snow told the tragic story! The trees seemed to sway before his eyes, a mistiness enveloped the trail ahead, and goodness, how weary he was! His limbs ached, his brain throbbed, a burning thirst racked his throat, yet just behind him were those red-eyed snarling dogs, ready to tear him asunder. Once he fell; it was at the crest of a deeply washed watercourse, and one dog was upon him in a trice. Down they went together, over the edge, rolling and sliding down the almost perpendicular bank of moving shale, to land with a thud and split asunder among the rocks sixty feet below. The fox fell lightly and was up in an instant, but the fall shattered the breath out of the dog and left him panting. Goldeye headed tottering down the rocky bed of the creek, at which the second dog came tobogganing down the bank of shale in savage, bristling pursuit.

Goldeye tottered. Could he make it – no! No! His own life's blood, teeming from a wound in his scalp, got into his eyes, his heart was thumping like a trip hammer, and behind him, not ten paces behind, came the leading hound. At the foot of the gorge, fifty yards ahead, he decided to turn at bay, to stand and fight for his life to the bitter end.

But as he neared this point there was a flash of gold and russet, and there, behind a windfall, stood Fireflank, white-fanged and prepared – a waiting, bright-eyed little fighter, ready to meet his foes on their own ground – ready to dare death on his friend's behalf. Goldeye slipped weakly past him, then as the hound came dashing up, Fireflank shot from his retreat like a bursting shell. His big tail struck the hound across the eyes, momentarily blinding him. Snap, click, snap went Fireflank's jaws, and the dog, thrown from the trail he was running, turned with dripping muzzle to face his assailant.

But Fireflank was up and away, sliding under the windfall, gliding in and out among the rocks, both hounds, bellowing their hatred, following by sight. Away down to the river he led them, then across from rock to rock, through the poultry yard of the farm he knew, scattering the hens like chaff, then up a little-frequented valley that led to a land of dead and abandoned lead mines in the heart of the Bentland Heights.

Fireflank was running easily, but for the hounds it was the stiffest chase they had ever known. Now and then the fox seemed almost within reach, then suddenly he would slide through a gate with bars so narrow that the dogs bruised their backs and their shoulder-blades trying to wriggle after him. Once he skimmed daintily down the sheer mountainside, leaping from rock to rock, but his heavy pursuers, hard behind him, set a veritable avalanche moving, and were almost annihilated by the crashing boulders. At the foot of the slope the fox looked round and leered at them, then down the valley again, back the way he had come, towards the river and the friendly Garolgome.

There was a breath of icy wind, the snowflakes began to fall, blotting out all objects thirty paces away. Through the whirling whiteness Fireflank ran, decoying on his pursuers, ready now to lose them in the blizzard, for his breath was giving out. Then harsh fate dealt a stunning blow to the hunted fox, robbing him, in the moment of triumph, of his glorious gifts, for, leaping the wall and landing on the high-road near the farm, Fireflank trod on something – on a pointed spike of glass, buried in the snow. It passed clean through his forepaw, all but stunning him with pain, and hearing his yelps the dogs redoubled their efforts, drew in behind him, encouraged to the utmost of their speed by his close proximity.

On three legs now, scarcely able to hold his own, sick with pain, panting for breath, Fireflank headed for home – straight and true, knowing that life lay in that direction only. He gained the river bank with not a yard to spare. He felt the hot breath of the hounds on his flanks and knew that they would catch him ere he could get across. Then he remembered another chase, glorious in its triumph. Quickly he turned and dashed downstream – down along the grassy bank till the thunder of the falls filled the air.

The single rock in midstream was covered with snow today, but beneath the snow was a coat of ice. Fantastic ice formations festooned every rock and clung in clusters from every beard of moss. Fireflank leaped, using his wounded paw and leaving a crimson imprint – he leapt and landed, light as a thistle-seed, buoyant as a russet leaf of autumn, landed and fled on towards the rocks of his secure home.

The hounds did not falter, and through the whirling white-ness they too leapt for the pointed rock in midstream. Instantly

the first lost his foothold, clawed desperately for a moment, but was caught by the tide and whirled away, uttering the cry of a dog which knows itself doomed. Unwaveringly, fearlessly, the second also leapt, gained a footing, slithered back, clawed to the top, slithered over into the current, lashing the water into foam. And it, too, was drawn over the brink of the fall, to be shattered lifeless among the rocks, caught by the eddies of the whirlpool, sucked into its vortex, and so, beaten and pulped, to become the sport of the waves.

Long after darkness had fallen the voice of a man could be heard along the river bank, calling, calling for his dogs as he searched the whirling whiteness. The snow had covered all signs, yet he could guess what had happened, and it was only the stubborn Celtic blood in his veins that bade him continue the search long after all hope was relinquished. He knew that his dogs had been decoyed to their doom, he knew that he would never see them again, yet far into the night he searched. And when at length he turned his steps wearily homewards he heard from the heart of Garolgome Wood a mocking 'yap-yap', which told him that he and his dogs were the sport of the wild creatures they had designed to kill.

The Eye of
the Eagle

Ruskin Bond

It was a high, piercing sound, almost like the yelping of a dog. Jai stopped picking the wild strawberries that grew in the grass around him, and looked up at the sky. He had a dog – a shaggy guard-dog called Motu – but Motu did not yet yelp, he growled and barked. The strange sound came from the sky, and Jai had heard it before. Now, realizing what it was, he jumped to his feet, calling to his dog, calling his sheep to start for home. Motu came bounding towards him, ready for a game.

'Not now, Motu!' said Jai. 'We must get the lambs home quickly.' Again he looked up at the sky.

He saw it now, a black speck against the sun, growing larger as it circled the mountain, coming lower every moment – a Golden Eagle, king of the skies over the higher Himalayas, ready now to swoop and seize its prey.

Had it seen a pheasant or a pine marten? Or was it after one of the lambs? Jai had never lost a lamb to an eagle, but recently some of the other shepherds had been talking about a golden eagle that had been preying on their flocks.

The sheep had wandered some way down the side of the mountain, and Jai ran after them to make sure that none of the lambs had gone off on its own.

Motu ran about, barking furiously. He wasn't very good at keeping the sheep together – he was often bumping into them and sending them tumbling down the slope – but his size and bear-like look kept the leopards and wolves at a distance.

Jai was counting the lambs; they were bleating loudly and staying close to their mothers. *One – two – three – four . . .*

There should have been a fifth. Jai couldn't see it on the slope below him. He looked up towards a rocky ledge near the steep path to the Tung temple. The golden eagle was circling the rocks.

The bird disappeared from sight for a moment, then rose again with a small creature grasped firmly in its terrible talons.

'It has taken a lamb!' shouted Jai. He started scrambling up the slope. Motu ran ahead of him, barking furiously at the big bird as it glided away over the tops of the stunted junipers to its eyrie on the cliffs above Tung.

There was nothing that Jai and Motu could do except stare helplessly and angrily at the disappearing eagle. The lamb had died the instant it had been struck. The rest of the flock seemed unaware of what had happened. They still grazed on the thick, sweet grass of the mountain slopes.

'We had better drive them home, Motu,' said Jai, and at a nod from the boy, the big dog bounded down the slope, to take part in his favourite game of driving the sheep homewards. Soon he had them running all over the place, and Jai had to dash about trying to keep them together. Finally they straggled homewards.

'A fine lamb gone,' said Jai to himself gloomily. 'I wonder what Grandfather will say.'

Grandfather said, 'Never mind. It had to happen some day. That eagle has been watching the sheep for some time.'

Grandmother, more practical, said, 'We could have sold the lamb for three hundred rupees. You'll have to be more careful in future, Jai. Don't fall asleep on the hillside, and don't read story-books when you are supposed to be watching the sheep!'

'I wasn't reading this morning,' said Jai truthfully, forgetting to mention that he had been gathering strawberries.

'It's good for him to read,' said Grandfather, who had never had the luck to go to school. In his days, there weren't any schools in the mountains. Now there was one in every village.

'Time enough to read at night,' said Grandmother, who did not think much of the little one-room school down at Maku, their home village.

'Well, these are the October holidays,' said Grandfather. 'Otherwise he would not be here to help us with the sheep. It will snow by the end of the month, and then we will move with the flock. You will have more time for reading then, Jai.'

At Maku, which was down in the warmer valley, Jai's parents tilled a few narrow terraces on which they grew barley, millets, and potatoes. The old people brought their sheep up to the Tung meadows to graze during the summer months. They stayed in a small stone hut just off the path which pilgrims took to the ancient temple. At 12,000 feet above sea level, it was the highest Hindu temple on the inner Himalayan ranges.

The following day Jai and Motu were very careful. They did not let the sheep out of sight even for a minute. Nor did they catch sight of the golden eagle. 'What if it attacks again?' wondered Jai. 'How will I stop it?'

The great eagle, with its powerful beak and talons, was more than a match for boy or dog. Its hindclaw, four inches round the curve, was its most dangerous weapon. When it spread its wings, the distance from tip to tip was more than eight feet.

The eagle did not come that day because it had fed well and was now resting in its eyrie. Old bones, which had belonged to pheasants, snow-cocks, pine martens, and even foxes, were scattered about the rocks which formed the eagle's home. The eagle had a mate, but it was not the breeding season and she was away on a scouting expedition of her own.

The golden eagle stood on its rocky ledge, staring majestically across the valley. Its hard, unblinking eyes missed nothing. Those strange orange-yellow eyes could spot a field-rat or a mouse-hare more than a hundred yards below.

There were other eagles on the mountain, but usually they kept to their own territory. And only the bolder ones went for lambs, because the flocks were always protected by men and dogs.

The eagle took off from its eyrie and glided gracefully, powerfully over the valley, circling the Tung mountain.

Below lay the old temple, built from slabs of grey granite. A line of pilgrims snaked up the steep, narrow path. On the meadows below the peak, the sheep grazed peacefully, unaware of the presence of the eagle. The great bird's shadow slid over the sunlit slopes.

The eagle saw the boy and the dog, but he did not fear them. He had his eye on a lamb that was frisking about on the grass, a few feet away from the other grazing sheep.

Jai did not see the eagle until it swept round an outcrop of rocks about a hundred feet away. It moved silently, without any movement of its wings, for it had already built up the momentum for its dive. Now it came straight at the lamb.

Motu saw the bird in time. With a low growl he dashed forward and reached the side of the lamb at almost the same instant that the eagle swept in.

There was a terrific collision. Feathers flew. The eagle screamed with rage. The lamb tumbled down the slope, and Motu howled in pain as the huge beak struck him high on the leg.

The big bird, a little stunned by the clash, flew off rather unsteadily, with a mighty beating of its wings.

Motu had saved the lamb. It was frightened but unhurt. Bleating loudly, it joined the other sheep, who took up the bleating. Jai ran up to Motu, who lay whimpering on the ground. There was no sign of the eagle. Quickly he removed his shirt and vest; then he wrapped his vest round the dog's wound, tying it in position with his belt.

Motu could not get up, and he was much too heavy for Jai to carry. Jai did not want to leave his dog alone, in case the eagle returned to attack.

He stood up, cupped his hand to his mouth, and began calling for his grandfather.

'Dada, dada!' he shouted, and presently Grandfather heard him and came stumbling down the slope. He was followed by another shepherd, and together they lifted Motu and carried him home.

Motu had a bad wound, but Grandmother cleaned it and applied a paste made of herbs. Then she laid strips of carrot over the wound – an old mountain remedy – and bandaged the leg. But it would be some time before Motu could run about again. By then it would probably be snowing and time to leave these high-altitude pastures and return to the valley. Meanwhile, the sheep had to be taken out to graze, and Grandfather decided to accompany Jai for the remaining period.

They did not see the golden eagle for two or three days, and, when they did, it was flying over the next range. Perhaps it had found some other source of food, or even another flock of sheep. 'Are you afraid of the eagle?' Grandfather asked Jai.

'I wasn't before,' said Jai. 'Not until it hurt Motu. I did not know it could be so dangerous. But Motu hurt it too. He banged straight into it!'

'Perhaps it won't bother us again,' said Grandfather thoughtfully. 'A bird's wing is easily injured – even an eagle's.'

Jai wasn't so sure. He had seen it strike twice, and he knew that it was not afraid of anyone. Only when it learnt to fear his presence would it keep away from the flock.

The next day Grandfather did not feel well; he was feverish and kept to his bed. Motu was hobbling about gamely on three legs; the wounded leg was still very sore.

'Don't go too far with the sheep,' said Grandmother. 'Let them graze near the house.'

'But there's hardly any grass here,' said Jai.

'I don't want you wandering off while that eagle is still around.'

'Give him my stick,' said Grandfather from his bed. Grandmother took it from the corner and handed it to the boy.

It was an old stick, made of wild cherry wood, which Grandfather often carried around. The wood was strong and well-seasoned; the stick was stout and long. It reached up to Jai's shoulders.

'Don't lose it,' said Grandfather. 'It was given to me many years ago by a wandering scholar who came to the Tung temple. I was going to give it to you when you got bigger, but perhaps this is the right time for you to have it. If the eagle comes near you, swing the stick around your head. That should frighten it off!'

Clouds had gathered over the mountains, and a heavy mist hid the Tung temple. With the approach of winter, the flow of pilgrims had been reduced to a trickle. The shepherds had started leaving the lush meadows and returning to their villages at lower altitudes. Very soon the bears and the leopards and the golden eagles would have the high ranges all to themselves.

Jai used the cherry wood stick to prod the sheep along the path until they reached the steep meadows. The stick would have to be a substitute for Motu. And they seemed to respond to it more readily than they did to Motu's mad charges.

Because of the sudden cold and the prospect of snow, Grandmother had made Jai wear a rough woollen jacket and a pair of high boots bought from a Tibetan trader. He wasn't used to the boots – he wore sandals at other times – and had some difficulty in climbing quickly up and down the hillside. It was tiring work, trying to keep the flock together. The cawing of some crows warned Jai that the eagle might be around, but the mist prevented him from seeing very far.

After some time the mist lifted and Jai was able to see the temple and the snow-peaks towering behind it. He saw the golden eagle, too. It was circling high overhead. Jai kept close to the flock – one eye on the eagle, one eye on the restless sheep.

Then the great bird stooped and flew lower. It circled the temple and then pretended to go away. Jai felt sure it would be back. And a few minutes later it reappeared from the other side of the mountain. It was much lower now, wings spread out and back, taloned feet to the fore, piercing eyes fixed on its target – a small lamb that had suddenly gone frisking down the slope, away from Jai and the flock.

Now it flew lower still, only a few feet off the ground, paying no attention to the boy.

It passed Jai with a great rush of air, and as it did so the boy struck out with his stick and caught the bird a glancing blow.

The eagle missed its prey, and the tiny lamb skipped away.

To Jai's amazement, the bird did not fly off. Instead it landed on the hillside and glared at the boy, as a king would glare at a humble subject who had dared to pelt him with a pebble.

The golden eagle stood almost as tall as Jai. Its wings were still outspread. Its fierce eyes seemed to be looking through and through the boy.

Jai's first instinct was to turn and run. But the cherry wood stick was still in his hands, and he felt sure there was power in it. He saw that the eagle was about to launch itself again at the lamb. Instead of running away, he ran forward, the stick raised above his head.

The eagle rose a few feet off the ground and struck out with its huge claws. Luckily for Jai, his heavy jacket took the force of the blow. A talon ripped through the sleeve, and the sleeve fell away. At the same time the heavy stick caught the eagle across its open wing. The bird gave a shrill cry of pain and fury. Then it turned and flapped heavily away, flying unsteadily because of its injured wing.

Jai still clutched the stick, because he expected the bird to return; he did not even glance at his torn jacket. But the golden eagle had alighted on a distant rock and was in no hurry to return to the attack.

Jai began driving the sheep home. The clouds had become heavy and black, and presently the first snow-flakes began to fall.

Jai saw a hare go lolloping down the hill. When it was about fifty yards away, there was a rush of air from the eagle's beating wings, and Jai saw the bird approaching the hare in a sidelong drive.

'So it hasn't been badly hurt,' thought Jai, feeling a little relieved, for he could not help admiring the great bird. 'Now it has found something else to chase for its dinner.'

The hare saw the eagle and dodged about, making for a clump of junipers. Jai did not know if it was caught or not, because the snow and sleet had increased and both bird and hare were lost in the gathering snow-storm.

The sheep were bleating behind him. One of the lambs looked tired, and he stooped to pick it up. As he did so, he heard a thin, whining sound. It grew louder by the second. Before he could look up, a huge wing caught him across the shoulders and sent him sprawling. The lamb tumbled down the slope with him, into a thorny bilberry bush.

The bush saved them. Jai saw the eagle coming in again, flying low. It was another eagle! One had been vanquished, and now here was another, just as big and fearless, probably the mate of the first eagle.

Jai had lost his stick and there was no way in which he could fight the second eagle. So he crept further into the bush, holding the lamb beneath him. At the same time he began shouting at the top of his voice – both to scare the bird away and to summon help. The eagle could not easily get at them now; but the rest of the flock was exposed on the hillside. Surely the eagle would make for them.

Even as the bird circled and came back in another dive, Jai heard fierce barking. The eagle immediately swung away and rose skywards.

The barking came from Motu. Hearing Jai's shouts and sensing that something was wrong, he had come limping out of the house, ready to do battle. Behind him came another shepherd and – most wonderful of all – Grandmother herself, banging two frying-pans together. The barking, the banging, and the shouting frightened the eagles away. The sheep scattered too, and it was some time before they could all be rounded up. By then it was snowing heavily.

'Tomorrow we must all go down to Maku,' said the shepherd.

'Yes, it's time we went,' said Grandmother. 'You can read your story-books again, Jai.'

'I'll have my own story to tell,' said Jai.

When they reached the hut and Jai saw Grandfather, he said, 'Oh, I've forgotten your stick!'

But Motu had picked it up. Carrying it between his teeth, he brought it home and sat down with it in the open doorway. He had decided the cherry wood was good for his teeth and would have chewed it up if Grandmother hadn't taken it from him.

'Never mind,' said Grandfather, sitting up on his cot. 'It isn't the stick that matters. It's the person who holds it.'

No Medal for Matt

Walter Macken

It was a beautiful morning. The cliff top, at the western edge of the island, which lay some miles off the Irish coast, was a green carpet of closely cropped grass. Five hundred feet below, the water broke indolently over black jagged rocks. Its sinister sound was almost soothing. Westward, the Atlantic stretched calmly away to a limitless light-blue horizon.

Matt came towards the cliff from the village, walking on the enormous slabs of flat rock that covered the fields, which sloped steeply upward. The rocks were warm to the soles of his bare feet. Homespun trousers ending at the shin and a heavy knitted red jersey were making him sweat under the June sun. A canvas schoolbag flopped up and down on his hip as he journeyed, reminding him and bringing a frown between his brown eyes.

The climb up the slope was hard enough. He had to leap at times, and try to dodge the briars lurking in the crevices of the rocks. Sometimes the thorns scraped at the brown skin of his feet, leaving behind a scarlet scratch of blood. On both sides of him, small black-faced sheep, the kind that make such tender mutton, raised their heads to look at him and then moved cautiously away, following him with their eyes for a little, after he had passed, and then resuming the search for their meagre forage.

Matt was filled with a sense of guilt and injustice, and between the two of them his heart was very heavy. You are in school, see, just as he was yesterday. Near the end of the day, the sleepy part, the fellow beside him in the desk, young Pat Mullen, suddenly gives him a fierce puck in the ribs. Matt turns to clatter him, but before he can land even one blow on him, down the master comes and belts Matt.

Matt protests that he is being belted in the wrong, and the master belts him again. Matt still protests, and the master, his face as red as the comb of a Christmas turkey, belts him once again and asks him does he want more. Matt says he doesn't want more. On his way home from school, burning with the injustice of it all, Matt tells himself that his father will right this wrong. His father is noted for his justice. 'All right,' says his father when Matt explains to him, 'so the master was in the wrong. What do you want me to do, go up and hit the man? If every father did that, there would be not a school left in the universe.' Couldn't he just tell him that he was in the wrong? Matt asks. No, he could not, his father says. Maybe the poor fellow was having trouble with his wife, or maybe he had an interior ailment that was persecuting him. Well, you will just have to tell him he was in the wrong, Matt says. His father gets angry then and shouts that he'll be damned if he will do anything of the sort, and even if this time Matt has been belted in the wrong, it will do him no harm, because there were times when he wasn't belted before and should have been. Matt denies this, and his father walks out of the house saying, 'If I don't go, I'll belt you, and where will you be then?' His father is upset, because he doesn't like to think of Matt's being belted, right or wrong, but, being civilized, he can't go and hammer the poor teacher.

So now Matt saw the whole world was a place of great injustice for boys; that there was no equity in it at all when even your father refused to stand up for you. That was why he had walked past the schoolhouse door this morning, just as if it wasn't there, and had headed for the tall cliffs. He had never done this before, because he liked school, except on Mondays and the first day after holidays. And even though he knew that he was right – it is necessary for every man to make some protest against injustice – he felt that he was wrong, and it seemed to him that some of the beauty had gone out of the day, and that this freedom he had chosen had, in some odd way, a chain on it.

When he had cleared the last obstacles barring his way to the cliff top, he stood there and looked back. He could see the whole island sloping away from his feet. It was shaped, he thought, like the kidney of a pig. He could see the golden beaches, and the sea beyond them reaching towards the distant mainland, which was hidden in a blue haze. He couldn't see his own house, but he could see the schoolhouse, and was sorry he was out of it, because just about now they would be chanting the multiplication tables, and he liked that. He also liked going into the yard at lunchtime and wolfing his jam sandwiches, so that he would have more time to play *capaillini conemara*, a game in which small boys, mounted on the backs of larger boys, raced each other.

He sighed and his heart was heavy, but his stomach was empty, so he sat on the grass and, after removing the books from his schoolbag, took the sandwiches his mother had made for his lunch and proceeded to eat them, and it was miraculous how the seagulls knew that there was food around. They thronged about him, screaming, from the sky and from the cliffs, and he amused himself by throwing crusts into the void and watching the wonderful swerving and twisting, the grace and the beauty of the gulls as they caught the crusts in flight.

My father will kill me, Matt thought then, and he looked over the water, thinking he might see his father's lobster boat if his father was doing this side of the island today. No boat was in sight. His father wouldn't actually kill him, Matt thought. He never raised a hand to him. It was his mother who always held the threat of him over Matt's head. Someday your father will kill you, Matt, she'd say. All the same, Matt knew that his father would be hurt by what he had done, and this made him feel a bit sad. He rolled on his stomach with his face over the cliff and looked down at the waves breaking on the rocks far, far below.

It was some while before he saw the movement – a fluttering movement, about fifty feet below him, on a ledge. He thought at

first it might be a young gull,
but then, as he watched closely,
he saw that what moved was a
rabbit, a plump young rabbit.
He raised himself to his knees in
surprise. A rabbit fifty feet
down the face of the cliff! How
could he have got there? Did
a big bird claw him and lose
him, or was he chased by a fox
so that he fell and landed on
that ledge below, or what?

Will I climb down and get
the rabbit? was the next
thought that came into his
head. A terrible thought. His
eyes narrowed as he looked
over every inch of the cliff to
the ledge. Suppose I fall, he
wondered, looking further,
to the cruel black rocks waiting
below. Who would miss me?
Isn't everyone against me?
Even so, his heart had begun to
thump excitedly. It would be a
famous climb. He stood up
straight now, his hands on his
hips, his eyes very bright. If the
rabbit was left there, he would die
and become a skeleton, or a
bird would scoop him. If Matt
saved his life, what a hero Matt
would be! I climbed down cliffs
when I was smaller, he thought,
but never this cliff. This was the
highest on the island.

He was still standing up when the boat came around a promontory behind him. He didn't see it, of course, and he didn't hear it. The chug-chug of its diesel engine was not loud, because the boat was going slowly as it negotiated a channel through some rocks towards a cluster of bobbing buoys that marked lobster pots.

The man at the tiller raised his eyes and saw the figure of the boy up there on the cliff top. He took his pipe out of his mouth, which remained open in amazement. 'Here, Tom!' he called to the other man, who was coiling a rope in the waist. 'For the love of God, is that my Matt up there?'

Tom came back to him, shaded his eyes with his hand, and said, 'By all that's holy, it is!'

'What's he doing up there?' Matt's father asked. 'He should be at school.'

Then Matt's father opened his lungs to let a shout out of them, but it was never emitted, because Tom suddenly clapped a hard hand over his mouth and the shout died in a strangled gurgle. Tom took his hand away, and the two of them stood there, looking up, petrified with fear, the hair rising on the back

of their necks at the sight of the boy casually letting himself down over the cliff.

'Oh, my God!' groaned Matt's father.

'If you shouted, you would have startled him,' Tom whispered.

'He'll fall! He's mad! What's come over him?' Matt's father asked in anguish, his eyes glued painfully to the small figure slowly descending the sheer face. In that red jersey of his, it was all too easy to see him.

'Birds' eggs or something,' said Tom. 'My God, I never saw anybody climbing that bit. He'll be kilt!'

Matt's father swung the tiller to bring the boat in towards the foot of the cliff. Tom struggled with him, and forced the tiller so that the boat turned out again. He switched off the engine.

'Are you mad?' he asked. 'You can't get within fifty yards of the place. The tide is low. Will you kill us as well?'

'He'll fall! He'll fall!' said Matt's father.

'Well, if he falls now,' said Tom, annoyed at the boy, 'you'll only get his body. The rocks are up.'

'Oh, my God!' said Matt's father.

Matt's heart was thumping and his mouth was dry. Even so, there was a soaring in his breast. He was glad he was in his bare feet. His big toes were wonderful, the way they could feel, gauge, and grip a narrow crevice. The cliff face was almost solid granite, which, for all its height, had many times been washed by enormous waves. The sea water had sought every weakness, and here and there had scooped out the poor spots in the stone. So there were cracks for Matt's thin fingers and his hardened toes. All the same, you could be frightened, he thought, if you hadn't climbed down cliffs before. He knew where he was going, but he didn't want to look down to see. Clinging like a fly, he lowered himself bit by bit, until below him, out of the corner of his right eye, he could see the end of the ledge where the rabbit crouched.

Down in the boat, Matt's father, who was in the middle of a prayer, thought he could feel the hairs turning grey on his head. He relaxed a little as he saw his son's feet feeling for a ledge and then resting there firmlv

Matt was happy to feel his feet on solid rock, though it was a very narrow ledge. The rabbit went to the far end of it, on the right, but he was still within reach of Matt's hand. Matt lowered his body slowly, gripping the surface of the cliff with the nails of his left hand and reaching for the rabbit with his right.

He grabbed the rabbit's fur. Don't struggle, don't struggle, Matt shouted at him in his heart, or you'll have the two of us over. He gripped him tightly. The animal stiffened. Slowly, Matt lifted him, and then carefully inserted him in the open school-bag on his hip and strapped the flap shut.

Matt rested for a moment. He felt good now. Then he took a few deep breaths and started the climb up. The rabbit remained very still in the bag.

By now, Matt's father was kneeling, his hands covering his eyes. 'What's he doing now, Tom?' he asked. 'What in the name of God is he doing now?'

'He's on his way up,' said Tom quietly. 'He'll likely make it. What scoundrels boys are! What did he do it for? He got something. I wouldn't do that to rescue a king. That fellow will be a famous man or he'll end up hung.'

'God bring him to the top,' said Matt's father.

On the cliffside, Matt whispered to himself, 'Going up is not as bad as going down.' Because you can see. It looked fierce far just the same. The granite had torn his fingers. The middle ones were bleeding. And the sides of his toes were bleeding, too. He could feel them. Above, he could see a few slivers of green grass on the very top, beckoning to him. I'm coming, he silently called up to them, laughing. Wait'll you see. But it seemed a long time to him, before his hand rested on the coolness of the grass, and he paused, breathless, and then pulled himself over the top.

It seemed a lifetime to his father before he heard Tom's pent-up breath expelled and his voice saying, with a sigh, 'He is over. He is over now.' Matt's father couldn't say anything.

Matt was now lying on the grass, feeling it with one cheek. His fist was beating the ground. 'I did it! I did it!' he said out loud.

What a tale to tell, he thought, but who will believe me? But what does it matter if nobody believes me? It was a great and famous climb, so it was.

Then, from the depths below, he heard a voice hailing and hailing, so he stood up and looked over the edge. Oh, it was his father and Tom. He hoped they hadn't seen him climbing down to the ledge. His father would murder him!

'What you doing? What the hell you think you're doing?' he faintly heard Tom saying.

So they *had* seen him! Then he remembered the rabbit. The rabbit would change things. Because of the rabbit, his father would be pleased with him. He'd be pleased, you'd see, and forget all about his dodging school. He opened the schoolbag and, reaching for the rabbit with his left hand, caught him by the hind legs and extracted him. Then he expertly hit him on the back of the neck with the edge of his right hand, so that the rabbit died, swiftly executed, in a second.

And Matt waved the body of the rabbit above his head, leaning out perilously over the cliff, and, with one hand curved around his mouth, shouted down, 'Hey, Father! Father! You'll have rabbit stew tonight. You hear that? Rabbit stew tonight!'

He laughed as he waved the rabbit, because his father loved rabbit stew, he really did. Then Matt gathered up his schoolbooks and put them back in his bag, along with the rabbit, and hurried down the slope, over the long fields of great flat rocks, towards home.

And his father still sat, completely drained, completely exhausted, in the bottom of the lobster boat.

The Truce

Charles G. D. Roberts

Too early, while yet the snow was thick and the food scarce, the big black bear had roused himself from his long winter sleep and forsaken his snug den under the roots of the pine tree. The thawing spring world he found an empty place, no rabbits to be captured, no roots to be dug from wet meadows; and his appetite was sorely vexing him. He would have crept back into his hole for another nap; but the air was too stimulatingly warm, too full of promise of life, to suffer him to resume the old, comfortable drowsiness. Moreover, having gone to bed thin the previous December, he had woken up hungry; and hunger is a restless bedfellow. In three days he had had but one meal – a big trout, clawed out half-dead from a rocky eddy below the Falls; and now, as he sniffed the soft, wet air with fiercely eager nostrils, he forgot his customary tolerance of mood and was ready to do battle with anything that walked the wilderness.

It was a little past noon, and the shadows of the tree-tops fell blue on the rapidly shrinking snow. The air was full of faint trickling noises, and thin tinklings where the snow veiled the slopes of little rocky hollows. Under the snow and under the rotting patches of ice, innumerable small streams were everywhere hurrying to swell the still ice-fettered flood of the river, the Big Fork, whose roomy valley lay about a half-mile eastward through the woods. Every now and then, when a soft gust drew up from the south, it bore with it a heavy roar, a noise as of muffled and tremendous trampling, the voice of the Big Fork Falls thundering out from under their decaying lid of ice. The Falls were the only thing which the black bear really feared. Often as he had visited them, to catch wounded fish in the ominous eddies at their foot, he could never look at their terrific plunge without a certain awed dilation of his eyes, a certain shrinking at his heart. Perhaps by reason of some association of his cubhood, some imminent peril and narrow escape at the age when his senses were most impressionable, in all his five years of life the Falls had never become a commonplace to him. And even now, while questing noiselessly and restlessly for food, he rarely failed to pay the tribute of an instinctive, unconscious turn of head whenever that portentous voice came up upon the wind.

Prowling hither and thither among the great ragged trunks, peering and sniffing and listening, the bear suddenly caught the sound of small claws on wood. The sound came apparently from within the trunk of a huge maple, close at hand. Leaning his head to one side, he listened intently, his ears cocked, eager as a child listening to a watch. There was, indeed, something half childish in the attitude of the huge figure, strangely belying the ferocity in his heart. Yes, the sound came, unmistakably, from within the trunk. He nosed the bark warily. There was no opening; and the bark was firm. He stole to the other side of the tree, his head craftily outstretched and reaching around far before him.

The situation was clear to him at once – and his hungry muzzle jammed itself into the entrance to a chipmunk's hole. The maple tree was dead, and partly decayed, up one side of the trunk. All his craft forgotten on the instant, the bear sniffed and snorted and drew loud, fierce breaths, as if he thought to suck the little furry tenant forth by inhalation. The live, warm smell that came from the hole was deliciously tantalizing to his appetite. The hole, however, was barely big enough to admit the tip of his black snout, so he presently gave over his foolish sniffings, and set himself to tear an entrance with his resistless claws. The bark and dead wood flew in showers under his efforts, and it was evident that the chipmunk's little home would speedily lie open to the foe. But the chipmunk, meanwhile, from the crotch of a limb overhead, was looking down in silent indignation. Little Stripe-sides had been wise enough to provide his dwelling with a sort of skylight exit.

Suddenly, in the midst of his task, the bear stopped and lifted his muzzle to the wind. What was that new taint upon the air? It was one almost unknown to him – but one which he instinctively dreaded, though without any reason based directly upon experience of his own. At almost any other time, indeed, he would have taken the first whiff of that ominous man-smell as a signal to efface himself and make off noiselessly down the wind. But just now, his first feeling was wrath at the thought of being hindered from his prospective meal. He would let no one, not even a man, rob him of that chipmunk. Then, as his wrath swelled rapidly, he decided to hunt the man himself. Perhaps, as the bear relishes practically everything edible under the sun except human flesh, he had no motive but a savage impulse to punish the intruder for such an untimely intrusion. However that may be, a red light came into his eyes, and he swung away to meet this unknown trespasser upon his trails.

On that same day, after a breakfast before dawn in order that he might make an early start, a gaunt trapper had set out from the Settlement on the return journey to his camp beyond the Big Fork. He had been in to the Settlement with a pack of furs, and was now hurrying back as fast as he could, because of the sudden thaw. He was afraid the ice might go out of the river and leave him cut off from his camp – for his canoe was on the other side. As the pelts were beginning to get poor, he had left his rifle at home, and carried no weapon but his knife. He had grown so accustomed to counting all the furry wild folk as his prey that he never thought of them as possible adversaries – unless it might chance to be some such exception as a bull-moose in rutting season. A rifle, therefore, when he was not after skins, seemed to him a useless burden; and he was carrying, moreover, a pack of camp supplies on his broad back. He was tall, lean, leather-faced, and long-jawed, with calm, light blue eyes under heavy brows; and he wore a stout, yellow-brown, homespun shirt, squirrel-skin cap, long leggings of deerhide, and oiled cowhide moccasins. He walked rapidly with a long, slouching stride that was almost a lope, his toes pointing straight ahead like an Indian's.

When, suddenly, the bear lurched out into his trail and confronted him, the woodsman was in no way disturbed. The bear paused, swaying in surly fashion, about ten paces in front of him, completely blocking the trail. But the woodsman kept right on. The only attention he paid to the big, black stranger was to shout at him authoritatively – 'Git out the way, thar!'

To his unbounded astonishment, however, the beast, instead of getting out of the way, ran at him with a snarling growl. The woodsman's calm blue eyes flamed with anger; but the life of the woods teaches one to think quickly, or rather, to act in advance of one's thoughts. He knew that with no weapon but his knife he was no match for such a foe, so, leaping aside as lightly as a panther, he darted around a tree, regaining the trail beyond his assailant, and ran on at his best speed towards the river. He felt sure that the bear had acted under a mere spasm of ill-temper, and would not take the trouble to follow far.

When, once in a long time, a hunter or trapper gets the worst of it in his contest with the wild kindreds, in the majority of cases it is because he had fancied he knew all about bears. The bear is strong in individuality and delights to set at nought the traditions of his kind. So it happens that every now and then a woodsman pays with his life for failing to recognize that the bear won't always play by rule.

To the trapper's disgusted amazement, this particular bear followed him so vindictively that before he realized the full extent of his peril he was almost overtaken. He saw that he must deliver up his precious pack, the burden of which was effectively handicapping him in the race for life. When the bear was almost upon him, he flung the bundle away, with angry violence, expecting that it would at once divert the pursuer's attention.

In about ninety-nine cases out of a hundred, perhaps, it would have done so, for among other things it contained bacon and sugar, dainties altogether delectable to a bear's palate. But as luck would have it, the bundle so bitterly hurled struck the beast full on the snout, making him grunt with pain and fresh fury. From that moment he was a veritable demon of vengeance. Well enough he knew it was not the bundle, but the man who had thrown it, upon whom he must wipe out the affront. His hunger was all forgotten in red rage.

Fortunate it was now for the tall woodsman that he had lived abstemiously and laboured sanely all that winter, and could depend upon both wind and limb. Fortunate, too, that on the open trail, cut years before by the lumbermen of the Big Fork Drive, the snow was already almost gone, so that it did not seriously impede his running. He ran almost like a caribou, with enough in reserve to be able to glance back over his shoulder from time to time. But seeing how implacable was the black bulk that pursued, he could not help thinking what would happen, there in the great, wet, shadow-mottled solitudes, if he should chance to trip upon a root, or if his wind should fail him before he could reach the camp. At this thought, not fear, but a certain disgust and impotent resentment, swelled his heart; and with a challenging look at the ancient trunks, the familiar forest aisles, the high, branch-fretted blue, bright with spring sunshine, he defied the wilderness, which he had so long loved and ruled, to turn upon him with such an unspeakable betrayal.

The wilderness loves a master; and the challenge was not accepted. No root tripped his feet, nor did his wind fail him; and so he came out, with the bear raging some ten paces behind his heels, upon the banks of the Big Fork. Once across that quarter-mile of sloppy, rotting ice, he knew there was good, clear running to his cabin and his gun. His heart rose, his resentment left him, and he grinned as he gave one more glance over his shoulder.

As he raced down the bank, the trampling of the Falls, a mile away, roared up to him on a gust of wind. In spite of himself he could not but notice how treacherous the ice was looking. In spite of himself he noticed it, having no choice but to trust it. The whole surface looked sick, with patches of sodden white and sickly lead-colour; and down along the shore it was covered by a lane of shallow, yellowish water. It appeared placid and innocent enough; but the woodsman's practised eye perceived that it might break up, or 'go out', at any moment. The bear was at his heels, however, and that particular moment was not the one for indecision. The woodsman dashed knee-deep through the margin water, and out upon the free ice; and he heard the bear, reckless of all admonitory signs, splash after him about three seconds later.

On the wide, sun-flooded expanse of ice, with the dark woods beyond and soft blue sky above, the threat of imminent death seemed to the woodsman curiously out of place. Yet there death was, panting savagely at his heels, ready for the first misstep. And there, too, a mile below, was death in another form, roaring heavily from the swollen Falls. And hidden under a face of peace, he knew that death lurked all about his feet, liable to rise in mad fury at any instant with the breaking of the ice. As he thought of all this besetting menace, the woodsman's nerves drew themselves to steel. He set his teeth grimly. A light of elation came into his eyes. And he felt himself able to win the contest against whatever odds.

As this sense of new vigour and defiance spurred him to a fresh burst of speed, the woodsman took notice that he was just about half-way across the ice. 'Good!' he muttered, counting the game now more than half won. Then, even as he spoke, a strange, terrifying sound ran all about him. Was it in the air, or beneath the ice? It came from everywhere at once – a straining grumble, ominous as the first growl of an earthquake. The woodsman understood that dreadful voice very well. He wavered for a second, then sprang forward desperately. And the bear, pursuing, understood also. His rage vanished in a breath. He stumbled, whimpered, cast one frightened glance at the too distant shore behind him, then followed the woodsman's flight – followed now, with no more heed to pursue.

For less than half a minute that straining grumble continued. Then it grew louder, mingled with sharp, ripping reports, and long, black lanes opened suddenly in every direction. Right

before the woodsman's flying feet one opened. He took it with a bound. But even as he sprang the ice went all to pieces. What he sprang to was no longer a solid surface, but a tossing fragment which promptly went down beneath the impact of his descent. Not for nothing was it, however, that the woodsman had learned to 'run the logs' in many a tangled boom and racing 'drive'. His foot barely touched the treacherous floe ere he leaped again and yet again, till he had gained, by a path which none but a riverman could ever have dreamed of traversing, an ice-cake broad and firm enough to give him foothold. Beyond this refuge was a space of surging water, foam, and ice-mush, too broad for the essay of any human leap.

The Big Fork, from shore to shore, was now a tossing, swishing, racing, whirling, and grinding chaos of ice-cakes, churning in an angry flood and hurrying blindly to the Falls. In the centre of his own floe the woodsman sat down, the better to preserve his balance. He bit off a chew from his plug of 'blackjack', and with calm eyes surveyed the doom towards which he was rushing. A mile is a very short distance when it lies above the inevitable. The woodsman saw clearly that there was nothing to be done but chew his 'blackjack', and wait on fate. That point settled, he turned his head to see what the bear was doing.

To his surprise, the animal was now a good fifty yards further up-stream, having evidently been delayed by some vagary of the struggling ice. He was now sitting up on his haunches on a floe, and staring silently at the volleying cloud which marked the Falls. The woodsman was aware of a curious fellow feeling for the great beast which, not five minutes ago, had been raging for his life. To the woodsman, with his long knowledge and understanding of the wild kindreds, that rage and that pursuit now appeared as lying more or less in the course of events, a part of the normal savagery of Nature, and no matter of personal vindictiveness.

Now that he and his enemy were involved in a common and appalling doom, the enmity was forgotten. 'Got cl'ar grit, too!' he murmured to himself, as he took note of the quiet way the bear was eyeing the Falls.

And now it seemed to him that the trampling roar grew louder every second, drowning into dumbness the crashing and grinding of the ice; and the volleying mist-clouds seemed to race up-stream to meet him. Then, with a sickening jump and turn of his heart, a hope came and shook him out of his stoicism. He saw that his ice-cake was sailing straight for a little rocky islet just above the fall. Two minutes more would decide his fate – at least for the time. He did not trouble to think what he would do on the island, if he got there. He rose cautiously and crouched, every sinew tense to renew the battle for life.

Another minute fled away, and the island was close ahead, wrapped in the roar and the mist-volleys. A cross-current seized the racing ice-cake, dragging it aside – and the man clenched his fists in a fury of disappointment as he saw that he would miss the refuge after all. He made ready to plunge in and at least die battling. Then fate took yet another whim, and a whirling mass of logs and ice, colliding with the floe, forced it back to its original course. Another moment and it grounded violently, breaking into four pieces, which rolled off on either side towards the abyss. And the woodsman, splashing into the turbulent shallows, made good his hold upon a rock and dragged himself ashore.

Fairly landed, he shook himself, spat coolly into the flood, and turned to see what was happening to his fellow in distress. To the roaring vortex just below him – so close that it seemed as if it might at any moment drag down the little island and engulf it – he paid no heed whatever, but turned his back contemptuously upon the tumult and the mists. His late enemy, alive, strong, splendid, and speeding to a hideous destruction, was of the keener interest to his wilderness spirit.

The bear was now about twenty paces above the island; but caught by an inexorable current, he was nearly that distance beyond it. With a distinct regret, a pang of sympathy, the man saw that there was no chance of his adversary's escape. But the bear, like himself, seeing a refuge so near, was not of the temper to give up without a struggle. Suddenly, like a gigantic spring uncoiling, he launched himself forth with a violence that completely up-ended his ice-cake, and carried him over a space of churned torrent to the edge of another floe. Gripping this with his mighty forearms till he pulled it half under, he succeeded in clawing out upon it. Scrambling across, he launched himself again, desperately, sank almost out of sight, rose and began swimming, with all the energy of courage and despair combined.

But already he was opposite the head of the island. Could he make it? The man's own muscles strained and heaved in unconscious sympathy with that struggle. The bear was a gallant swimmer, and for a moment it looked as if there might be the ghost of a chance for him. But no, the torrent had too deadly a grip upon his long-furred bulk. He would *just* miss that last safe ledge!

In his eagerness, and without any conscious thought of what he was doing, the man stepped down into the water knee-deep, bracing himself, and clinging with his left hand to a tough projecting root. Closer came the bear, beating down the splintered refuse that obstructed him, his long, black body labouring dauntlessly. Closer he came – but not quite close enough to get his strong paws on the rock. A foot more would have done it – but that paltry foot he was unable to make good.

The man could not stand it. It was quite too fine a beast to be dragged over the Falls before his eyes, if he could help it. Reaching out swiftly with his right hand, he caught the swimmer by the long fur of his neck, and heaved with all his strength.

For a moment he wondered if he could hold on. The great current drew and sucked, almost irresistibly. But his grip was of steel, his muscles sound and tense. For a moment or two the situation hung in doubt. Then the swimmer, stroking desperately, began to gain. A moment more, and that narrow, deadly foot of space was covered. The animal got first one paw upon the rocks, then the other. With prompt discretion, the woodsman dropped his hold and stepped back to the top of the island, suddenly grown doubtful of his own wisdom.

Drawing himself just clear of the torrent, the bear crouched panting for several minutes, exhausted from the tremendous struggle; and the man, on the top of the rock, waited with his hand upon his knife-hilt to see what would come of his reckless act. In reality, however, he did not look for trouble, knowing the natures of the wild kindreds. He was merely holding himself on guard against the unexpected. But he soon saw that his caution was unnecessary. Recovering breath, the bear clambered around the very edge of the rocks to the further side of the island, as far as possible from his rescuer. There he seated himself upon his haunches, and devoted himself to gazing down, as if fascinated, at the cauldron from which he had been snatched.

During the next half-hour the woodsman began to think. For the present, he knew that the bear was quite inoffensive, being both grateful and over-awed. But there was no food on the island for either, except the other. So the fight was bound to be renewed at last. And after that, whoever might be the victor, what remained for him? From that island, on the lip of the fall and walled about with wild rapids, there could be no escape. The situation was not satisfactory from any point of view. But that it was clear against his principles to knuckle down, under any conditions, to beast, or man, or fate, the woodsman might have permitted himself to wish that, after all, his ice-cake had

missed the island. As it was, however, he took another bite from his plug of 'blackjack', and set himself to whittling a stick.

With a backwoodsman's skill in the art of whittling, he had made good progress towards the shaping of a toy hand-sled, when, looking up from his task, he saw something that mightily changed the face of affairs. He threw away the half-shaped toy, thrust the knife back into his belt, and rose to his feet. After a long, sagacious survey of the flood, he drew his knife again, and proceeded to cut himself a stout staff, a sort of alpenstock. He saw that an ice-jam was forming just above the falls.

The falls of the Big Fork lie at the sharp elbow of the river, and cross the channel on a slant. Immediately above them the river shoals sharply; and though at ordinary seasons there is only one island visible, at times of low water huge rocks appear all along the brink. It chanced, at this particular time, that after the first run of the ice had passed there came a second run that was mixed with logs. This ice, moreover, was less rotten than that which had formed near the falls, and it came down in larger cakes. When some of these big cakes, cemented with logs, grounded on the head of the island, the nucleus of a jam was promptly formed. At the same time some logs, deeply frozen into an ice-floe, caught and hung on one of the unseen mid-stream ledges. An accumulation gathered in the crook of the elbow, over on the further shore; and then, as if by magic, the rush stopped, the flood ran almost clear from the lip of the falls, and the river was closed from bank to bank.

The woodsman sat quietly watching, as if it were a mere idle spectacle, instead of the very bridge of life, that was forming before his eyes. Little by little the structure welded itself, the masses of drift surging against the barrier, piling up and diving under, till it was compacted and knit to the very bottom – and the roar of the falls dwindled with the diminishing of the stream. This was the moment for which the man was waiting. Now, if ever, the jam was solid, and might hold so until he gained the further shore. But beyond this moment every second of delay only served to gather the forces that were straining to break the obstruction. He knew that in a very few minutes the rising weight of the flood must either sweep all before it, or flow roaring over the top of the jam in a new cataract that would sweep the island bare. He sprang to his feet, grasped his stick, and scanned the tumbled, precarious surface, choosing his path. Then he turned and looked at the bear, wondering if that animal's woodcraft were subtler than his own to distinguish when the jam was secure. He found that the bear was eyeing him anxiously, and not looking at the ice at all; so he chuckled, told himself that if he didn't know more than a bear he'd no business in the woods, and stepped resolutely forth upon the treacherous pack. Before he had gone ten paces the bear jumped up with a whisper, and followed hastily, plainly conceding that the man knew more than he.

In the strange, sudden quiet, the shrunken falls clamouring thinly and the broken ice swishing against the upper side of the jam, the man picked his way across the slippery, chaotic surface of the dam, expecting every moment that it would crumble with a roar from under his feet. About ten or a dozen yards behind him came the bear, stepping hurriedly, and trembling as he looked down at the diminished cataract. The miracle of the vanishing falls daunted his spirit most effectively, and he seemed to think that the whole mysterious phenomenon was of the man's creating. When the two reached shore, the flood was already boiling far up the bank. Without so much as a thank you, the bear scurried past his rescuer, and made off through the timber like a scared cat. The man looked after him with a slow smile, then turned and scanned the perilous path he had just traversed. As he did so, the jam seemed to melt away in mid channel. Then a terrific, rending roar tortured the air. The mass of logs and ice, and all the incalculable weight of imprisoned waters hurled themselves together over the brink with a stupefying crash, and throbbing volumes of spray leapt skyward. The woodsman's lean face never changed a muscle; but presently, giving a hitch to his breeches under the belt, he muttered thoughtfully:

'Blame good thing we come away when we did!'

Then, turning on his larriganed heels, he strode up the trail till the great woods closed about him, and the raving thunders gradually died into quiet.

A Tiger in
the House

Ruskin Bond

T imothy, the tiger-cub, was discovered by Grandfather on a hunting expedition in the Terai jungle near Dehra.

Grandfather was no *shikari*, but as he knew the forest of the Siwalik hills better than most people, he was persuaded to accompany the party – it consisted of several Very Important Persons from Delhi – to advise on the terrain and the direction the beaters should take once a tiger had been spotted.

The camp itself was sumptuous – seven large tents (one for each *shikari*), a dining-tent, and a number of servants' tents. The dinner was very good, as Grandfather admitted afterwards; it was not often that one saw hot-water plates, finger-glasses, and seven or eight courses, in a tent in the jungle! But that was how things were done in the days of the Viceroys . . . There were also some fifteen elephants, four of them with howdahs for the *shikaris*, and the others especially trained for taking part in the beat.

The sportsmen never saw a tiger, nor did they shoot anything else, though they saw a number of deer, peacock, and wild boar. They were giving up all hope of finding a tiger, and were beginning to shoot at jackals, when Grandfather, strolling down the forest path at some distance from the rest of the party, discovered a little tiger about eighteen inches long, hiding among the intricate roots of a banyan tree. Grandfather picked him up, and brought him home after the camp had broken up. He had the distinction of being the only member of the party to have bagged any game, dead or alive.

At first the tiger cub, who was named Timothy by Grand-mother, was brought up entirely on milk given to him in a

220

feeding-bottle by our cook, Mahmoud. But the milk proved too rich for him, and he was put on a diet of raw mutton and cod liver oil, to be followed later by a more tempting diet of pigeons and rabbits.

Timothy was provided with two companions – Toto the monkey, who was bold enough to pull the young tiger by the tail, and then climb up the curtains if Timothy lost his temper; and a small mongrel puppy, found on the road by Grandfather.

At first Timothy appeared to be quite afraid of the puppy, and darted back with a spring if it came too near. He would make absurd dashes at it with his large forepaws, and then retreat to a ridiculously safe distance. Finally, he allowed the puppy to crawl on his back and rest there!

One of Timothy's favourite amusements was to stalk anyone who would play with him, and so, when I came to live with Grandfather, I became one of the tiger's favourites. With a crafty look in his glittering eyes, and his body crouching, he would creep closer and closer to me, suddenly making a dash for my feet, rolling over on his back and kicking with delight and pretending to bite my ankles.

He was by this time the size of a full-grown retriever, and when I took him out for walks, people on the road would give us a wide berth. When he pulled hard on his chain, I had

difficulty in keeping up with him. His favourite place in the house was the drawing-room, and he would make himself comfortable on the long sofa, reclining there with great dignity, and snarling at anybody who tried to get him off.

Timothy had clean habits, and would scrub his face with his paws exactly like a cat. He slept at night in the cook's quarters, and was always delighted at being let out by him in the morning.

'One of these days,' declared Grandmother in her prophetic manner, 'we are going to find Timothy sitting on Mahmoud's bed, and no sign of the cook except his clothes and shoes!'

Of course, it never came to that, but when Timothy was about six months old a change came over him; he grew steadily less friendly. When out for a walk with me, he would try to steal away to stalk a cat or someone's pet Pekinese. Sometimes at night we would hear frenzied cackling from the poultry house, and in the morning there would be feathers lying all over the veranda. Timothy had to be chained up more often. And finally, when he began to stalk Mahmoud about the house with what looked like villainous intent, Grandfather decided it was time to transfer him to a zoo.

The nearest zoo was at Lucknow, two hundred miles away. Reserving a first class compartment for himself and Timothy – no one would share a compartment with them – Grandfather took him to Lucknow where the zoo authorities were only too glad to receive as a gift a well-fed and fairly civilized tiger.

About six months later, when my grandparents were visiting relatives in Lucknow, Grandfather took the opportunity of calling at the zoo to see how Timothy was getting on. I was not there to accompany him, but I heard all about it when he returned to Dehra.

Arriving at the zoo, Grandfather made straight for the particular cage in which Timothy had been interned. The tiger was there, crouched in a corner, full-grown and with a magnificent striped coat.

'Hello, Timothy!' said Grandfather and, climbing the railing with ease, he put his arm through the bars of the cage.

The tiger approached the bars, and allowed Grandfather to put both hands around his head. Grandfather stroked the tiger's forehead and tickled his ears, and, whenever he growled, smacked him across the mouth, which was his old way of keeping him quiet.

It licked Grandfather's hands and only sprang away when a leopard in the next cage snarled at him. Grandfather 'shooed' the leopard away, and the tiger returned to lick his hands; but every now and then the leopard would rush at the bars, and he would slink back to his corner.

A number of people had gathered to watch the reunion when a keeper pushed his way through the crowd and asked Grandfather what he was doing.

'I'm talking to Timothy,' said Grandfather. 'Weren't you here when I gave him to the zoo six months ago?'

'I haven't been here very long,' said the surprised keeper. 'Please continue your conversation. But I have never been able to touch him myself, he is always very bad tempered.'

'Why don't you put him somewhere else?' suggested Grandfather. 'That leopard keeps frightening him. I'll go and see the Superintendent about it.'

Grandfather went in search of the Superintendent of the zoo, but found that he had gone home early; and so, after wandering about the zoo for a little while, he returned to Timothy's cage to say goodbye. It was beginning to get dark.

He had been stroking and slapping Timothy for about five minutes when he found another keeper observing him with some alarm. Grandfather recognized him as the keeper who had been there when Timothy had first come to the zoo.

'*You* remember me,' said Grandfather. 'Now why don't you transfer Timothy to another cage, away from this stupid leopard?'

'But – sir —' stammered the keeper. 'It is not your tiger.'

'I know, I know,' said Grandfather testily. 'I realize he is no longer mine. But you might at least take a suggestion or two from me.'

'I remember your tiger very well,' said the keeper. 'He died two months ago.'

'Died!' exclaimed Grandfather.

'Yes, sir, of pneumonia. This tiger was trapped in the hills only last month, and he is very dangerous!'

Grandfather could think of nothing to say. The tiger was still licking his arm, with increasing relish. Grandfather took what seemed to him an age to withdraw his hand from the cage.

With his face near the tiger's he mumbled, 'Goodnight, Timothy,' and giving the keeper a scornful look, walked briskly out of the zoo.

The Tiger

Alan Devoe

Noiselessly, on cushioned paws, he padded around the cage. His movement was as soundless and flowing as the glide of water; under the sleek-furred hide of his fulvous flanks and shoulders the great muscles scarcely rippled. Around and around and around he circled, pacing as rhythmically as a slow and silent metronome. On the wooden floor of the cage was stained a circular track, signature of his rhythmic pacing circuit, day upon day, month upon month, year upon year.

In one corner of the cage there was a cunningly simulated tree, cast in iron and made fast with rivets to the floor; and in another corner was a kind of kennel, fashioned of concrete and reinforced with steel, to serve as lair. These were the furniture of his world; this was the universe around which he prowled in his unceasing circuit. The iron tree was coated, at the height of his shoulder, with tawny hairs rubbed from him as he passed it on his million rounds; the white concrete of the kennel showed a smeary stain, where with unvarying ritual he voided his musky urine.

The interruptions of his measured purposeless pacing were only three. They were when he slept, with his great velvety forepaws outstretched before him; and when the strange sounds and movements from that uncomprehended world which lay outside the bars became too insistent to be ignored; and when there reached his silky tufted ears the faint and far-off rumble which meant that the blood-smeared butcher-cart, piled with the day's meat, had been trundled into the building and was approaching him.

He slept as a kitten does, in utter relaxation. In the dark interior of his concrete kennel, warm with the heat of his flesh

225

and pungent with his jungle smell, he could enter into the sanctuary of sleep, of refuge from an alien world and from bewilderment. As he slept his great curved claws would glide forth sometimes and retract again in their soft sheaths, and sometimes his tail would stir and twitch a little, and tiny growls and whimpers would mingle with the harsh rhythmic rattle of his snore. Such stirrings were the witness to his dreams, to those dim race-memories which would not be effaced except by death. In that dreaming skull were the vague elusive stuffs of recollection . . . of the whipping of bamboo stalks against his flesh, of the feel of the Sumatran sun at noon, of the scent of deer-dung on a forest path.

Most of the time, in his waking hours, he gave no heed to that uncomprehended world, full of shuffling steps and meaningless speech-sounds and peering eyes, which existed outside the bars of his cage. He had been here three years, more than a thousand risings of the sun, until now the unintelligible procession which endlessly shuffled and stared and gibbered outside the bars had come to be hardly more than a dim blur on the rim of his awareness.

At first it had been different, when he was still trembling and disorientated by the quickness of his transition from his old life. The old life had ended very suddenly, when, on a moonless night, he had plunged through the cunning plaiting which hid a pit dug in the jungle path which led to his water-hole. He had been put in a wooden crate, bound with hoops, and had journeyed in a long darkness across an ocean, and then he had been set loose in his new world of the iron tree and the concrete kennel and the endless unmeaning faces outside the bars. During those first weeks and months here he had rushed often to the bars, and pressed his great muzzle against them, and loosed roar after roar to frighten away the peering faces and silence the shuffling steps. Once upon a time his roar had silenced the heavy-beaked hornbills in the forest, and the bands of chattering gibbons in the tree tops had grown hushed at the sound of it. But here, in this new world, the strange waxy-white faces outside the bars only grew more numerous, and peered more intently, when he made his sound. Now, after three years, he seldom roared; and his old bewilderments were mostly resolved into a kind of dull uncaring.

Only rarely now – when the stridence of the uncomprehended voices grew too shrill to be endured, or the stench of the white bifurcated bodies too sour in his delicate cat's nostrils – did he come padding silently to the front of his cage and stand there staring out, a tumult of baffled fury in his heart.

He got his daily meat at half-past two. He had not liked it at first, had scarcely known that it was meat, this cold juiceless fibre with no smell and quiver of life in it. There was no spurt of scarlet blood when he tore at it with his teeth, no hot and salt-sweet trickle passing over his tongue as he licked and sucked at the torn flesh. When he pinned it to the floor with a great paw, as was his way with prey, it did not squirm or scream. But it did quiet the hurting hunger in his belly, that ache which once had sent him gliding stealthily through the tropical night, smelling the heavy jungle air and cocking his tawny head and listening, and so at last he came to accept it as his food, and to await its coming with a kind of lower-pitched rekindling of the old ecstacy that once had possessed him as he awaited, beside a water-hole, the coming of the little spotted deer.

By noon the fever would begin to infect him, and he would pad around his endless circle with a quicker pace, his long tail writhing and thrashing like a great furred snake, his claws involuntarily extruded a little from their sheaths and clicking against the floor. As the minutes passed he would move faster and faster, and a fire of excitement would consume him, so that often as his frenzy grew he would void a jet of urine or a dropping of dung, and would not even heed the consequent rumble of sound which came from outside the bars and which he could not know was human laughter. And then suddenly he would hear, faint and far away, the clang and clatter of the hand-truck that meant the approaching of his meat. Silently he would pad to the bars and crouch down beside the little slot-like aperture through which, day after day, his meal was thrust to him. All his fury would have subsided now, giving place to a taut quiet, and he would crouch as motionless as stone.

He was crouching thus now. Intently, with unwinking eyes, he was watching while the truck was trundled to a halt outside his cage, and while the chunks of cold flesh were sorted over. Most especially he watched, in absorbed fascination, the white human hand and arm which performed these things. He did not know what it was, this curious five-pronged whitish thing that each day flickered just outside the slot of his cage for just a few seconds and then whisked away. More than a thousand times he had stared at it, rapt and uncomprehending. He watched it as a kitten watches a white butterfly, or as a sparrow studies a grub.

He watched it now as it pawed over the meat, and then as it lifted a chunk and slid it through the slot. It was hovering inside the aperture for a second longer than usual. He reached out a paw, quickly as the dart of a cobra, and pinioned the white flesh with his claws. And, as his claws hooked into it, there reached his silky ears a sound he had not heard for more than a thousand risings of the sun. It was the sound of screaming.

He put forth all his curved claws to their full length, and raked at the white skin. As he ripped at it, scarlet blood spurted in great jets against his muzzle, and the smell of hot blood was in his nostrils and his lungs. He took the quivering meat between his jaws, and the bones cracked and snapped, and on his tongue was a warm salt-sweetness. There rushed into him a flooding exultation, and in an instant the world of the iron tree and the concrete kennel and the latticed bars was dissolved and vanished away. In his skull raced dim-formed remembrances, evocations of the flower-heavy sweetness of the jungle night, of the pattern of wild hog's tracks in an oozy stream-bank, of the chatter of finches when the sun was rising. His cage did not exist now, and there were no bars around him, or stained boards under his cushioned feet.

He had gone from there. He had re-entered into his ancient kingdom.

They drove him off at last, with pitchforks and pointed iron rods. And early in the morning, before the zoo was opened to the public for the day, they put a bullet through his brain.

6
*In Field
and Home*

The Great Lad

Joyce Stranger

It had been a wicked day. Snow lay deep in crack and crevice and gully, drifted against the drystone walls, and hid the shape of the land beneath it. A wind whipped across the steeps, whining as it came, and the trees were heavy and doom laden, branches cracking under the sullen weight.

The dog had been uneasy all day. Restless as they quartered the ground, digging out the ewes, and trying to guide them back to the farm through snow that came tail high, so that the beasts plunged miserably, each step a struggle.

He could not tell his master his fears. The snowfilled sky lay dark and leaden, sulphur yellow on the far horizon, eerie with light that made the dog shiver. The hill grumbled to itself, too softly for the shepherd to hear, but loud enough to panic the sheep and make the dog unbiddable.

Twice he crouched and whined, refusing to move on, and the man shouted at him, hating the weather and annoyed that his dog should choose such a day to play him up. He wanted to get back to the farmhouse, to scalding tea and a blazing fire. He cursed the sheep.

Once he used his crook to drag a beast down from a rocky plateau where it stood stupefied, never having seen such weather before in its short life. Once he had to use it to help the dog out of a drift that covered a deep gully, and into which the animal plunged with a yelp of terror.

A moment later, the dog was clear. The man used his crook to judge the depth of the snow, and found a way to the other side, but before he reached it the hill shuddered, and a weight of snow and rock and earth came tumbling from the heights, gathering momentum in a tide that came faster and faster, straight for the man.

The dog barked and ran. The man followed, clumsy in his thick clothing. He missed the main tide, but a rock struck his shoulder, and another, hurling itself downwards, pinned his arm as he fell. Try as he would, he could not move, but lay helpless as an insect pinned on a collector's board.

He whistled the dog and Moss came doubtfully, tail moving slowly, not in greeting, but in bewilderment. He was too young to have seen snow before, and he was well drilled. He knew he must never move without his master's command.

Now Wyn Jones cursed the gruelling training he had given the dog. Training that ensured that if told to sit he would sit for two days if not given a counter order, training that ensured he would watch other dogs herd sheep, and never interfere. Training that ensured he would rely on his master's brains and never on his own.

'Home, lad,' the shepherd said.

He could think of no other command. If the dog came alone they would come out and look for him. If it did not snow they might be able to follow his tracks. If it did snow . . . Wyn Jones closed his eyes and prayed to his Maker, sweat darkening his skin in spite of the cold that seeped through his clothes and the damp that soaked him.

The dog was puzzled. 'Home' was a command for unruly pups, not for a grown dog out with his master on the hill. He crept forward, whining.

'Home, you fool.'

The voice was testy, but not yet a shout. The dog looked at the sheep, grey against the dazzling white, huddled in misery, woolly fleeces close packed, as they waited patiently for someone to herd them.

Wyn Jones cursed to himself, for one of the ewes was due to lamb and any lamb born in the snow and the cold was doomed unless he could get them to safety.

'Home, dog,' he yelled, with all the strength he could muster, and watched anxiously as Moss's tail went between his legs, and crouching, hangdog, punished unknowingly, he turned away.

But Moss could still not believe his ears. There was work to be done, and his master had no right to lie in the snow. He ran back and tried to dig at the rock that held him prisoner. Jones sighed. The poor beast was trying his best, but help must come from men.

'No,' he said sharply, and the dog backed away, head on one side, ears half-cocked, puzzled.

'Home!' the shepherd roared.

This time the dog started, but kept looking back, eyes anxious, as if hoping to see his master stand and follow him. Soon, persuaded that this was not going to happen, he gave his whole mind to following the trail back to the farm.

He knew the way, by scent and sight, and by the feel of the ground, but scent was masked, landmarks had vanished, and the unbroken hummocked snow lay all around him. He plunged and floundered, afraid of the quietness, of the absence of birds, and the dimming light, and the sultry glow in the sky.

Much was hidden because he was small. Each crest was a mountain to be traversed with difficulty. Once he fell into a small drift and struggled out again, panting. Once he dropped to the ground to rest, but the command given him was too powerful. His duty was to obey, and he had to go home.

The shepherd, lying where he had fallen, wiped tears of cold away from his eyes with gloved fingers, and looked at the sheep. They stood listlessly, heads hanging, tails into the wind. When he moved one of them turned towards him, and perhaps seeking shelter under the lee of the snow that partly covered him, came and stood beside him.

The other sheep followed, breaking the wind, unknowing that their coming offered the shepherd a longer grip on life. He pulled at the nearest fleece, and the ewe lay in the snow against him, the presence of the familiar man giving her comfort. He pushed his hands into the rank smelling wool, and dozed, dreaming uneasily of hot coffee and steak and kidney pudding, rich with warm gravy, and the warmth and comfort of the farmyard. Each waking was a small agony.

The sheepdog was half-way home. The wind caused his eyes to water, stung his eyeballs, and froze his muzzle so that there was ice clinging to the fur around his jaws.

He hungered more for men than for food. Men who encouraged him and brought him comfort and gave him warmth. He could not bear the dismal landscape where nothing moved, and he was too low on the ground to see the far away plume of welcoming smoke from the farmhouse chimneys.

He struck the track, worn by the passing of sheep and men, and ran more jauntily, the freer movement bringing warmth.

236

When he paused, weary, his breath plumed on the air and he shook his head, not liking this sudden surprising manifestation of something he could not understand.

The track ended, as the men had turned away to a farm lower down the valley. His own, the sheep still on the hill, caught by the sudden early unseasonable November snowfall, lay trapped and white, the only path cleared round the yard so that the cows could be brought for milking and pigs and chickens fed.

The dog was almost home when the blizzard struck, coming without, for him, any warning. One moment he was plunging, able to see, through hardpacked snow in which were the tracks of fox and stoat and weasel, and of foraging birds. The next, blindness came on him as the great flakes swirled on the wind and fell on eyes and muzzle, on shoulder and back, and on his head and neck, so that he shook himself repeatedly and then sat in the clammy snow using first one paw and then another to try and clear away the clinging uncanny stuff that prevented sight and movement.

It was useless to go on. He crouched where he lay, listening to the wind keening from the North and the now close and familiar sounds from below. The clank of a bucket, oddly muffled, the low of a cow as she was led to shelter, the yelp of a dog.

That gave him his clue. He barked, sharp and loud, calling to the dog below and Rex heard his companion and answered, a welcome barking that went on even after the farmer had shouted at him.

When Rex stopped for breath Moss barked again.

'Dammit, that's Moss out there,' the farmer called to his wife, and he stood in the doorway, staring at the swirling flakes. 'What's happened to Wyn, then?'

Mair Thomas could only stare at him, white-faced. The dog had never come home alone before, not since he was a pup. Wyn had trained him too well to have sent him off in punishment for disobedience. Nor would he send the animal home alone on a night like this.

'What can you do?' she asked Dai, almost whispering, fear taking away her voice.

The farmer was already huddled into his coat, dialling at the telephone that was the only link with neighbours too far to see or call on casually.

'Damme, the line's dead,' he said, after futile jerkings at the receiver rest.

'You can't go out in this.' Mair pushed her dark hair back with her hands, a gesture of extreme worry that Dai recognized. He halted at the door, and called.

'Moss, here Moss. Come then, good dog.'

The dog barked, and, given the guidance of a voice, crawled over the ridge, slipping on ice that had formed on top of a trickle of water coming out of the spring.

Dai stared out into the night. Gathering darkness had hidden the world. A tree, normally stark, was a blurred outline, soft with snow, fairylike by day, but now inimical, a symbol of the weather that paralysed all movement on the hill.

The dog barked again. It was dark, and he was too low to see the farmhouse lights, which, for him, were hidden behind the low wall that lay, humped and unrecognizable, blocking his view.

'Moss. Good lad, here then.'

The voice was welcome, a warmth in the night. He plunged towards it and came to grief, with a yelp of fright, in the ditch, hidden and deep. He tried to claw his way out, but the soft snow was loose and fell away, leaving him beyond the wall, whimpering.

Dai Thomas brought the big torch that he used in the byre at calving time. It threw a feeble circle of light on the packed snow, beaten by the hooves of the cows into a flat and sodden mush that had thawed and frozen again until now it was glacierlike, threatening a man with sudden disaster if he failed to watch his step.

The dog whined again and Dai walked cautiously towards the sound, his voice reassuring.

He leaned over the wall, feeling it hard beneath the snow that gave beneath his weight, and saw the dog, a dark patch against the glitter. He moved, leaned down, gripped the loose scruff and heaved, and Moss, wild with pleasure at being once more with men, whined and wagged his tail and licked the man's hand in an ecstasy of welcome.

'Don't usually do that,' Dai said, as he brought the dog into the warmth. He set food before it. Moss stared at him, whimpered and refused to eat.

'Well then, you'd best be eating. We can't find shepherd now,' the man said, looking out into the darkness where the flakes swirled, feather light, drifting and clinging to byre and barn and stable. Beyond the patch of light one of the ponies yickered a complaint, afraid of the weather as snowflakes drifted in through his half open stable door.

Dai went out to shut it, sliding and cursing. He turned in time to see the dog, half a leg of lamb in its mouth, streak out into the night.

'Damned little thief,' he said in fury. 'Wouldn't touch his own food. Had to take mine.'

'Are you going out on the hill?' Mair asked, busy at the sink.

Dai moved restlessly, looking out into the night. The snow came thickly, swirling towards him, eddying upwards as the wind blew, and he listened unhappily to the scream of the gale and the bluster in the chimney.

'Be two of us lost out there,' he said at last, unwilling to face the truth, yet aware of his responsibility to his wife and the three lads safely asleep upstairs.

'First light,' he said. 'I'll get help from the Williams. Can't even track the dog in the snow. All tracks will be covered.'

He was too restless for sleep. The thought of the shepherd irked him. Perhaps the man was dead, but more likely, buried in some drift, or fallen on the ice, to die by little inches in the wicked cold.

Long after his wife had gone upstairs he sat by the fire, watching the kittens play with a straw brought in from the yard on somebody's shoe, thinking of the wildness beyond the windows, and wishing that he had a warm job in town, not tied to the cattle and the bitter bleak hills, working for a pittance grubbed from the ground while other men fattened on the food he grew and played with their money, earned much more easily than his.

He forgot about Moss, and the stolen meat.

The dog was trying to retrace his path, back to the hill and the man that meant more to him than food and warmth. The meat held in his jaws made his mouth slaver, but he did not take a single bite. He picked his way carefully out of the farmyard, and back on to the hill.

The wind was behind him and in spite of the snow, the going was easier. A faint trace of scent lay on the ground, and he tracked back, with difficulty because the smell of mutton was strong in his nose, but it did not mask his own familiar trail, nor the rankness of the fox that caught a whiff of dog and meat and came running, only to find disaster as it met a drift that covered it completely and left it hungry and tantalized, buried until the thaw that found it thinner and wiser, not to be caught that way a second time.

The snow stopped. The moon broke through a layer of cloud, and shone on whiteness that covered all tracks, that hid the shepherd and the sheep that sheltered him, and hid the path.

Moss went on. In places he struggled, neck deep, dragging each leg from the snow, jumping and bounding on, more and more weary. Once he rested by a humped tree, and the meat tempted him badly, but he left it alone. It made his jaws ache, but he went on gamely.

He came to the patch where the shepherd lay, and stopped and looked in surprise at the unbroken snow. Carefully, he put the meat down, sniffed around and then began to dig. He found sheep and man in a hollow made by their breath, and the man, glad of fresh air, felt overwhelming disappointment when he saw the dog.

'Moss, Moss. You damned old fool. We'll both die out here now,' he said, and the dog wagged a forlorn tail, unable to understand why he was not greeted with fervour.

He went back for the meat.

This time, he approached more cautiously, afraid of a cuff for his trouble. The shepherd, watching him with dull eyes, saw the half leg of lamb and stared at it, unbelieving.

'You durned old fool. You been back? I hope they saw you,' he said, and reached out a hand to pat the wet coat. The dog dropped beside him, and licked his face. The sheep, too exhausted by snow and cold, were too apathetic to move. They watched Moss, eyes wary, but did not move. The lambing ewe struggled to bring her lamb to birth.

The shepherd took the meat. It was slimed and snowy, but he dragged at it with his teeth and spat the outer parts to the dog, who took his reward greedily, while the man gnawed at the bone, too hungry to care what he ate.

The farmer, tracking the dog through the snow two hours later, with the men from the farm in the hollow, found the pair of them asleep, the lamb cuddled between them, the ewe under the shepherd's head, acting as a pillow, her own head stretched to lick her son.

Dai Thomas stared at them, at the dog, which came to greet them, and at the bone that lay, gnawed clean, beside them.

'Moss brought me some dinner,' the shepherd said, his eyes proud on the dog, as they dug the rock and snow away from his arm and helped him to stand, rolling him in blankets to go on the stretcher that the second farmer had provided. Hot coffee laced with rum quickly restored him, and the damage to his arm, apart from bruising, was not bad.

That night, bedded in the warm farmhouse on Mair Thomas's settee, which she thought a better bed than his own above the cow byre until he was well and rested, Wyn watched his dog eat a meal fit for a king.

'Eh, Moss, you're a great lad,' he said, and the dog turned and looked at him, and his tail beat a steady thunder on the hard floor before he returned to the dish that Mair had given him as his right.

241

Zlateh the Goat

Isaac Bashevis Singer

At Hanukkah time the road from the village to the town is usually covered with snow, but this year the winter had been a mild one. Hanukkah had almost come, yet little snow had fallen. The sun shone most of the time. The peasants complained that because of the dry weather there would be a poor harvest of winter grain. New grass sprouted, and the peasants sent their cattle out to pasture.

For Reuven the furrier it was a bad year, and after long hesitation he decided to sell Zlateh the goat. She was old and gave little milk. Feyvel the town butcher had offered eight gulden for her. Such a sum would buy Hanukkah candles, potatoes and oil for pancakes, gifts for the children, and other holiday necessaries for the house. Reuven told his oldest boy Aaron to take the goat to town.

Aaron understood what taking the goat to Feyvel meant, but he had to obey his father. Leah, his mother, wiped the tears from her eyes when she heard the news. Aaron's younger sisters, Anna and Miriam, cried loudly. Aaron put on his quilted jacket and a cap with earmuffs, bound a rope around Zlateh's neck, and took along two slices of bread with cheese to eat on the road. Aaron was supposed to deliver the goat by evening, spend the night at the butcher's, and return the next day with the money.

While the family said good-bye to the goat, and Aaron placed the rope around her neck, Zlateh stood as patiently and good-naturedly as ever. She licked Reuven's hand. She shook her small white beard. Zlateh trusted human beings. She knew that they always fed her and never did her any harm.

242

When Aaron brought her out on the road to town, she seemed somewhat astonished. She'd never been led in that direction before. She looked back at him questioningly, as if to say, 'Where are you taking me?' But after a while she seemed to come to the conclusion that a goat shouldn't ask questions. Still, the road was different. They passed new fields, pastures, and huts with thatched roofs. Here and there a dog barked and came running after them, but Aaron chased it away with his stick.

The sun was shining when Aaron left the village. Suddenly the weather changed. A large black cloud with a bluish centre appeared in the east and spread itself rapidly over the sky. A cold wind blew in with it. The crows flew low, croaking. At first it looked as if it would rain, but instead it began to hail as in summer. It was early in the day, but it became dark as dusk. After a while the hail turned to snow.

In his twelve years Aaron had seen all kinds of weather, but he had never experienced a snow like this one. It was so dense it shut out the light of the day. In a short time their path was completely covered. The wind became as cold as ice. The road to town was narrow and winding. Aaron no longer knew where he was. He could not see through the snow. The cold soon penetrated his quilted jacket.

At first Zlateh didn't seem to mind the change in weather. She too was twelve years old and knew what winter meant. But when her legs sank deeper and deeper into the snow, she began to turn her head and look at Aaron in wonderment. Her mild eyes seemed to ask, 'Why are we out in such a storm?' Aaron hoped that a peasant would come along with his cart, but no one passed by.

The snow grew thicker, falling to the ground in large, whirling flakes. Beneath it, Aaron's boots touched the softness of a ploughed field. He realized that he was no longer on the road. He had gone astray. He could no longer make out which was east or west, which way was the village, the town. The wind whistled, howled, whirled the snow about in eddies. It looked as if white imps were playing tag on the fields. A white dust rose above the ground. Zlateh stopped. She could walk no

longer. Stubbornly she anchored her cleft hooves in the earth and bleated as if pleading to be taken home. Icicles hung from her white beard, and her horns were glazed with frost.

Aaron did not want to admit the danger, but he knew just the same that if they did not find shelter they would freeze to death. This was no ordinary storm. It was a mighty blizzard. The snowfall had reached his knees. His hands were numb, and he could no longer feel his toes. He choked when he breathed. His nose felt like wood, and he rubbed it with snow. Zlateh's bleating began to sound like crying. Those humans in whom she had so much confidence had dragged her into a trap. Aaron began to pray to God for himself and for the innocent animal.

Suddenly he made out the shape of a hill. He wondered what it could be. Who had piled snow into such a huge heap? He moved towards it, dragging Zlateh after him. When he came near it, he realized that it was a large haystack which the snow had blanketed.

Aaron saw immediately that they were saved. With great effort he dug his way through the snow. He was a village boy and knew what to do. When he reached the hay, he hollowed out a nest for himself and the goat. No matter how cold it may be outside, in the hay it is always warm. And hay was food for

Zlateh. The moment she smelled it she became contented and began to eat. Outside the snow continued to fall. It quickly covered the passageway Aaron had dug. But a boy and an animal need to breathe, and there was hardly any air in their hideout. Aaron bored a kind of window through the hay and snow and carefully kept the passage clear.

Zlateh, having eaten her fill, sat down on her hind legs and seemed to have regained her confidence in man. Aaron ate his two slices of bread and cheese, but after the difficult journey he was still hungry. He looked at Zlateh and noticed her udders were full. He lay down next to her, placing himself so that when he milked her he could squirt the milk into his mouth. It was rich and sweet. Zlateh was not accustomed to being milked that way, but she did not resist. On the contrary, she seemed eager to reward Aaron for bringing her to a shelter whose very walls, floor, and ceiling were made of food.

Through the window Aaron could catch a glimpse of the chaos outside. The wind carried before it whole drifts of snow. It was completely dark, and he did not know whether night had already come or whether it was the darkness of the storm. Thank God that in the hay it was not cold. The dried grass and field flowers exuded the warmth of the summer sun. Zlateh ate frequently; she nibbled from above, below, from the left and right. Her body gave forth an animal warmth, and Aaron cuddled up to her. He had always loved Zlateh, but now she was like a sister. He was alone, cut off from his family, and wanted to talk. He began to talk to Zlateh. 'Zlateh, what do you think about what has happened to us?' he asked.

'Maaaa,' Zlateh answered.

'If we hadn't found this stack of hay, we would both be frozen stiff by now,' Aaron said.

'Maaa,' was the goat's reply.

'If the snow keeps on falling like this, we may have to stay here for days,' Aaron explained.

'Maaaa,' Zlateh bleated.

'What does "Maaaa" mean?' Aaron asked. 'You'd better speak up clearly.'

'Maaaa. Maaaa,' Zlateh tried.

'Well, let it be "Maaaa" then,' Aaron said patiently. 'You can't speak, but I know you understand. I need you and you need me. Isn't that right?'

'Maaaa.'

Aaron became sleepy. He made a pillow out of some hay, leaned his head on it, and dozed off. Zlateh, too, fell asleep.

When Aaron opened his eyes, he didn't know whether it was morning or night. The snow had blocked up his window. He tried to clear it, but when he had bored through to the length of his arm, he still hadn't reached the outside. Luckily he had his stick with him and was able to break through to the open air. It was still dark outside. The snow continued to fall and the wind wailed, first with one voice and then with many. Sometimes it had the sound of devilish laughter. Zlateh, too, awoke, and when Aaron greeted her, she answered, 'Maaaa.' Yes, Zlateh's language consisted of only one word, but it meant many things. Now she was saying, 'We must accept all that God gives us – heat, cold, hunger, satisfaction, light, and darkness.'

Aaron had awakened hungry. He had eaten up his food, but Zlateh had plenty of milk.

For three days Aaron and Zlateh stayed in the haystack. Aaron had always loved Zlateh, but in these three days he loved her more and more. She fed him with her milk and helped him keep warm. She comforted him with her patience. He told her many stories, and she always cocked her ears and listened. When he patted her, she licked his hand and his face. Then she said, 'Maaaa,' and he knew it meant, I love you, too.

The snow fell for three days, though after the first day it was not as thick and the wind quieted down. Sometimes Aaron felt that there could never have been a summer, that the snow had always fallen, ever since he could remember. He, Aaron, never had a father or mother or sisters. He was a snow child, born of the snow, and so was Zlateh. It was so quiet in the hay that his ears rang in the stillness. Aaron and Zlateh slept all night and a good part of the day. As for Aaron's dreams, they were all about warm weather. He dreamed of green fields, trees covered with blossoms, clear brooks, and singing birds. By the third night the snow had stopped, but Aaron did not dare to find his way home in the darkness. The sky became clear and the moon shone, casting silvery nets on the snow. Aaron dug his way out and looked at the world. It was all white, quiet, dreaming dreams of heavenly splendour. The stars were large and close. The moon swam in the sky as in a sea.

On the morning of the fourth day Aaron heard the ringing of sleigh bells. The haystack was not far from the road. The peasant who drove the sleigh pointed out the way to him – not to the town and Feyvel the butcher, but home to the village. Aaron had decided in the haystack that he would never part with Zlateh.

Aaron's family and their neighbours had searched for the boy and the goat but had found no trace of them during the storm. They feared they were lost. Aaron's mother and sisters cried for him; his father remained silent and gloomy. Suddenly one of the neighbours came running to their house with the news that Aaron and Zlateh were coming up the road.

There was great joy in the family. Aaron told them how he had found the stack of hay and how Zlateh had fed him with her milk. Aaron's sisters kissed and hugged Zlateh and gave her a special treat of chopped carrots and potato peel, which Zlateh gobbled up hungrily.

Nobody ever again thought of selling Zlateh, and now that the cold weather had finally set in, the villagers needed the services of Reuven the furrier once more. When Hanukkah came, Aaron's mother was able to fry pancakes every evening, and Zlateh got her portion too. Even though Zlateh had her own pen, she often came to the kitchen, knocking on the door with her horns to indicate that she was ready to visit, and she was always admitted. In the evening Aaron, Miriam, and Anna played dreidel. Zlateh sat near the stove watching the children and the flickering of the Hanukkah candles.

Once in a while Aaron would ask her, 'Zlateh, do you remember the three days we spent together?'

And Zlateh would scratch her neck with a horn, shake her white bearded head and come out with the single sound which expressed all her thoughts, and all her love.

Rikki-Tikki-Tavi

Rudyard Kipling

This is the story of the great war that Rikki-tikki-tavi fought single-handed, through the bathrooms of the big bungalow in Segowlee cantonment. Darzee, the tailor-bird, helped him, and Chuchundra, the musk-rat, who never comes out into the middle of the floor, but always creeps round by the wall, gave him advice; but Rikki-tikki did the real fighting.

He was a mongoose, rather like a little cat in his fur and his tail, but quite like a weasel in his head and his habits. His eyes and the end of his restless nose were pink; he could scratch himself anywhere he pleased, with any leg, front or back, that he chose to use; he could fluff up his tail till it looked like a bottle-brush, and his war-cry, as he scuttled through the long grass, was: '*Rikk-tikk-tikki-tikki-tchk!*'

One day, a high summer flood washed him out of the burrow where he lived with his father and mother, and carried him, kicking and clucking, down a road-side ditch. He found a little wisp of grass floating there, and clung to it till he lost his senses. When he revived, he was lying in the hot sun on the middle of a garden path, very draggled indeed, and a small boy was saying: 'Here's a dead mongoose. Let's have a funeral.'

'No,' said his mother; 'let's take him in and dry him. Perhaps he isn't really dead.'

They took him into the house, and a big man picked him up between his finger and thumb, and said he was not dead but half choked; so they wrapped him in cotton-wool, and warmed him, and he opened his eyes and sneezed.

'Now,' said the big man (he was an Englishman who had just

moved into the bungalow); 'don't frighten him, and we'll see what he'll do.'

It is the hardest thing in the world to frighten a mongoose, because he is eaten up from nose to tail with curiosity. The motto of all the mongoose family is, 'Run and find out'; and Rikki-tikki was a true mongoose. He looked at the cotton-wool, decided that it was not good to eat, ran all round the table, sat up and put his fur in order, scratched himself, and jumped on the small boy's shoulder.

'Don't be frightened, Teddy,' said his father. 'That's his way of making friends.'

'Ouch! He's tickling under my chin,' said Teddy.

Rikki-tikki looked down between the boy's collar and neck, snuffed at his ear, and climbed down to the floor, where he sat rubbing his nose.

'Good gracious,' said Teddy's mother, 'and that's a wild creature! I suppose he's so tame because we've been kind to him.'

'All mongooses are like that,' said her husband. 'If Teddy doesn't pick him up by the tail, or try to put him in a cage, he'll run in and out of the house all day long. Let's give him something to eat.'

They gave him a little piece of raw meat. Rikki-tikki liked it immensely, and when it was finished he went out into the veranda and sat in the sunshine and fluffed up his fur to make it dry to the roots. Then he felt better.

'There are more things to find out about in this house,' he

said to himself, 'than all my family could find out in all their lives. I shall certainly stay and find out.'

He spent all that day roaming over the house. He nearly drowned himself in the bath-tubs, put his nose into the ink on a writing-table, and burnt it on the end of the big man's cigar, for he climbed up in the big man's lap to see how writing was done. At nightfall he ran into Teddy's nursery to watch how kerosene-lamps were lighted, and when Teddy went to bed Rikki-tikki climbed up too; but he was a restless companion, because he had to get up and attend to every noise all through the night, and find out what made it. Teddy's mother and father came in, the last thing, to look at their boy, and Rikki-tikki was awake on the pillow. 'I don't like that,' said Teddy's mother; 'he may bite the child.' 'He'll do no such thing,' said the father. 'Teddy's safer with that little beast than if he had a bloodhound to watch him. If a snake came into the nursery now —'

But Teddy's mother wouldn't think of anything so awful.

Early in the morning Rikki-tikki came to early breakfast in the veranda riding on Teddy's shoulder, and they gave him banana and some boiled egg; and he sat on all their laps one after the other, because every well-brought-up mongoose always hopes to be a house-mongoose some day and have rooms to run about in, and Rikki-tikki's mother (she used to live in the General's house at Segowlee) had carefully told Rikki what to do if ever he came across white men.

Then Rikki-tikki went out into the garden to see what was to be seen. It was a large garden, only half cultivated, with bushes as big as summer-houses of Marshall Niel roses, lime and orange trees, clumps of bamboos, and thickets of high grass. Rikki-tikki licked his lips. 'This is a splendid hunting-ground,' he said, and his tail grew bottle-brushy at the thought of it, and he scuttled up and down the garden, snuffing here and there till he heard very sorrowful voices in a thorn-bush.

It was Darzee, the tailor-bird, and his wife. They had made a beautiful nest by pulling two big leaves together and stitching them up the edges with fibres, and had filled the hollow with cotton and downy fluff. The nest swayed to and fro, as they sat on the rim and cried.

'What is the matter?' asked Rikki-tikki.

'We are very miserable,' said Darzee. 'One of our babies fell out of the nest yesterday, and Nag ate him.'

'H'm!' said Rikki-tikki, 'that is very sad – but I am a stranger here. Who is Nag?'

Darzee and his wife only cowered down in the nest without answering, for from the thick grass at the foot of the bush there came a low hiss – a horrid cold sound that made Rikki-tikki jump back two clear feet. Then inch by inch out of the grass rose up the head and spread hood of Nag, the big black cobra, and he was five feet long from tongue to tail. When he had lifted one-third of himself clear of the ground, he stayed balancing to and fro exactly as a dandelion-tuft balances in the wind, and he looked at Rikki-tikki with the wicked snake's eyes that never change their expression, whatever the snake may be thinking of.

'Who is Nag?' said he. '*I* am Nag. The great god Brahm put his mark upon all our people when the first cobra spread his hood to keep the sun off Brahm as he slept. Look, and be afraid!'

He spread out his hood more than ever, and Rikki-tikki saw the spectacle-mark on the back of it that looks exactly like the eye part of a hook-and-eye fastening. He was afraid for the minute; but it is impossible for a mongoose to stay frightened for any length of time, and though Rikki-tikki had never met a live cobra before, his mother had fed him on dead ones, and he knew that all a grown mongoose's business in life was to fight and eat snakes. Nag knew that too, and at the bottom of his cold heart he was afraid.

'Well,' said Rikki-tikki, and his tail began to fluff up again, 'marks or no marks, do you think it is right for you to eat fledglings out of a nest?'

Nag was thinking to himself, and watching the least little movement in the grass behind Rikki-tikki. He knew that mongooses in the garden meant death sooner or later for him and his family, but he wanted to get Rikki-tikki off his guard. So he dropped his head a little, and put it on one side.

'Let us talk,' he said. 'You eat eggs. Why should not I eat birds?'

'Behind you! Look behind you!' sang Darzee.

Rikki-tikki knew better than to waste time in staring. He jumped up in the air as high as he could go, and just under him whizzed by the head of Nagaina, Nag's wicked wife. She had crept up behind him as he was talking, to make an end of him; and he heard her savage hiss as the stroke missed. He came down almost across her back, and if he had been an old mongoose he would have known that then was the time to break her back with one bite; but he was afraid of the terrible lashing return-stroke of the cobra. He bit, indeed, but did not bite long enough, and he jumped clear of the whisking tail, leaving Nagaina torn and angry.

'Wicked, wicked Darzee!' said Nag, lashing up as high as he could reach towards the nest in the thorn-bush; but Darzee had built it out of reach of snakes, and it only swayed to and fro.

Rikki-tikki felt his eyes growing red and hot (when a mongoose's eyes grow red, he is angry), and he sat back on his tail and hind legs like a little kangaroo, and looked all round him, and chattered with rage. But Nag and Nagaina had disappeared into the grass. When a snake misses its stroke, it never says anything or gives any sign of what it means to do next. Rikki-tikki did not care to follow them, for he did not feel sure that he could manage two snakes at once. So he trotted off to the gravel path near the house, and sat down to think. It was a serious matter for him.

If you read the old books of natural history, you will find they say that when the mongoose fights the snake and happens to get bitten, he runs off and eats some herb that cures him. That is not true. The victory is only a matter of quickness of eye and quickness of foot, – snake's blow against mongoose's jump, – and as no eye can follow the motion of a snake's head when it strikes, that makes things much more wonderful than any magic herb. Rikki-tikki knew he was a young mongoose, and it made him all the more pleased to think that he had managed to escape a blow from behind. It gave him confidence in himself, and when Teddy came running down the path, Rikki-tikki was ready to be petted.

But just as Teddy was stooping, something flinched a little in the dust, and a tiny voice said: 'Be careful. I am death!' It was Karait, the dusty brown snakeling that lies for choice on the dusty earth; and his bite is as dangerous as the cobra's. But he is so small that nobody thinks of him, and so he does the more harm to people.

Rikki-tikki's eyes grew red again, and he danced up to Karait with the peculiar rocking, swaying motion that he had inherited from his family. It looks very funny, but it is so perfectly balanced a gait that you can fly off from it at any angle you please; and in dealing with snakes this is an advantage. If Rikki-tikki had only known, he was doing a much more dangerous thing than fighting Nag, for Karait is so small, and can turn so quickly, that unless Rikki bit him close to the back of the head, he would get the return-stroke in his eye or lip. But Rikki did not know: his eyes were all red, and he rocked back and forth, looking for a good place to hold. Karait struck out. Rikki jumped sideways and tried to run in, but the wicked little dusty grey head lashed within a fraction of his shoulder, and he had to jump over the body, and the head followed his heels close.

Teddy shouted to the house: 'Oh, look here! Our mongoose is killing a snake'; and Rikki-tikki heard a scream from Teddy's mother. His father ran out with a stick, but by the time he came up, Karait had lunged out once too far, and Rikki-tikki had sprung, jumped on the snake's back, dropped his head far between his fore-legs, bitten as high up the back as he could get hold, and rolled away. That bite paralysed Karait, and Rikki-tikki was just going to eat him up from the tail, after the custom of his family at dinner, when he remembered that a full meal makes a slow mongoose, and if he wanted all his strength and quickness ready, he must keep himself thin.

He went away for a dust-bath under the castor-oil bushes, while Teddy's father beat the dead Karait. 'What is the use of that?' thought Rikki-tikki. 'I have settled it all'; and then Teddy's mother picked him up from the dust and hugged him, crying that he had saved Teddy from death, and Teddy's father said that he was a providence, and Teddy looked on with big scared eyes. Rikki-tikki was rather amused at all the fuss, which, of course, he did not understand. Teddy's mother might just as well have petted Teddy for playing in the dust. Rikki was thoroughly enjoying himself.

That night, at dinner, walking to and fro among the wine-glasses on the table, he could have stuffed himself three times over with nice things; but he remembered Nag and Nagaina, and though it was very pleasant to be patted and petted by Teddy's mother, and to sit on Teddy's shoulder, his eyes would get red from time to time, and he would go off into his long war-cry of '*Rikk-tikk-tikki-tikki-tchk!*'

Teddy carried him off to bed, and insisted on Rikki-tikki sleeping under his chin. Rikki-tikki was too well-bred to bite or scratch, but as soon as Teddy was asleep he went off for his nightly walk round the house, and in the dark he ran up against Chuchundra, the musk-rat, creeping round by the wall. Chuch-undra is a broken-hearted little beast. He whimpers and cheeps all the night, trying to make up his mind to run into the middle of the room, but he never gets there.

'Don't kill me,' said Chuchundra, almost weeping. 'Rikki-tikki, don't kill me.'

'Do you think a snake-killer kills musk-rats?' said Rikki-tikki scornfully.

'Those who kill snakes get killed by snakes,' said Chuch-undra, more sorrowfully than ever. 'And how am I to be sure that Nag won't mistake me for you some dark night?'

'There's not the least danger,' said Rikki-tikki; 'but Nag is in the garden, and I know you don't go there.'

'My cousin Chua, the rat, told me —' said Chuchundra, and then he stopped.

'Told you what?'

'H'sh! Nag is everywhere, Rikki-tikki. You should have talked to Chua in the garden.'

'I didn't – so you must tell me. Quick, Chuchundra, or I'll bite you!'

Chuchundra sat down and cried till the tears rolled off his whiskers. 'I am a very poor man,' he sobbed. 'I never had spirit enough to run out into the middle of the room. H'sh! I mustn't tell you anything. Can't you *hear*, Rikki-tikki?'

Rikki-tikki listened. The house was as still as still, but he thought he could just catch the faintest *scratch-scratch* in the world, – a noise as faint as that of a wasp walking on a window-pane, – the dry scratch of a snake's scales on brick-work.

'That's Nag or Nagaina,' he said to himself; 'and he is crawling into the bath-room sluice. You're right, Chuchundra; I should have talked to Chua.'

He stole off to Teddy's bath-room, but there was nothing there, and then to Teddy's mother's bath-room. At the bottom of the smooth plaster wall there was a brick pulled out to make a sluice for the bath-water, and as Rikki-tikki stole in by the masonry curb where the bath is put, he heard Nag and Nagaina whispering together outside in the moonlight.

'When the house is emptied of people,' said Nagaina to her husband, '*he* will have to go away, and then the garden will be our own again. Go in quietly, and remember that the big man who killed Karait is the first one to bite. Then come out and tell me, and we will hunt for Rikki-tikki together.'

'But are you sure that there is anything to be gained by killing the people?' said Nag.

'Everything. When there were no people in the bungalow, did we have any mongoose in the garden? So long as the bungalow is empty, we are king and queen of the garden; and remember that as soon as our eggs in the melon-bed hatch (as they may tomorrow), our children will need room and quiet.'

'I had not thought of that,' said Nag. 'I will go, but there is no need that we should hunt for Rikki-tikki afterward. I will kill the big man and his wife, and the child if I can, and come away quietly. Then the bungalow will be empty, and Rikki-tikki will go.'

Rikki-tikki tingled all over with rage and hatred at this, and then Nag's head came through the sluice, and his five feet of cold body followed it. Angry as he was, Rikki-tikki was very frightened as he saw the size of the big cobra. Nag coiled himself up, raised his head, and looked into the bath-room in the dark, and Rikki could see his eyes glitter.

'Now, if I kill him here, Nagaina will know; and if I fight him on the open floor, the odds are in his favour. What am I to do?' said Rikki-tikki-tavi.

Nag waved to and fro, and then Rikki-tikki heard him drinking from the biggest water-jar that was used to fill the bath. 'That is good,' said the snake. 'Now, when Karait was killed, the big man had a stick. He may have that stick still, but when he comes in to bathe in the morning he will not have a stick. I shall wait here till he comes. Nagaina – do you hear me? – I shall wait here in the cool till daytime.'

There was no answer from outside, so Rikki-tikki knew Nagaina had gone away. Nag coiled himself down, coil by coil, round the bulge at the bottom of the water-jar, and Rikki-tikki stayed still as death. After an hour he began to move, muscle by muscle, toward the jar. Nag was asleep, and Rikki-tikki looked at his big back, wondering which would be the best place for a good hold. 'If I don't break his back at the first jump,' said Rikki, 'he can still fight; and if he fights – oh, Rikki!' He looked at the thickness of the neck below the hood, but that was too much for him; and a bite near the tail would only make Nag savage.

'It must be the head,' he said at last; 'the head above the hood; and when I am once there, I must not let go.'

Then he jumped. The head was lying a little clear of the water-jar, under the curve of it; and, as his teeth met, Rikki braced his back against the bulge of the red earthenware to hold down the head. This gave him just one second's purchase, and he made the most of it. Then he was battered to and fro as a rat is shaken by a dog – to and fro on the floor, up and down, and round in great circles; but his eyes were red, and he held on as the body cart-whipped over the floor, upsetting the tin dipper and the soap-dish and the flesh-brush, and banged against the tin side of the bath. As he held he closed his jaws tighter and tighter, for he made sure he would be banged to death, and, for the honour of his family, he preferred to be found with his teeth locked. He was dizzy, aching, and felt shaken to pieces when something went off like a thunderclap just behind him; a hot wind knocked him senseless, and red fire

singed his fur. The big man had been wakened by the noise, and had fired both barrels of a shot-gun into Nag just behind the hood.

Rikki-tikki held on with his eyes shut, for now he was quite sure he was dead; but the head did not move, and the big man picked him up and said: 'It's the mongoose again, Alice; the little chap has saved *our* lives now.' Then Teddy's mother came in with a very white face, and saw what was left of Nag, and Rikki-tikki dragged himself to Teddy's bedroom and spent half the rest of the night shaking himself tenderly to find out whether he really was broken into forty pieces, as he fancied.

When morning came he was very stiff, but well pleased with his doings. 'Now I have Nagaina to settle with, and she will be worse than five Nags, and there's no knowing when the eggs she spoke of will hatch. Goodness! I must go and see Darzee,' he said.

Without waiting for breakfast, Rikki-tikki ran to the thorn-bush where Darzee was singing a song of triumph at the top of his voice. The news of Nag's death was all over the garden, for the sweeper had thrown the body on the rubbish-heap.

'Oh, you stupid tuft of feathers!' said Rikki-tikki angrily. 'Is this the time to sing?'

'Nag is dead – is dead – is dead!' sang Darzee. 'The valiant Rikki-tikki caught him by the head and held fast. The big man brought the bang-stick, and Nag fell in two pieces! He will never eat my babies again.'

'All that's true enough; but where's Nagaina?' said Rikki-tikki, looking carefully round him.

'Nagaina came to the bath-room sluice and called for Nag,' Darzee went on; 'and Nag came out on the end of a stick – the sweeper picked him up on the end of a stick and threw him upon the rubbish-heap. Let us sing about the great, the red-eyed Rikki-tikki!' and Darzee filled his throat and sang.

'If I could get up to your nest, I'd roll all your babies out!' said Rikki-tikki. 'You don't know when to do the right thing at the right time. You're safe enough in your nest there, but it's war for me down here. Stop singing a minute, Darzee.'

'For the great, the beautiful Rikki-tikki's sake I will stop,' said Darzee. 'What is it, O Killer of the terrible Nag?'

'Where is Nagaina, for the third time?'

'On the rubbish-heap by the stables, mourning for Nag. Great is Rikki-tikki with the white teeth.'

'Bother my white teeth! Have you ever heard where she keeps her eggs?'

'In the melon-bed, on the end nearest the wall, where the sun strikes nearly all day. She hid them there weeks ago.'

'And you never thought it worth while to tell me? The end nearest the wall, you said?'

'Rikki-tikki, you are not going to eat her eggs?'

'Not eat exactly; no. Darzee, if you have a grain of sense you will fly off to the stables and pretend that your wing is broken, and let Nagaina chase you away to this bush. I must get to the melon-bed, and if I went there now she'd see me.'

Darzee was a feather-brained little fellow who could never hold more than one idea at a time in his head; and just because he knew that Nagaina's children were born in eggs like his own, he didn't think at first that it was fair to kill them. But his wife was a sensible bird, and she knew that cobra's eggs meant young cobras later on; so she flew off from the nest, and left Darzee to keep the babies warm, and continue his song about the death of Nag. Darzee was very like a man in some ways.

She fluttered in front of Nagaina by the rubbish-heap, and cried out: 'Oh, my wing is broken! The boy in the house threw a stone at me and broke it.' Then she fluttered more desperately than ever.

Nagaina lifted up her head and hissed: 'You warned Rikki-tikki when I would have killed him. Indeed and truly, you've chosen a bad place to be lame in.' And she moved toward Darzee's wife, slipping along over the dust.

'The boy broke it with a stone!' shrieked Darzee's wife.

'Well, it may be some consolation to you when you're dead to know that I shall settle accounts with the boy. My husband lies on the rubbish-heap this morning, but before night the boy in the house will lie very still. What is the use of running away? I am sure to catch you. Little fool, look at me!'

Darzee's wife knew better than to do *that*, for a bird who looks at a snake's eyes gets so frightened that she cannot move. Darzee's wife fluttered on, piping sorrowfully, and never leaving the ground, and Nagaina quickened her pace.

Rikki-tikki heard them going up the path from the stables, and he raced for the end of the melon-patch near the wall. There, in the warm litter about the melons, very cunningly hidden, he found twenty-five eggs, about the size of a bantam's eggs, but with whitish skin instead of shell.

'I was not a day too soon,' he said; for he could see the baby cobras curled up inside the skin, and he knew that the minute they were hatched they could each kill a man or a mongoose.

He bit off the tops of the eggs as fast as he could, taking care to crush the young cobras, and turned over the litter from time to time to see whether he had missed any. At last there were only three eggs left, and Rikki-tikki began to chuckle to himself, when he heard Darzee's wife screaming:

'Rikki-tikki, I led Nagaina toward the house, and she has gone into the veranda, and – oh, come quickly – she means killing!'

Rikki-tikki smashed two eggs, and tumbled backward down the melon-bed with the third egg in his mouth, and scuttled to the veranda as hard as he could put foot to the ground. Teddy and his mother and father were there at early breakfast; but Rikki-tikki saw that they were not eating anything. They sat stone-still, and their faces were white. Nagaina was coiled up on the matting by Teddy's chair, within easy striking-distance of Teddy's bare leg, and she was swaying to and fro singing a song of triumph.

'Son of the big man that killed Nag,' she hissed, 'stay still. I am not ready yet. Wait a little. Keep very still, all you three. If you move I strike, and if you do not move I strike. Oh, foolish people, who killed my Nag!'

Teddy's eyes were fixed on his father, and all his father could do was to whisper: 'Sit still, Teddy. You mustn't move. Teddy, keep still.'

Then Rikki-tikki came up and cried: 'Turn round, Nagaina; turn and fight!'

'All in good time,' said she, without moving her eyes. 'I will settle my account with *you* presently. Look at your friends, Rikki-tikki. They are still and white; they are afraid. They dare not move, and if you come a step nearer I strike.'

'Look at your eggs,' said Rikki-tikki, 'in the melon-bed near the wall. Go and look, Nagaina.'

The big snake turned half round, and saw the egg on the veranda. 'Ah-h! Give it to me,' she said.

Rikki-tikki put his paws one on each side of the egg, and his eyes were blood-red. 'What price for a snake's egg? For a young cobra? For a young king-cobra? For the last – the very last of the brood? The ants are eating all the others down by the melon-bed.'

Nagaina spun clear round, forgetting everything for the sake of the one egg; and Rikki-tikki saw Teddy's father shoot out a big hand, catch Teddy by the shoulder, and drag him across the little table with the tea-cups, safe and out of reach of Nagaina.

'Tricked! Tricked! Tricked! *Rikk-tck-tck!*' chuckled Rikki-tikki. 'The boy is safe, and it was I – I – I that caught Nag by the hood last night in the bath-room.' Then he began to jump up and down, all four feet together, his head close to the floor. 'He threw me to and fro, but he could not shake me off. He was dead before the big man blew him in two. I did it. *Rikki-tikki-tck-tck!* Come then, Nagaina. Come and fight with me. You shall not be a widow long.'

Nagaina saw that she had lost her chance of killing Teddy, and the egg lay between Rikki-tikki's paws. 'Give me the egg, Rikki-tikki. Give me the last of my eggs, and I will go away and never come back,' she said, lowering her hood.

'Yes, you will go away, and you will never come back; for you will go to the rubbish-heap with Nag. Fight, widow! The big man has gone for his gun! Fight!'

Rikki-tikki was bounding all round Nagaina, keeping just out of reach of her stroke, his little eyes like hot coals. Nagaina gathered herself together, and flung out at him. Rikki-tikki jumped up and backward. Again and again and again she struck, and each time her head came with a whack on the matting of the veranda, and she gathered herself together like a watch-spring. Then Rikki-tikki danced in a circle to get behind her, and Nagaina spun round to keep her head to his head, so that the rustle of her tail on the matting sounded like dry leaves blown along by the wind.

He had forgotten the egg. It still lay on the veranda, and Nagaina came nearer and nearer to it, till at last, while Rikki-tikki was drawing breath, she caught it in her mouth, turned to the veranda steps, and flew like an arrow down the path, with Rikki-tikki behind her. When the cobra runs for her life, she goes like a whip-lash flicked across a horse's neck.

Rikki-tikki knew that he must catch her, or all the trouble would begin again. She headed straight for the long grass by the thorn-bush, and as he was running Rikki-tikki heard Darzee still singing his foolish little song of triumph. But Darzee's wife was wiser. She flew off her nest as Nagaina came along, and flapped her wings about Nagaina's head. If Darzee had helped they might have turned her; but Nagaina only lowered her hood and went on. Still, the instant's delay brought Rikki-tikki up to her, and as she plunged into the rat-hole where she and Nag used to live, his little white teeth were clenched on her tail, and he went down with her – and very few mongooses, however wise and old they may be, care to follow a cobra into its hole. It was dark in the hole; and Rikki-tikki never knew when it might open out and give Nagaina room to turn and strike at him. He held on savagely, and struck out his feet to act as brakes on the dark slope of the hot, moist earth.

Then the grass by the mouth of the hole stopped waving, and Darzee said: 'It is all over with Rikki-tikki! We must sing his death-song. Valiant Rikki-tikki is dead! For Nagaina will surely kill him underground.'

So he sang a very mournful song that he made up on the spur of the minute, and just as he got to the most touching part the grass quivered again, and Rikki-tikki, covered with dirt, dragged himself out of the hole leg by leg, licking his whiskers. Darzee stopped with a little shout. Rikki-tikki shook some of the dust out of his fur and sneezed. 'It is all over,' he said. 'The widow will never come out again.' And the red ants that live between the grass-stems heard him, and began to troop down one after another to see if he had spoken the truth.

Rikki-tikki curled himself up in the grass and slept where he was – slept and slept till it was late in the afternoon, for he had done a hard day's work.

'Now,' he said, when he awoke, 'I will go back to the house. Tell the Coppersmith, Darzee, and he will tell the garden that Nagaina is dead.'

The Coppersmith is a bird who makes a noise exactly like the beating of a little hammer on a copper pot; and the reason he is always making it is because he is the town-crier to every Indian garden, and tells all the news to everybody who cares to listen. As Rikki-tikki went up the path, he heard his 'attention' notes like a tiny dinner-gong; and then the steady 'Ding-dong-tock!

Nag is dead – *dong!* Nagaina is dead! *Ding-dong-tock!*' That set all the birds in the garden singing, and the frogs croaking; for Nag and Nagaina used to eat frogs as well as little birds.

When Rikki got to the house, Teddy and Teddy's mother (she still looked very white, for she had been fainting) and Teddy's father came out and almost cried over him; and that night he ate all that was given him till he could eat no more, and went to bed on Teddy's shoulder, where Teddy's mother saw him when she came to look late at night.

'He saved our lives and Teddy's life,' she said to her husband. 'Just think, he saved all our lives!'

Rikki-tikki woke up with a jump, for all the mongooses are light sleepers.

'Oh, it's you,' said he. 'What are you bothering for? All the cobras are dead; and if they weren't, I'm here.'

Rikki-tikki had a right to be proud of himself; but he did not grow too proud, and he kept that garden as a mongoose should keep it, with tooth and jump and spring and bite, till never a cobra dared show its head inside the walls.

Patch

Patch was my dog. Well, he was in a way. When the family next door moved out, a widow woman came to live there. The gossip was she used to run a pub and was a bit fed up with always having people round her. So she never went out but sat in her front room in her best dark velvet dress all day with her two dogs stretched out on the carpet. One dog was like the old lady. He never went further than the back door and then only when desperate.

But Patch, her second dog, liked people and liked to be out of doors. So I took him for walks. Or rather he took me. He was a kind of cross between an Airedale and a Labrador, brown as a fox (in fact a farmer nearly shot him once) with a patch over one eye. If I went out in the yard and whistled, he'd shoot out of next door on to the pavement and then leap our front gate, stopping in mid-jump, all four paws balanced on the pointed gate posts, before jumping down. I was always scared he'd trip, but he never did.

He'd go anywhere with you, charge after a stick, leap a hedge or ditch, swim a stream. When we ran in the woods on the hill above the Works, where the garlic plants grew by thousands in spring time, he'd roll in them down the slope and come up smelling like a pizza. Or he'd jump in the canal to get at his own reflection and come up smelling like nothing on earth.

His eyes were big and brown and he was so full of good will it's a wonder his tail stayed on his body. If you had a wrestle on the grass, he'd join in, though sometimes he got over-enthusiastic and bit everyone. It was lucky he did it gently, Mam said, or he'd have your leg off. We were in no danger, though, because Patch never bit anyone in anger in his life (except once). To tell you the truth I began to think he was a bit too easy going, a bit of a coward in fact.

One day, when we were out walking, as we passed a farm a great black dog charged out of the yard, barking furiously. Patch immediately moved over and put me between himself and the black one. Not only that, he suddenly started limping and looking sorry for himself. We drove off the black dog with a few well-aimed sticks while I examined Patch. As it happened he had a thorn in one of his pads, so he wasn't putting on an act. But I felt he hadn't really matched up to my expectations. He was big enough to look after himself, I reckoned.

The truth was, of course, that he didn't like fighting. If he was in the road and saw the whacking great white-grey Alsatian who belonged to Hicksie, round the corner, Patch would slip over to the other pavement and look for a hole in the hedge.

He preferred small dogs, and when Jammy got a puppy, Patch was delighted. It was about as mixed as he was, a kind of spaniel cum dachshund, very low on the ground with floppy ears and appealing eyes. They took to each other as soon as they met and always stuck together when we were out in the country, though Flip, Jammy's dog, hated water as much as Patch loved it. But it was a treat to watch them rolling about together when we came to a clover field or going mad racing in circles and barking when we went to Rabbit Hollow. They were real mates.

In the middle of Tarcroft there was this open space, in front of the Co-op, with the ice-cream shop on the corner, where Joe sold ice cream in summer and fish and chips in winter. When he drove his van round the streets you could hear his handbell ringing and everyone came running. On the other side of the square was a blacksmith's and when the farmers brought their horses in to be shod, we used to gather round to see the sparks fly and the water boil when the hot iron was plunged in. Everybody came there at some time or other, and it was a kind of Tom Tiddler's Ground: nobody ever started a fight there. We used to leave each other alone. The trouble was, dogs didn't know this.

One Saturday morning we were hanging about waiting for Joe's to open, when I noticed Patch behaving in a funny manner, walking round my legs, twisting his lead round my arm, as if he were trying to hide. I looked round. Sure enough, there was Freddie's mob from round the corner, about six of them, standing by the blacksmith's. The big Alsatian was wandering about loose, scratching the ground and making horrible snuffling noises.

Just then his tail went up, he sniffed the air and came trotting over to us. Flip, no more than a puppy still, and innocent with it, pulled loose from Jammy's grip and went up to sniff at the big dog. It was the worst thing he could have done, for the next moment he was rolled over on his back as the Alsatian went for him.

'Hey, call your stupid dog off,' yelled Jammy. He was as scared as Flip. But across the square they only laughed while their dog got on with eating Jammy's.

But right then I felt a tremendous jerk on my wrist – it almost pulled my hand off. Then another wrench. The loop of the leash came off and like a brown streak, Patch went for the Alsatian.

There was a snapping and a snarling, a rolling and a cloud of dust, and a yowl from one of them. I couldn't see which, because now one of them was on top and now the other.

Then the bigger dog was running for his life, tail between his legs. From across the square came an agonized shout.

'Hey, he's bitten a lump out of his nose. That dog of yours ought to be shot.'

'Your dog ought to pick somebody his own size,' yelled Jammy, who was holding Flip in his arms and trying to pat Patch at the same time. I couldn't help it. I burst out laughing. Bella and Harold joined in.

I called across the square. 'My dog's going in for an ice cream. When he comes out, he's going to eat yours for afters.'

When we came out of Joe's with our ice-cream cornets, the square was empty.

The Foal

A faint whinny, penetrating her dreams, woke the little girl on the veranda. When she opened her eyes it was still not quite light and the tall gums crowding the steep rise to the road loomed up darkly over the house, only leaving a pale strip of sky. Dew lay heavy on everything – the bark woodshed, the wheelbarrow by the stump, the bracken on the edge of the bush. From the spouting trickled beads of water, dimming the fly-wire that netted the veranda.

Warm in her blankets, the little girl looked drowsily up at the dark shape that always frightened her at bedtime; it had the beard and hunched shoulders of an old man and stretched out a dead hand. Now, in the growing light, it was only a tree, no different from the other trees. Noises were beginning to seep through the woolly mist – the yellow robin's plucked string, clop-clop and jingle of a farmer's cart on the road above, snort of the pony that was always brought into the paddock near the house at night-time.

And then again the queer whinny! She sat up in bed, a flicker at her heart, staring out through the fly-netting. Near the woodheap she could see the thick form of Dozy, standing quite still and looking enormous against the rising ground in the dim light, her winter coat puffed out with cold. Her head was sunk low, her heavy forelock had fallen over her eyes, she seemed rooted in the waxy earth. But round her flickered something wavery and uncertain, a small, glimmering shape like her shadow in water, and from it came a light whickering.

Fully awake now, the little girl sprang out of bed and pressed her nose against the netting. She was beside herself with

269

excitement. Sunk in a dream, Dozy stood with her head drooping, as if quite unconscious of what was going on round her. The little girl wanted to cry out and tell her what had happened.

Instead, she rushed inside through the dark kitchen and banged on the door of her father's bedroom.

'Dad! Dad! Come and see, Dad! Dozy's got a foal.'

There came a stirring from inside, the sound of a struck match. His eyes heavy with sleep, her father appeared at the door holding a candle.

'Eh? What's this?'

'A foal,' she stuttered. 'Dozy's got a foal. I saw it.'

'That's all right,' he told her. 'Don't wake the house now. Get back to bed till your aunt calls you for breakfast.'

Rebuffed, she went back to bed, but sleep was miles away from her. She did not know how she could wait for the day to begin. Dozy and her foal were no longer by the woodheap, and she sat up to listen for sound of them. Had they gone up the track between the thick bush to the gate? Or were they round at the front of the house where the sliprails led into the big paddock?

Now that it was near daylight she was terribly afraid she had only dreamed about the foal. She had not really seen it; merely a dancing, wavery shape at Dozy's side. When the sun came out there might be nothing left of it.

The sun was beginning to gild the tops of the tall trees now. Everything glistened with dew – the filmy wattles, the out-house roof, a new kerosene-tin by the woodheap. Blundering out in his heavy boots the little girl's father began to light the fire in the kitchen range. He filled the big kettle at the tap and then went to the other room to call her aunt.

'That mare's had her foal,' she heard him say.

'Oh?'

'Th' kid's worked up about it. Ran in to tell me half an hour ago.'

'She would. Always looking for something fresh to go crazy over, that child.'

'Well, can you blame her? No other youngster her age to play with ... I'll give the mare a good feed of warm mash and turn her into the open paddock.'

He mixed the mash by the stove and then, taking the winkers from a nail on the veranda, went off for the plough-horses. He had to be at work in the big orchard a mile away by eight. There came a clatter of crockery as his sister, trailing about in her down-at-heel slippers, began to lay the table for breakfast.

He was away up the track, trudging along behind the plough-horses, before the little girl had washed and dressed, for she was waiting at the front window in her knickers to catch a sight of the foal. Yes, there it was by the sliprails, dancing round its mother on thin, spindly legs, its baby hoofs prodding the soft earth. It seemed to have to move like that to keep its balance; it wobbled painfully when it stood still. She feasted her eyes on its short head and long ears, its rusty brown coat that turned whitish under the belly. Like a ruff, its crisp little mane ran along its neck; its tail was a small curly mop.

She could hardly eat at breakfast; all her thoughts were on the foal. But she didn't want to talk about it to her aunt. Her aunt thought she was crazy about her pony and dolls. Her aunt was never crazy about anything but the chance of a trip back to town. She could sit through the meal without a word, except to tell her her porridge would get cold if she dawdled over it, and when the morning's work was done she would sit silently in the rocking-chair on the veranda poring over the big catalogue from some shop in town.

All that morning the little girl left her dolls untended in the fire-blackened butt of the big tree that was their secret home. She could do nothing but follow Dozy and her foal, standing in the mud by the sliprails to stare at them, climbing on the rails when they came near the fence, trailing after them over the mushroom-spotted turf when they moved to the far corner of the paddock. It was only a small paddock, and it was safe for them now the draught-horses were gone. Yet there was a steep slope falling to the head of the creek: what if Dozy tried to go down there to drink? The foal could not follow on its thin spidery legs.

'Keep up by the fence, Dozy,' she wanted to warn her. 'There's no need to go down there. There's plenty water in the tank – plenty.'

But Dozy showed no signs of going down the slope. She stood brooding in the warm sun while the foal teetered round her, making odd movements with its head, mixing up the long legs that looked as if they might snap at any moment like dry twigs. Now and then she curved her neck to look round at it with moist eyes, her nostrils vibrating in a faint whinny. Her back was sunk in a hollow. She looked very old.

Yet when a dog came out of the bush and trotted across a corner of the paddock she sprang to life in a moment. Her head jerked up, a light flashed through her eyes. Moving towards the dog with brisk steps she laid back her ears and made a sudden rush. The dog slunk away through the wires.

Something in that quick action awed the little girl. She had never before seen Dozy all stirred-up and savage. She had been used to crawling under her belly, playing round her heels, jogging on her back to the store. So gentle was she that it seemed cruel to kick your heels into her and make her trot. Dozy was bone-lazy, her father said; she wouldn't even snap at the bot-flies that buzzed round her to lay their eggs in her long fur. But there was this new quality that had come to her; she seemed strange.

Don't come too near, her eyes said.

The sun climbed high over the tops of the trees, the dew vanished from the grass, the rabbits that had been squatting in furry balls along the line of ferns faded into their burrows. In the shade of the paddock's one tree Dozy went to sleep with her head over the foal's back.

'Lena!' called a shrill voice. 'Are you going to stay out there staring all day? There's plenty little things to do in the house here.'

Reluctantly, walking backwards part of the way, she sidled towards the house till she was swallowed up in the kitchen's darkness.

When she came back from the messages, late in the afternoon, something was going on in the paddock. Dozy, sedate but a little flustered, was trying to lead the foal down the steep grassy slope to water. Patiently she guided it along the side of the slope, edging down gradually and waiting for it to follow. But the foal, moving shakily on its high legs, had become scared. It baulked, tossing its little head up and down in a queer, sulky way. It cantered forwards a few steps and propped, falling on its knees. It picked itself up whinnying, and turned back, making up the hill again.

Dozy seemed to lose her head. She gave a throaty grunt as she lumbered up the hill after it and at the top she threw back her head and neighed wildly, a distracted look in her eyes. The foal was scampering uncertainly across the paddock. She flung up her heels and went after it.

Suddenly other horses appeared on the far side of the fence, their heads held high, their manes windblown, their glittering eyes fastened on the foal. A flurry of excitement spread through them; they whinnied and snorted, plunging off with mad bucks and returning to look over the fence again.

Come and see this strange creature, they seemed to be urging one another. Come and see!

The taut wires strummed with the pressure of their bodies, the lunging of their shod hoofs as they turned to gallop away.

The world had suddenly become filled with waving manes, staring eyes, threatening heels; and in all this tumult the foal's body seemed small and fragile, liable to be beaten into the earth. It cantered about crazily, as if blown here and there like a feather by the violent snorting on the other side of the fence; no sooner had Dozy come up with it than it skittered away again.

Danger for it increased when the plough-horses clumped down the track through the dusk, jangling their chains. They jostled one another over their feed-boxes by the fence, laying back their ears and making ugly motions with their heels, their huge rumps looming up like whales in the lantern's pool of light as the little girl's father let down the rails and brought Dozy and her foal back into the paddock by the house.

Another day over! He stood watching the feeding horses, his body heavy, the weight of the turned furrows upon him. At the door he flashed his lantern on the mare and foal, as if giving them close scrutiny for the first time.

'Bit of a brumby,' he muttered with a dry grin. 'But its mother's no show-piece, either. Couldn't expect a young Phar Lap, I guess . . . Going to break it in yourself, girlie?'

She said soberly, as if she had been thinking the matter over, 'Not yet. Not for a long time yet.'

'It'll soon grow. Grow into a big, rangy brute, like as not, with a hammer head and the gait of a camel. You'll be cantering into the township on it in a couple of years.'

She didn't want that: she wanted it to stay a foal. There were three of them now, she was thinking dreamily – Dozy, herself, and this soft-eyed thing, her little sister, who was already nearer to her than any human being around. Some morning, when spring came, they might wander off together, out through the gate, along the road a little way and then across to where there were no houses and fences but only grassy flats lying gold in the sun. On and on they would go, Dozy taking her on her back when she was tired and the foal scampering ahead. Then suddenly they would find they were talking together.

She dreamed about the foal as she sat on her low stool by the fire after the evening meal, staring into the coals. It was somewhere out there in the dark, following its mother through the wet ferns, stumbling over hidden logs, pricking its ears in fright, perhaps, when a night-bird swooped low or a possum scuttled for a tree. His stockinged feet in front of him, her father drowsed in his padded chair, and her aunt sewed on without speaking, threading her needle against the flare of the lamp.

The dark closed in on her with its strange sounds as she lay on her bed on the veranda, keeping her head buried in the clothes. From far away on the sapling-covered hill came the bark of a fox like something torn from the earth's throat; then a night-owl hooted close at hand, the sound of its voice echoing back across the gully. The heavy trees moved closer, pressing on the roof. She crept deeper and deeper into the nest of blankets.

Gradually the trees changed to horses, heavy draught-horses, lumbering one by one through the sliprails and plunging about wildly as they entered the paddock. Their huge rumps shut out the sky as they kicked up their heels; they cut great flakes out of the turf; the ground quivered beneath their hoofs. Sometimes they fought in the middle of the paddock, crashing into one another with the sound of thunder. They were not horses now, but unicorns; steel horns jutted from their foreheads and their eyes were fiery coals.

Fearful, she wandered among them, dodging the nightmare hoofs, looking for the foal. There was no sign of it and yet from somewhere near at hand came a thin cry like a snared rabbit's. Her own voice, when she tried to call out, was only a thread of sound. She strained and strained, but could not make herself heard.

Then at the bottom of the steep slope to the creek she found it, its thin legs snapped like matches, its crushed body no bigger than a bird's. And Dozy was nowhere near. She must have turned away and left it; she must have gone to join the great brutes thundering about the paddock above.

In agony the little girl threw herself down beside the foal. Her voice, so long dammed back, broke out in a deep, convulsive sob that shook her whole body and burst open the misty veil covering her eyes.

She found herself sitting up in bed staring at the wire-netting. The terror of her nightmare was still trembling through her, but outside the daylight world was already taking shape – the dark woodshed, the blur of wattles, the stump with the axe in it. And there on the dewy rise, not ten yards away, was the foal tugging at its mother's teats, its long legs stretched out and firmly braced, its tiny mop of a tail flicking from side to side, its head butting into the sleepy flanks as if an urge for power and mastery were driving through it – as if it was the one thing fully alive on the whole earth.

The Donkey

Alan Marshall

The donkey was a very ordinary donkey, shabby and abstracted, and he stood with drooping head and half-closed eyes at the entrance to a circus tent that had been erected on the only patch of green land left close to the big city.

This was the first circus the city had seen for a year, and along the roads that led to the vacant plot of ground, long lines of cars moved and stopped, then moved again. People, walking rapidly, crossed footpaths and stepped over kerbs. They moved in groups and lines that met and converged till, when the plot was reached, a mass of people advanced across it, their heads lifted to see over shoulders ahead of them.

'Way down beneath this layer of lifted, superior faces, down to where big hands gripped little hands, were other faces, excited and smeared with ice-cream, that peered ahead through a bush of legs to where other legs were moving like those around them. In this world of trousers and silk stockings the little girls and boys who owned the faces could not see the tent or the elephants moving loosely near the painted wagons; they just had to wait till powerful arms came down to them and they emerged to a lift that raised them above the heads of the people. And there, confronting them, was the wonder of the donkey standing just inside the entrance to the circus tent.

The tent was a large one. The bright posters that for some weeks had been halting people in front of stained brick walls in back streets and alleys announced that the tent was the biggest in the world and held four thousand people. Since the donkey, tethered to a peg by a worn rope, was directly in the pathway of the people hurrying towards the tiers of seats that rose back from the lighted ring, they all had to pass him after they had purchased their tickets. Each Saturday three separate shows were held. Thus twelve thousand people passed the donkey on each of those two days.

At least three-quarters of those twelve thousand people patted or touched him as they passed. Thus nine thousand hands beat a tattoo somewhere upon the donkey in the course of the day. It would be hard to calculate how many tiny blows fell upon him during a week.

The pattings took various forms. Some were demonstrations of superiority, others were apprehensive gestures of need. There were pats that denoted love of self, and some that denoted love of donkeys. Some were the boastful displays of fathers wishing to impress their children, while others were gentle pats transformed by imagination into magical experiences.

A mother being dragged along by an excited little boy would stop while he moved a timid hand gently on the donkey's shoulder. Smaller children, held aloft by proud fathers, bent, and scraped their pudgy fingers along his back, or scratched the top of his head, or pulled his ears. Unaccompanied children, with no parents to restrain them, exhibited a hastily manufactured bravery by leaning on the donkey or rubbing his nose while they looked round for approval.

Sometimes kind people would try and force peanuts or lollies between the donkey's lips but this was hard to do since he kept his teeth firmly closed and shook his head when he felt their hands on his mouth.

About every ten minutes a Man Who Understood Donkeys came along.

'Ah, a donk!' he would say with an impressive familiarity that made the patting people withdraw their hands and look at him. The Man Who Understood Donkeys would then slip his arm round the animal's neck and address it in terms that established him as an authority.

'So you've come to this, old chap, eh! No more hard work for you! Well, that's how it is!' Then, in a change of tone, he would explain to the listening people, 'In the East they carry more than their own weight, you know – regular beasts of burden.'

The people murmured their understanding and gave the donkey a final pat of sympathy before they passed on.

The donkey accepted the attention of this multitude of people with a submissiveness that suggested he was reconciled to a lifetime of pats. If there were times when he felt the stirrings of rebellion within him he never showed it. He stood on three legs, one hip dropped, his unkempt hair disordered by hands that failed to disturb the dream in which he was lost.

On the final day of the circus a stout man with a navy blue suit stretched tightly upon him came confidently through the entrance. He paused in front of the donkey and subjected the animal to a critical survey. He pursed his lips and shook his

head, then moved back so that he could look at him from the rear. He moved round to the other side of the donkey and examined him from there. He completed the encircling of the donkey by a long contemplation of his head. Now there was nothing more he wished to know about this donkey. In the same movement he made to turn away he let his hand fall heavily on the animal's back. It was the eight thousandth pat of the day.

The donkey had seemed asleep but the sudden weight of the man's hand upon him affected him as if it were some signal for which he had been long waiting. He lifted his heavy head with a jerk, turned, and snapped at the man's arm with teeth that went off like a rabbit trap. They closed on the sleeve of the man's coat and ripped from the material a ragged patch of blue cloth that remained projecting from the donkey's mouth as the animal turned his head away to continue his dreams.

The man was astounded. He staggered back amongst the people with startled eyes and open mouth. He clutched his arm with his hand and looked at the people for confirmation of the amazing thing that had happened to him.

'He bit me!' he exclaimed in horrified tones, then added, as he looked unbelievingly at the donkey, 'What a vicious brute!'

The people passing had all stopped to look at the man and at the donkey with the piece of cloth in its mouth. They all nodded approval at the man's words. This donkey was indeed a vicious brute. He had bitten the stout man on the arm and all the man had done was to pat him. What an ungrateful, vicious creature!

For quite five minutes after that no one patted the donkey. It must have been his first taste of peace for years.

Fly Back to Me

A. N. Forde

Jerry opened the door of the pigeon loft. The pigeons came flocking out into the cool morning. They were greedy for their feed.

They flew crazily in the air waiting for him to throw the feed upon the ground. Jerry flung his hand in a careless arc and let the broken scrap corn fall through his fingers. From all angles they came towards the corn, slapping him unwarily with their wings.

But Jerry was not happy this morning.

Two days had passed since his best pigeon had disappeared. He had called it Wonder after the name of an aeroplane he had seen in a *Boy's Own Magazine*. Yes, Wonder had disappeared.

Jerry looked up into the sky more from habit than anything else. A small school of gauldings were soaring high over his head.

But there was no sign of Wonder.

He had never realized before how much this pigeon meant to him. He hadn't reared it. It was really a stranger that had arrived months ago out of the blue. Since then it came and went, day after day, and had become a fixture as casual as the rise and set of the sun. He had taken a fancy to it and accepted it as theirs – his and his mother's. Strangely enough his mother liked it, too – and she usually hated the sight of any pigeon trespassing in her yard. But with Wonder it was different. You couldn't help liking that pigeon.

It was a beautiful pigeon. The most delicate shades of green, blue, and fawn, bright and dull, blended on its breast; and when it shook its head the colours on neck and wings merged in a delightful shifting harmony. Its tail was black and white like a draught-board in pattern and its feet were a fragile pink.

Jerry looked back up into the sky. A few scattered pieces of corn still lay on the ground, exciting the eager contention of the pigeons. The gaudlings were out of sight, but there was still no sign of Wonder.

Two days! Perhaps he might never see it again!

His heart felt heavy and the chucklings of the pigeons near him went unnoticed. He hardly thought of them today; and when his mother called, he answered listlessly.

'Yes, Mom.'

'Wonder come?'

'No, Mom.'

'Where he could be?'

'I doan' know, Mom.'

Perhaps it had died, he thought. Or had been killed!

Then his mother spoke again.

'I bet you anyt'ing one of them boys hit it with a catapult. That is why I always stop you from using one. You all does kill people's chicken and things just for fun. I will brek your hand if I see yo' with one.'

Jerry did not answer. He could not. He felt uneasy. For he had a catapult – though his mother did not know it. He had made it himself with his scout knife and was very proud of it. Its edges were smooth and well-turned. And the fork tapered neatly down into the stem. He had made it shine with some stolen varnish, and the clean red rubber which he had got by swapping the face of a watch for it was tied with thin wire to the branches of the fork. He had made the catapult in moments of quiet, always out of sight of his mother.

Two days ago he had had his first hit with the catapult, had drawn his first blood.

He remembered it as if it were now. The head and upper breast of the dove peeping out over the house-top. The challenge it presented. His trembling eagerness to try his luck. The catapult sticking in his pocket and giving him trouble to get it out. The 'heffing' of the weapon when he raised it for the shot.

The breathless ecstasy of taking aim. The suspended moment. And then he had loosed the tight straining length of rubber and the stone flew from the sling.

The bird toppled over backwards out of sight.

He stood stunned with the rapture of it all, unable to gather his thoughts together. He was a hero. But he must get the bird, he said to himself. He wanted to run around into the person's yard and ask if he could climb the house and take it off the roof. But he dared not. His mother would hear of it and he was sure to get a 'cussing.' He stifled his eagerness to see the dead bird and went on home, carrying the keen satisfaction of a deed well done. Now he could speak with authority. This was the first of many – perhaps he would become a better bird-catcher than any other boy in the district. At least, he had shown his mastery. He had made the grade.

But he should have got the bird as testimony. Those boys were sure to question and suspect something shady if they didn't see the bird themselves. He could almost hear Dan's sarcastic laugh:

'Who yo' think yo' can fool? Ha! Ha! Ha! With your mother watching every step you make, what bird you can shoot?'

And whatever Dan said was sure to be echoed by his pals.

Still, he knew he had shot it. What more? And with the freshness of triumph in his heart he had walked lightly home. He was just in time to hear his mother calling him loudly to feed the pigeons. He fed them but, surprisingly, Wonder had not turned up. He found it strange but it was not till evening that he began to think seriously about Wonder's absence. Where was the pigeon?

Suppose he had killed it!

The next day came and the absence of the bird became more perplexing.

And two days had now passed.

Yes, it was quite possible. He wasn't sure it was a dove he had shot. It might have been a pigeon for that matter. And why not Wonder? And the irony of it! His first catapult, his first shot, his first bird had deprived him of the creature dearest to him. What a nasty thing to happen.

He moved away from the pigeon roost meditatively. Almost in a trance he heard the pigeons suddenly rush out of the loft and knew by the whirring sound that they were wheeling in the air above. They didn't feel like him, he thought. Without interest, he turned and followed them with slow eyes as they circled above.

And then he saw it! There could be no doubt about it!

Moving slowly from the upper air, a pigeon was coming down to earth. Instinctively he knew. It was Wonder.

His eyes clung to the small moving creature.

It seemed in danger of toppling over into space and one wing was paddling inexpertly, but there was greatness in the way it came – like a torn fishing vessel limping into harbour.

Jerry stood and watched, amazed and heartened in the same breath. He felt the pressure of a new joy rising inside him and he shouted with all his might!

'Mom, here it is!'

The bird descended slowly – majestically, and the other pigeons flew restlessly about it. It was sheer joy to watch the act. They flew around and before like excited guards of honour, and the bird at last landed safely at Jerry's feet. He stood and looked down at it, not yet sure of himself, not quite sure what to do with the joy in his heart.

Then in a childish but masterful impulse he took something from his pocket in haste and broke it in two. It fell a yard or two from the bird.

When his mother ran out, Jerry was fondling the fluttering bird and at his feet was a smooth, well-polished, but now useless catapult.

285

The Poacher's Narrow Shave

Dan Russell

Miss Pemberton's cottage was a good half mile from the village. It stood well back from the road in an acre of well-tended garden, half of which was given over to vegetables. In front were two narrow lawns, dotted with beds of frostbitten dahlias.

Behind the cottage, reaching right down to the garden fence, were the strictly preserved coverts which were famous for their high-flying pheasants.

On this December afternoon Miss Pemberton sat reading before her parlour fire. Every now and then she lifted her eyes from the page to gaze at the cat which lay on the rug.

He was an enormous beast, a large tabby, as big as a Pekinese dog. He lay there stretched at full length, purring gently, full-fed and lazy, a picture of domestic ease.

At length she closed her book and rose. 'I shan't be long,' she said, 'be a good boy, Tiger.'

The cat lay quietly basking in the gentle warmth; but when he heard the click of the garden gate he rose to his feet. He stretched lazily until the claws of his feet stuck out like tacks. Then he shook himself and padded out into the little hall.

The window was ajar, and he leaped easily on to the sill and looked out on to the back garden. Then with easy haste he jumped down to the cinder path and trotted down towards the coverts.

He came to the fence and passed under a broken paling with the certainty of long usage. Inside the covert all was still, save for the rustling of the crimson leaves as they drifted gently earthwards.

286

The cat trotted down a narrow pathway. He moved now with the slinking caution of the born hunter. Gone was the lazy, stupid animal which had lain before Miss Pemberton's fire; in its place was a keen, ferocious killer, his yellow eyes blazing with the lust for blood.

At the end of the path was a small clearing in which the grass grew thickly. Here were many rabbits, hopping and humping themselves to feed.

When the cat drew near the clearing he proceeded more slowly; belly touching the ground and ears flattened to his skull, he crawled forward, an inch at a time, taking advantage of every bit of cover to conceal his advance.

Fringing the clearing were hazel-bushes, and behind one of these the cat waited, motionless and patient. Only the fire in his yellow eyes betrayed the excitement within him.

At length a young buck rabbit drew near to the hazel. Eagerly the cat watched him with an unblinking stare. The rabbit hopped nearer, but still the cat waited with the uncanny patience of his kind.

Another hop, and the rabbit was near enough. Slowly the cat flexed his hind legs and tensed himself for the leap. Then he sprang.

The rabbit saw him coming in mid-air, but was too late. The cruel claws hooked into his back and shoulders, and the needle teeth sank into the neck behind the skull.

The rabbit struggled and kicked convulsively, but it was soon over; the tabby cat was no bungler.

He stood over his kill, kneading it with his forepaws and growling ferociously. More than ever it was difficult to reconcile this beast of the woods with the gentle animal of which Miss Pemberton was so proud.

He left the body of the rabbit and sauntered on, the first keen edge of his desire blunted by the kill.

Beyond the clearing was another narrow path. He was trotting easily along this path when he swerved sharply. From the bushes by his side came the rattling of iron and a scrambling of feet. The cat peered round the bush.

There, caught by both forefeet in an iron trap was a young rat. It was struggling desperately; both its legs were broken and its face was a mask of dried blood. When it saw the cat it redoubled its efforts and squealed piteously. But not for long. Claws and teeth soon gave it relief from its long agony.

He soon left the rat, for the iron trap made him suspicious. He came back to the little pathway which led to Miss Pemberton's garden, and sat down to clean himself.

He was washing his paws when there was a hissing whistle all around him, leaves and twigs were cut off by some invisible agency; a fraction of a second later came the ear-shattering report of a gun.

The cat looked up and saw the keeper standing in the pathway with a smoking gun.

Instantly he acted. With a sideways jump he landed in the undergrowth. Then like a thunderbolt he raced for home. He crashed through the brushwood regardless of noise until he reached the garden. Then he slowed his pace. He trotted sedately up the garden path and entered by the open window.

Miss Pemberton, returning from the village, met the keeper at her front gate. 'Your cat, Miss,' he cried, 'been in my coverts an' disturbin' everything.'

'My cat!' Miss Pemberton bridled. 'Nonsense, he never goes near your coverts. Why, I left him asleep in front of the fire.'

'T'was your cat, Miss,' persisted the keeper.

'Don't be ridiculous. He hasn't been out all day. Come and see for yourself.'

And, sure enough, fast asleep before the fire, basking in the warm glow, lay Miss Pemberton's cat. As she spoke he opened one yellow eye and gave a little purr of content; then, once more, he curled up to sleep in front of the little log fire.

Poor Arthur

Gene Kemp

After Dennis, the cat, had caught the white mouse one day when the cage was being cleaned out – by Bloggs, my stupid sister, of course – I wouldn't have let it happen, only she's so slow, she didn't see Dennis coming like a streak of death across the floor, up on to the table, and to where that white mouse was just running round and round, then Mum said there weren't to be any more animals, because she couldn't stand the smell, and she was the only one that fed them.

Well, we took to moaning about having no animals except the cat, Dennis, you remember, and he's so old I'm sure he was never a kitten, older than me and always asleep except when he's hunting defenceless birds and mice, and being all streaky and murderous, and then we took to hanging around petshops and looking at the creatures. I fancied a yellow spotted snake and Bloggs a Great Dane, but we didn't have much hopes of either, really, not with our mum.

Then, just at the right moment, our next door neighbour said she'd got gerbils, and they were very nice, and you didn't have to clean them out often as they didn't smell.

'All animals smell,' said Mum.

The next door neighbour took us all round to the gerbillery, I suppose you could call it, as there were two couples and two sets of baby gerbils.

'I'll give you one for your birthday,' she said, as I stood there letting them run over me, with my inside swimming with joy at the feel of their fur and their little soft claws. And Mum said all right, then, providing you look after them, not me.

So we cleaned up the old mouse cage, then rushed off to buy sawdust and gerbil food.

And so came Chuchi.

Not that we called her Chuchi at first. We tried Polly, and Nosey, and Cleo, but nothing fitted. She wasn't much to look at, a bit tatty, really, with ruffled fur and a big hooked nose which she poked into everything. But she had bright black eyes and she ran to us whenever we came near, head cocked on one side, chattering furiously, hiding nuts, eating nuts, tearing up toilet rolls, kicking angrily with her back feet when she was in a temper. Dad called her the little rat. He was always chatting to her or tempting her with peanuts so that she'd jump really high. Even Mum took to her. She let me have her in my bedroom because the cage didn't smell, and at night I'd let her run round my bed and snuggle in my pyjama pocket.

And she still hadn't got a name.

Only one day Mum said, out of the blue, 'Let's go and get some grass seeds for Chuchi. She likes grass seeds.'

'Chuchi?'

'Yes, Chuchi, of course,' as if we ought to have known all along. 'That's the sound we make when we want her to come to us, and it's her funny chatter noise as well.'

So there she was. Chuchi. Named at last.

Now all this time we'd kept an eye on Dennis, that hunting cat. There was no smell to tempt him, but he knew something very interesting was going on. Dennis is a clever cat. Watches and waits. Sometimes we'd find him outside my room, washing himself very innocently. Chuchi grew bad-tempered. Straw and shredded toilet rolls flew through the air.

'She needs a mate,' Dad announced at tea-time.

'Babies,' Bloggs cried, stupid eyes shining.

'I like Chuchi, but enough is enough,' Mum said.

'Females need mating,' Dad said. 'That's why she's irritable. Females do get irritable.'

'Humph,' snorted Mum, banging down scrambled eggs on the table. I thought for a minute she was going to bang them on his head.

We bought another gerbil.

Dad built a second cage in case they didn't get on, and for the babies later.

This turned out to be a good thing, because Chuchi took a violent dislike to the new gerbil, and chased him out, biting and kicking like fury. He was terrified and squealed pitifully, poor little thing, only half her size. We called him Arthur.

The next day we tried to put him in with her again, but it was no good. The cage was her territory and she wasn't having Arthur in it.

Then Dad thought of putting the cages together, and soon they were sniffing each other through the wire.

A week later they were both living happily in Chuchi's cage. Arthur grew bigger and braver but she was still the boss. They looked very alike now, though Chuchi still had the longer tail and the bigger nose, and a more untidy look.

Dennis the hunter waited, licking his tabby fur. Patient, wicked Dennis.

'I do wish she'd have babies,' sighed Bloggs.

'Well, she's getting fatter,' Mum said.

My dad drives a bus and works different shifts. That day he'd gone to work very early, returned at ten in the morning, and gone out again at three. We came home with Mum, who's a teacher, at four. There was a note for us on the table. Dad in a temper is like Vesuvius erupting. The note said:

'If I find out who left the cage door open this morning, you'll wish you'd never been born, for that murdering cat has killed Chuchi. I've tried to catch him but he was too fast, which is just as well for him.'

He'd put her on the sideboard, and she was stiff and cold, but her fur was as soft as ever. Mum was sobbing, and tears were streaming down Blogg's face. I didn't cry. I just stood there, stroking her over and over again.

'We must bury her,' Mum said, at last.

I found a Dinky car-container with a transparent top, and Bloggs put her inside, wrapped in cotton wool. Mum fetched some little flowers from the garden and put them in with her, and Bloggs drew a cross on a card and wrote, 'Here lies Chuchi, the Beloved.'

We dug a hole and placed her inside. The ground was hard. It hadn't rained for a long time.

Dad came home, face pale, anger gone.

'I loved the little rat,' he said.

Mum stirred. 'We ought to go and see if Arthur's all right. He must have been terrified when Dennis came out of nowhere and seized Chuchi.'

We all trooped up to my bedroom, and Arthur was there, nervous and jittery; not surprising. Bloggs felt in the dark room Dad had built on above the cage, as a nursery, still crying.

'Now there'll never be any babies,' and then: 'I can feel

something. There's something here. The babies!'

'Let me see!' we all cried. But we couldn't, for it had been made specially dark and quiet for the babies and the only way to see inside was to take the top off.

I fetched the screwdriver. Dad unscrewed the screws. Bloggs chewed her fingers. It seemed to take hours, but at last, there they lay, naked, pink, squirming, beautiful, four of them.

'But how can they survive,' Mum whispered, 'without Chuchi to feed them? I can't feed anything as small as that. They'll starve . . .'

Dad's face had turned even paler. Bloggs was crying again.

'No, I'll put them to sleep, first,' he said.

At that moment Arthur jumped out of my hand, where I'd been stroking him for comfort, and ran across the room. We watched him. Perhaps Bloggs isn't so stupid as I've been saying all along, for she got it first.

'Look! Look! That's not Arthur! The tail's too long and the nose is too big, and he's . . . she's heading for the babies! Dennis killed Arthur, not Chuchi! It's Chuchi! She's alive!'

Chuchi had reached the cage and the babies. She pulled them to her, and then all her blue and pink toilet paper, covered herself and the babies with it, and sat, glaring out of the heap, very angrily indeed, as if she didn't think much of us.

We were all grinning from ear to ear.

'Everything's going to be all right. The babies will live now.'

'I'll put the roof back on so that they can be quiet,' Dad said.

As he screwed in the screws, he started to laugh, a funny sort of laugh.

'What is it, Dad?'

'It's just that, well, poor old Arthur—he didn't have much of a life because Chuchi bullied him all the time, and when he dies he gets buried with someone else's name over him, and all of us smiling and happy because he's dead and not Chuchi. Poor old Arthur, I say.'

'Poor Arthur,' we all echoed, but we still didn't feel sad. Chuchi and the babies were going to live. Everything would be all right. Except for Arthur. Poor Arthur.

The King of Beasts

Philip José Farmer

The biologist was showing the distinguished visitor through the zoo and laboratory.

'Our budget,' he said, 'is too limited to re-create all known extinct species. So we bring to life only the higher animals, the beautiful ones that were wantonly exterminated. I'm trying, as it were, to make up for brutality and stupidity. You might say that man struck God in the face every time he wiped out a branch of the animal kingdom.'

He paused, and they looked across the moats and the force fields. The quagga wheeled and galloped, delight and sun flashing off his flanks. The sea otter poked his humorous whiskers from the water. The gorilla peered from behind bamboo. Passenger pigeons strutted. A rhinoceros trotted like a dainty battleship. With gentle eyes a giraffe looked at them, then resumed eating leaves.

'There's the dodo. Not beautiful but very droll. And very helpless. Come, I'll show you the re-creation itself.'

In the great building, they passed between rows of tall and wide tanks. They could see clearly through the windows and the jelly within.

'Those are African Elephant embryos,' said the biologist. 'We plan to grow a large herd and then release them on the new government preserve.'

'You positively radiate,' said the distinguished visitor. 'You really love the animals, don't you?'

'I love all life.'

'Tell me,' said the visitor, 'where do you get the data for re-creation?'

'Mostly, skeletons and skins from the ancient museums. Excavated books and films that we succeeded in restoring and then translating. Ah, see those huge eggs? The chicks of the giant moa are growing within them. There, almost ready to be taken from the tank, are tiger cubs. They'll be dangerous when grown but will be confined to the preserve.'

The visitor stopped before the last of the tanks.

'Just one?' he said. 'What is it?'

'Poor little thing,' said the biologist, now sad. 'It will be so alone. But I shall give it all the love I have.'

'Is it so dangerous?' said the visitor. 'Worse than elephants, tigers, and bears?'

'I had to get special permission to grow this one,' said the biologist. His voice quavered.

The visitor stepped sharply back from the tank. He said, 'Then it must be . . . But you wouldn't dare!'

The biologist nodded.

'Yes. It's a man.'

If You Want A Story About . . .

299

Turtles

Wolverines

Wolves and Coyotes

Acknowledgements

Allison & Busby: 'The Old Woman's Animals', retold by John Mercer, from *The Stories of Vanishing Peoples* (1982).

Aitken & Stone Ltd: 'The Great Lad' from *A Dog Called Gelert and Other Stories* (Corgi, 1973). © Joyce Stranger 1973.

Angus & Robertson Publishers Australia: 'The Foal' by Vance Palmer from Allan Edwards (comp.), *The Rainbow-Bird and Other Stories by Vance Palmer*, first published in *Let the Birds Fly* (1955); 'The Donkey' by Alan Marshall from H. Drake Brockman (ed.), *Coast to Coast—Australian Stories 1955–1956* (1956).

Eleanor Brockett: 'The Deceitful Heron', retold by Eleanor Brockett in *Burmese and Thai Fairy Tales* (Frederick Muller, 1965). © 1965 Eleanor Brockett.

Laura Cecil Literary Agency: 'Lion, Goat, and Vulture' and 'Hare and Tortoise' from *Fables From Aesop* by James Reeves (Blackie & Son Ltd.). © James Reeves, 1961. Reprinted by permission of the James Reeves Estate.

The University of Chicago Press: 'Cat, Lion, and Man' from Georgios A. Megas (ed.), *Folktales of Greece*, trans. Helen Colaclides (1970). Reprinted by permission.

Jack Cope: 'Drinker of the Bitter Water' from *Alley Cat and Other Stories* by Jack Cope. © 1973 Jack Cope.

Columbia University Press: 'Kitten and Little Rat' from *Suriname Folk-Lore*, ed. Melville J. & Frances S. Herskovit, copyright © Columbia University Press, New York, 1954. Reprinted by permission of the publisher.

Coward McCann Inc.: Alan Devoe, 'The Tiger', reprinted from Frances Brentano (ed.), *Big Cats* (Ernest Benn, 1949).

J. M. Dent & Sons Ltd., Publishers: 'The Sea Beast and the *Queen of Heaven*' from *Hath the Rain a Father?* by Juanita Casey. Reprinted by permission of the publisher.

Faber & Faber Ltd./Laurence Pollinger Ltd.: 'Poor Arthur' from *Dog Days and Cat Naps* by Gene Kemp. Reprinted by permission of the publisher and author's agent.

A. N. Forde: 'Fly Back to Me', © A. N. Forde 1982.

Fulcrum Publishing, Inc., 350 Indiana St., #350, Golden, CO 80401: 'Sedna, the Woman Under the Sea' from *Native American Stories* by Joseph Bruchac. Reprinted by permission.

Arthur Gordon: 'The Sea Devil' from *Through Many Windows* (Fleming H. Revall Co.), © 1983 Arthur Gordon. Reprinted with the author's permission.

Hamish Hamilton Ltd.: 'The Fox, the Wolf, and the Mule', trans. Eilís Dillon, from *A Book of Wise Animals*, © 1975 Eilís Dillon. Reprinted with permission.

302

Hamish Hamilton Ltd./Rosemary Thurber: 'The Tortoise and the Hare' from *Fables for our Time* by James Thurber, © James Thurber, 1940, 1968 Helen Thurber. Reprinted with permission.

Harper Collins Publishers: 'Zlateh the Goat' from *Zlateh the Goat and Other Stories* by Isaac Bashevis Singer, © 1966 by Isaac Bashevis Singer. Reprinted by permission of the publisher.

A. M. Heath & Co./The Estate of Henry Williamson: 'The Meal' from *Collected Nature Stories* by Henry Williamson (Macdonald & Jane's, 1970).

Robert Leeson: 'Patch' from *Harold and Bella, Jammy and Me* (Fontana Lions, 1980). © Robert Leeson 1980.

Little Brown & Co.: 'Think Before You Jump' from J. Frank Dobie, *The Voice of the Coyote*, © 1949 J. Frank Dobie.

Little Brown & Co. (UK), Ltd.: 'The Wisdom of Crows' from *Tales of the Amber Ring* by Miloš Malý (Orbis Books, 1985). Reprinted with permission.

Macmillan London Ltd.: 'No Medal for Matt' from *God Made Sunday and Other Stories* by Walter Macken. Reprinted with permission.

Scott Meredith Literary Agency and the author: 'The King of Beasts' by Philip José Farmer, © 1964 Galaxy Publishing Corporation. Reprinted with permission.

D'Arcy Niland: 'The Parachutist' from *Dadda Jumped Over Two Elephants*, © 1961 D'Arcy Niland.

Harold Ober Associates Incorporated: 'The Snapping Turtle and the Wisteria Vine' from *99 Fables* by William March. © 1960 by The University of Alabama Press, copyright renewed 1988 by The Merchants National Bank of Mobile and Patty C. Maxwell. Reprinted with permission.

Eileen O'Faolain: 'The Wren, the King of the Birds', translated by Eileen O'Faolain, from *Children of the Salmon and Other Irish Folktales*, translation © Eileen O'Faolain 1965.

Oxford University Press: 'The Hyena and the Dead Ass' from *The Children of the Wind* by René Guillot, trans. Gwen Marsh, English translation © 1964 OUP. Reprinted with permission.

Penguin Books India Pvt Ltd.: 'The Eye of the Eagle' from Ruskin Bond: *Panther's Moon and Other Stories* (Puffin, 1991); 'A Tiger in the House' from Ruskin Bond: *Times Stops at Shamli and Other Stories* (1989). Reprinted by permission of the author and publisher.

Penguin USA: 'Brer Rabbit and the Tar Baby', retold by Julius Lester from *The Tales of Uncle Remus* (Dial Books), © 1987 Julius Lester. Used by permission of Dial Books for Young Readers, a division of Penguin Books USA Inc.

Peters Fraser & Dunlop Group Ltd.: 'The Seal' from *Two Lovely Beasts and Other Stories* (Victor Gollancz). Reprinted with permission.

Random House UK Ltd./Harcourt Brace Jovanovich, Inc.: 'The Rockfish' from *Spring Sowing* by Liam O'Flaherty (1924). Reprinted with permission.

A. H. & A. W. Reed: 'The Oyster Brothers and the Shark' from *Aboriginal Fables and Legendary Tales*, © 1965 A. W. Reed. Reprinted with permission.

Dan Russell: 'The Poacher's Narrow Shave', © 1948 Dan Russell.

Robert Scott: 'Coyote and the Making of the People'; 'How Raven Brought the Light'; 'How Beaver Stole the Fire'; 'Why the Bat Flies at Night'; 'Why Bear Has a Stumpy Tail'; 'The Sleep Test'; 'Rabbit and King Lion'; 'The Big Drought'; 'Bear says "North"'; 'The Wolf and the Lamb'; 'The Turtle and the Swans'; and 'Anancy and Commonsense': all © 1994 Robert Scott. Reprinted with permission.

George Vukelich: 'The Turtle', originally appeared in *The University of Kansas City Review*, Summer 1958 (Volume XXIV, no. 4). It is reprinted here with the permission of New Letters/The University of Kansas City

ACKNOWLEDGEMENTS

Review and the Curators of The University of Missouri-Kansas City.
Barbara Ker Wilson: 'The Tiger, the Elephant, and the Monkey', retold by
Barbara Ker Wilson; 'The Fox and the Lion in Partnership', retold by
Barbara Ker Wilson, from *Animal Folk Tales* (Hamlyn, 1968).
Any errors or omissions in the above list are entirely unintentional. If
notified, the publisher will be pleased to correct any entries at the earliest
opportunity.

The Artists

Pages 4, 5, 7, 15, 20, 28, 57, 193, 221, 279, 287, 289   **Adam Stower**
Pages 11, 37, 43, 112, 212, 213, 217, 231, 272, 274   **Nicky Cornwell**
Pages 23, 26, 35, 63, 76, 137, 158   **Susie Skinner**
Pages 32, 33, 45, 51, 67, 78, 89, 91, 103, 115, 117, 128, 131, 134, 160, 171, 179,
183, 188, 189, 267, 291, 294   **William Geldart**
Pages 40, 48, 94, 98, 108, 144, 148, 227, 284, 285   **Chris Price**
Pages 54, 61, 70, 86   **Nick Harris**
Pages 80, 83, 203, 234, 241, 244   **Heribert Schulmeyer**
Page 141   **Ken Taylor**
Pages 249, 257, 261   **Martin Knowlden**
Page 298   **Neil Evans**